The Walnut Tree

An Autobiography of Kindness

By the author of

THE CHRONICLES OF CHURCH FARM
ROMANY COTTAGE, SILVERLAKE
RURAL REFLECTIONS
HUNDREDFOLD

Author (*right*) *and Belgian cousin*

The Walnut Tree

An Autobiography of Kindness

By
Monica M. Hutchings

London
Hodder and Stoughton

First Printed 1951

MADE AND PRINTED IN GREAT BRITAIN FOR
HODDER AND STOUGHTON LIMITED LONDON
BY C. TINLING & CO., LTD., LIVERPOOL, LONDON
AND PRESCOT

To my Two Friends

Littleton C. Powys & Anthony Essex-Lopresti

who have alternately helped and

hindered the production

of this book—

in gratitude and affection

M.M.H.

Acknowledgements

Passages from the late Mr. John Gort's letters are quoted by kind permission of his son, Mr. Albert Gort.

I am grateful to H. J. Massingham, Doris Langley Moore, Alyse Gregory and living members of the Powys family for giving me their kind permission to quote from their writings.

I also acknowledge my indebtedness to the following authors and publishers for permission to quote from their works :—

J. R. Robertson-Scott and Penguin books.
Vera Brittain and Victor Gollancz.
Malcolm Elwin and John Lane, the Bodley Head.
Arthur Mee's Executors and Hodder and Stoughton.
W. J. Perry and Methuens.
A. R. Wallace and Macmillans.

Finally, I want to thank Eclipse Film Productions Ltd., for permission to reproduce pictures from the documentary film, " New Face of Britain," opposite pages 80, 81, 144, 161, 240, 256 and 257.

Contents

Illustrations

Introduction

ONCE upon a time Three Princes and a Goose-Girl were jour-
neying across the magic vale called Taunton Dene.

It was the month of July and the oat-crop was set in pale gold
stooks beside the dusty highway. There were poppies in the corn and
the Goose-Girl loved their vagabond colour, yet she did not like to see
too many of them, for the better the corn, the fewer the poppies.
Being only a Goose-Girl she knew what it was to go hungry for bread,
so she both loved and feared the poppies and all the other lovely weeds
that made the summer magnificent.

Behind her was the sacred Vale of Avilion, and ahead, the dim blue
hills that guard the western sea. And in all that stretch of land,
appeared nothing untoward nor vexing. Yet the Goose-Girl's mind
was unquiet, for it was busy with the problem of which of the Three
Princes she should marry—always supposing they asked her.

It was a grave problem, for they were all good and all rich and all
handsome, and, in so far as she knew, brave and worthy in every
respect. It was indeed a problem.

Steadily the coach crossed the Vale, the blue hills drawing nearer.
And then a honey-bee blundered into their midst, disconcerting at
least two of the Three Princes.

The Goose-Girl observed it delightedly, for she loved most living
creatures, with the possible exception of bulls and slugs, which she
tolerantly supposed were all right in their proper place, but all wrong
out of it.

The First Prince waxed aggressive. He brandished a roll of parchment crying, " Kill the thing! Kill the thing! "

The Goose-Girl was horrified. Why should he want to kill such a
beneficial creature?

" Oh no," she cried, " It's a BEE and useful, you mustn't kill it! "
The Second Prince had covered his face with his hands.

" I don't fancy getting stung," was all *he* said.

" It won't hurt you," explained the Goose-Girl.

" So YOU say," retorted the Second Prince, rather rudely.

" Bees are so useful and harmless, please leave it alone, Your High-ness," begged the Goose-Girl of the First Prince, who was still hunting the bee up and down the coach, with his roll of parchment.

The Third Prince, who so far had not spoken (he was at all times a man of few words), had begun reining in, and now lowered the coach-window to give the bee a clear passage to the sunlit fields beyond.

"What in the world are you stopping for?" demanded the First Prince peevishly.

" If you do have to shoo the thing out so it can live to sting someone else, you don't have to *stop* to do it."

The Third Prince smiled ever so slightly.

"We must let the little fellow out near his home, or he will not be able to find his way back to the hive, and will die."

" Fancy stopping just for a bee! " exploded the Second Prince. " Now you've let that other coach get in front of us and we shall never pass it this side of the Turnpike."

The bee flew away, and the Goose-Girl watched it out of sight as the carriage started forward again. She said nothing, but she pitied the First and Second Prince because although they were witty and clever and all those other things, they really knew very little about the things that mattered.

" Do you like honey? " the Third Prince asked the other two.

They answered somewhat sulkily in the affirmative.

No further comment was made by any of them.

The Vale of Taunton Dene asleep in the sunshine, the blue fields of the cloudless sky and the gold fields of the ripening corn sang together, and in her heart the Goose-Girl thanked the bee for having made her choice for her.

I

Preliminaries

THIS autobiography is commenced in my thirtieth year. There are many reasons for writing it. Mainly because I want to, and a book written for that reason stands a better chance of being readable than one written for almost any other. Another reason is that I have been asked to write it by those kind people who have taken the time and trouble to tell me that they enjoyed *Romany Cottage, Silverlake,* and to ask me for " more of your life ".

Perhaps the last reason is, that I feel if I do not write it now, it may never be written. And yet there must be those who will say:

" But your thirtieth year is much too soon for you to be writing an autobiography—you have hardly lived long enough to have much to say."

To which I reply:

" To have lived at all, with open eyes and attentive ears, is to know of a tale worth telling. The world is full of wonders."

Above all, however, I write now because I feel there is an added need for kindness. It is the virtue to distinguish us from the very animals we tend to despise and often persecute. Kindness springs from understanding, cruelty from ignorance. This is always being proven both in the lives of individuals and of communities. It is expressed most clearly in man's attitude to the other creatures which share the earth with him. To observe, to learn, to know, to understand, begets tolerance and kindness, virtues always needed if Man is to survive, and never more than now.

Why do I not wait until I am sixty or ninety? Why do some people never grow really old in their minds, while others are never really young?

Here, you may wave your hand at me and say, " Ah well, perhaps this young lady has had a most adventurous life—been cast away on a Desert Island, fought alongside the Maquis, or circumnavigated the world in a rowing-boat." (And even on the thought, you may stifle a yawn and mentally add " Another of Them.")

For the world today is rife with sensations. They are too frequent and too numerous to be grasped. The news bludgeons us into a feeble acceptance of myriad marvels, just one of which would have served to stagger less sensational ages. Each week some item of colossal magnitude out-shoulders the last one, until we are too satiated to take any notice, and our minds too saturated to retain any recollection. What was last year's headline, or last month's—or even last night's?

War is, of course, the arch sensation-provider, but even when it ceased, the wonders did not. We discovered that this Clerk or that Salesgirl had lived through Arabian Nights adventures. We found rivals to the Roland and Oliver legend, we learned of new Inquisitions, modern Ghenghis Khans, up-to-date Attilas.

Wonderful and terrible, beautiful and heroic are things done and written about in our time, but not by the author of this autobiography.

For me there is only the adventure of being alive, of waking up and going to bed, the impact of each new spring which always seems better than the last, the glory of every succeeding autumn, the majesty of every maligned winter, the surprises of every uncertain summer. For me there is the high adventure of living on a farm, where life is never still and something is always happening.

For me there is the supreme adventure of living in some of the loveliest countryside the earth has to offer—not spectacular perhaps, not as capricious and cruel as some, but which contains all that is necessary to support life and make that life full and happy.

Yet all my adventures, humble though they are, have been threatened with extinction. The first by Man's madness in warfare and his new and dangerous weapons, the second by his disregard for the things that matter, and the third by his unthinking ignorance which permits progress to be bought at the cost of beauty and a gracious way of life.

The "Great Wen" of London spreads out over the surrounding country-side, while much of its very heart lies neglected and rotten. The old houses are left empty or derelict, the bombed acres are left to the rubble and rosebay willow herb, while the families that might have populated them, spread further and further over the face of the farmlands.

The Home Counties disappear beneath a plague of dormitories and garden-cities which no more resemble the real country (as their occupants appear to imagine) than the commercialised "resort" resembles the real sea-coast of Britain, or what remains yet free from asphalt and concrete, "solarium" and rhododendron.

The great downs, once so beautiful in their generous curves and subdued tones, are scarred with camps and battle-schools, firing-ranges and derelict hutments. Whole villages lie rotting, inhabited now by rabbits, rusty cans and barbed wire. Woods are denuded of their timber, and the undergrowth left to riot over once well-kept rides. Great houses are now the homes of only the bat and the rat, airfields sprawl across fertile farm-lands, camps and institutions occupy fine estates.

Since the Industrial Revolution, progress has been almost entirely synonymous with ugliness, and this last war has accelerated this rate of " progress " beyond the pace of all other ages. So that those who like myself, love and admire their heritage and know its worth economically and aesthetically, see it threatened and attacked on every side.

My country is being lost, damaged or altered so rapidly that I find I must write of it soon or not at all.

I have been unable to forget the lesson of my first visit to Norfolk. I knew it for a great agricultural country. I had also heard of the Broads.

Here I found exquisite newly-painted summer palaces fringing the still waters. How beautiful and pretentious they were, complete with gazebos, loggias, arbours, fairy-lights, and in one case, tame deer. And how wonderfully some of them were thatched, with that fine long-lasting Norfolk reed. Never have I seen better thatching, points and eaves and gables, even the boat-houses and garages were thatched to match.

At the back of these sylvan retreats, this paradise of smooth lawns, and shining motor-launches, I found the unpainted cottages, the derelict windmills, and the farms, roofed as cheaply as possible, which ruled out thatch.

I found the farm-workers who drew their water-supply from wells into which the age-old silt of the Broads had percolated, so that the sediment never clears how ever long the water is left in the glass or jug. I saw tiny children walking long distances to school, spattered with mud from army-lorries transporting men from one college of destruction to another.

And I wondered (as I have done all over England) at the neglect that wears the badge of indifference or unconcern and manifests itself in waste and destruction of something at once irreplaceable and unparalleled.

Yet much remains that is beautiful, significant and enduring, but it only serves to emphasise the ugly, the unimportant and the transitory.

A few feet from where I write there is a window. It opens on to a vista of garden, barn, and gentle slope of meadow, there are plenty of trees and a variegated sky. I can see a bunch of rough-coated young heifers and my dog is sitting alertly watching them. Down the garden path two little kittens are taking their first staggering steps, while an agitated Mama purrs encouragement and mews admonitions. I can see wild flowers and tame. It is spring once more, and the season is firmly advanced. The syringa is breaking forth into its waxy orange-blossom, by the farm gate-way a gnarled old withy tree is breaking into delicate new green. Away from the window, on the other side of me is a newspaper. It carries the headline—

" Budapest White Paper accuses Britain and the U.S."

Which is reality, this announcement in plain black and white or the black and white plumage of a magpie flying straight as an arrow for the orchard trees, lovely with blossom ?

How can a White Paper " accuse " ? What IS a White Paper? Can one wear it, eat it, build with it? What business have Men to be afraid of it? Am I just a very simple person or an idiot? I naturally prefer to think the former, but I fail to see how a collection of buildings forming the two cities of Buda and Pest, or the black letters on a White Paper can accuse anyone.

At the same time there is a semi-facetious article about " flying-saucers ". Behind the nonchalance I can detect that the reporter is just a little apprehensive. What new secret-weapon is this? What is going on ? He belittles it, but should he fear it ? It might turn out to be something after all. Only yesterday we were making jokes about " pilotless planes " which eventually became such a menace that we had to belittle them by christening them " doodle-bugs", or the equally contemptuous " buzz-bombs".

The reporter of the flying-saucer incidents is plainly hinting that the Russians are " up to something". If they are, it is a criminal waste of time, effort and Man's resources. Why aren't the White Paper men, and the Flying Saucer men out in the fields, are they yet unaware there is a world food shortage—surely they must have read *that* in their news-paper columns somewhere? Do they not realise that in spite of the depredations of war, populations are increasing with enormous rapidity the world over, while from overstocking, erosion, neglect or exploita-tion, the productive acreage is ever shrinking.

" Whole villages lie rotting "—Imber, 1948

Municipal Buildings, Cardiff

Of what can they be thinking, playing a child's game of make-believe while the world is threatened with starvation? Or is it we, the farmers who are futile, being somewhat in the position of a housewife, busily preparing a meal in the kitchen, while we well know the remainder of the house is on fire?

Perhaps some of the people on the Norfolk Broads who were paying twenty guineas a day for a house-boat should have wandered just over the border into the Hilgay Fen area, to see what avail is money and leisure in the face of nature. Here the floods broke through and crops and steadings were lost. Man's wealth and time should be spent on fighting disease, famine and flood, drought, plague and fire.

The same paper that tells me of political outrages, and secret weapons, makes light of the new race of " Spivs " and racketeers, making their " corners " in some scarce commodity; and I find myself reflecting that if farmers and farm-workers the world over went " on strike " for a year or two (less time than it took to perfect the atomic bomb) we should all revert to the age of hunters and food-gatherers. In the case of this reversion we should be less well-off than our cave-dwelling ancestors for there would be less both to hunt and gather in proportion to the world's population, owing to the brick and concrete wildernesses from which all nature has been ruthlessly exterminated.

If we continue to pay more regard to " White Papers " and " Flying Saucers " than food production, the lot of our ancestors in their cave-shelters will be enviable when compared with our " things to come."

When I think of H. G. Wells' book *The Shape of Things to Come,* I remember how he taught for a time in the village school of Wookey Hole, set in the shadow of the frowning Mendip range, which holds so many records of Early Man in Britain. I cannot help wondering if he penetrated into the great Cave at Wookey Hole, or explored the rock shelters of nearby Ebbor Gorge, looking backward as well as forward. The " grisly folk " described in one of his stories may well have roamed the great plateau above the Vale of Avalon. For the scientific Wells knew the danger of science—few better.

He also knew the value of agriculture and a healthy countryside. In *The New Machiavelli* he describes the village and countryside of Bromley in Kent, being swallowed up to make a suburb for greater London. As a boy he had seen the farms, fields and brooks he knew and loved, ruthlessly overtaken and destroyed by a tide of ugliness, and it bit deeply.

Even forty years before the death of H. G. Wells, George Gissing in *The Private Papers of Henry Ryecroft*, wrote:—

"I hate and fear science because of my conviction that, for long to come if not for ever, it will be the remorseless enemy of mankind. I see it destroying all simplicity and all gentleness of life, all the beauty in the world; I see it restoring barbarism under a mask of civilisation; I see it darkening men's minds and hardening their hearts; I see it bringing a time of vast conflicts, which will pale into significance the 'thousand wars of old,' and as likely as not, will whelm all the laborious advances of mankind in blood-drenched chaos."

Written over forty years ago, and how have we fulfilled the worst fears of this author! But the fault lies not in science alone, but in men's minds that can turn powers for good into powers for evil, that can increase suffering and the sum of human unhappiness and fear when they might seek only to diminish it.

There is only one hope, that we return to common sense and reality. This means putting food, clothing and shelter for all the world, before plastic ashtrays and nylon stockings. This means thinking first of nature as reality, of fields and crops as fundamentals, and White Papers and bombs as matters of unreality, belonging to a nightmare world.

I have nothing to give to this book but a love of nature and a consciousness of the importance of the land. As fortunately there are still millions who are of my way of thinking, I can but endeavour to show how I arrived at my conclusions, and what kind of road took me to them, and whether the signposts were by accident or design.

If it makes one solitary new recruit to the importance of the countryside, it will not be in vain nor time wasted; if it adds one crumb to the sum of human happiness or understanding, I shall be satisfied.

At thirty I have lived long enough to know I can stem no tides, change no universes, motivate no revolutions. At thirty I have not lived long enough not to wish to try.

I love my country and its people, and yet patriotism has nothing to do with it, for the further I travel the more I shall see that those who till the soil have a freemasonry the world over. Cattle and corn are the same in any language, I should but change the Plough for the Southern Cross, the Peon for the Moujik, the Coolie for the Tractor-Driver.

They all know that the man cast away on a barren desert island with only a roll of banknotes or a crock of gold, is poor indeed.

II

Childhood in Wales

> "Ah, it wouldn' be bad for some of us
> If we'd never gone furder, and never fared wuss;
> If we were skippin' and scamprin' and cap'rin' still
> On the sand that lies below the hill.
> Crunchin' its grey ribs with the beat
> Of our little patt'rin' naked feet;
> If we'd just keep childer upon the shore
> For ever and ever and ever more."
>
> T. E. BROWN. *Betsy Lee.*

WHEN Captain Scott, bound for the Antarctic, sailed from Cardiff in the *Terra Nova*, my mother was among the crowd who waved him God speed from the shores of Wales.

We too were Scotts, though not so far as I am aware related to the great explorer, and my mother who followed the fate of the *Terra Nova* keenly, decided that her expected child should be christened after the Captain's baby son, Peter. As we know, he was not to see either his son or our shores again, but Peter Scott grew up in the worthy tradition of his father, honoured as naturalist, painter and author of histories of the war at sea.

My earliest memories are of a great garden and a small house, I almost lived in the garden and was almost born in it, for my mother was picking gooseberries and currants, when, as the Elizabethans would have had it, " she was brought to bed of a female child ".

To turn the name Peter into something feminine taxed even my mother's ingenuity, so she compromised on the name Monica, which went well enough with Scott and did not lend itself to unsightly shortenings.

Her only other child was my sister Kathleen, almost twelve years old when I was born. Fourteen months after I arrived the Armistice of 1918 was signed, and shortly afterwards my father saw me for the first time. His remarks are not recorded, but if a brother was required for Kathleen I must have been something of a disappointment all round.

Such health as I have known, and certainly my first love of nature, I owe to my mother who left me in the garden at all hours and seasons.

When weather forced me indoors, my favourite playing places were the wide, deep window-sills of our old cottage from where I could watch the rain on the box-hedge " maze ", or the snow piling up round the blue-tits' home in a hollow in the walnut tree.

This ancient tree was the pride of the garden and gave the cottage its name. Once tree and cottage had stood in the real country, now the old house and the oasis of garden comprising nearly half an acre were surrounded by surburban houses while not far away was a very poor locality teeming with slum life.

Our home was part of what was known in those days as " a gentleman's estate ", much of which appeared to have been swallowed by the encroaching city, but there were still parts which remained outside the built-up areas; and visits to a gamekeeper's cottage on the edge of the estate are a happy memory of my earlier days.

Now, although I was born in the Principality, let it not be thought that I am Welsh—no more that is than the rest of you. If your ancestors fled with mine before the English invasion, or stayed and intermarried with them, we may all have some "Welsh" in our make-up somewhere.

My parents hailed from Yorkshire and Nottinghamshire respectively. The name Scott suggests Scotland but all I know is that there was some Irish in the family about Great-grandfather's time, which makes me of just about the kind of mongrel stock to be found all over Britain today.

I like to think there is more Celtic than Saxon in me. My colouring is Celtic and so are my sympathies. I love the hills and am at home among mountains and until my recent illness had a " balanced " kind of head for climbing. I feel more affinity with the races who terraced our Western hills than with the Saxons who settled the lowlands.

To draw nearer the present day, however, Mr. Littleton Powys insists that I have Stuart blood in me. He finds in me a resemblance to Charles II, and more still to his son Monmouth. In one portrait of Monmouth at the age of seven and a photograph of myself at the age of six the resemblance is plain enough for even me to see. Monmouth's mother was Lucy Walters whose distant kinsman, Lord George Scott, has recently decided that she was married to Charles II after all.

An independent witness in the form of a lady belonging to one of the oldest families in Somerset recently discovered the supposed likeness and declared that brow, chin and colouring were absolutely " Stuart ".

This amused me very much after Mr. Powys's remarks on the subject and I thereupon ceased to treat him with the deference due to his age and learning, pointing out that if his family were once Kings of Wales, I was a relative (albeit shady and distant!) of the rightful kings of England.

Be this as it may, such " illusions of grandeur " besides buttering no parsnips do not alter my initial preference for an ancestor peering over the ramparts of Maiden Castle, Eggardon or Hod Hill for sight of the infiltrating Saxons with their alien colouring and alien ways—so soon to stand for things " typically English ".

Memory paints the garden of Walnut Tree Cottage much larger than it really is, it also throws upon it the almost never failing brightness of sunny summers. The only knowledge I have of wet weather is going out where the tent had stood and watching the wriggly worm " casts " in the square of bare soil left amid the green of the lawn.

This lawn was the scene of many of my games, not quite long enough for a tennis-court it was used for games of out-door badminton. Beside the lawn was an untidy vegetable garden, a small hen run and a pair of beautiful ducks known as Egbert and 'Erbert.

The other side of the lawn was bordered by a path and then a high hedge which shut out our neighbours. The part of the garden that lay in front of the house was composed of box hedges set in mazy patterns interspersed with flower-beds and crowned splendidly by the walnut tree.

The old hedges round the garden contained many treasures, sycamore saplings, with wonderfully shaped ruddy-green leaves, a young ash-tree, some elder bushes which leaned over to form a cave-like arbour, real wild blackberry bushes, and wonder of wonders, a crab-apple tree. The fruit of this was too bitter to be eaten with anything like abandon, but it was just possible by taking a small nibble at a time (plentifully sweetened with demerara sugar out of a glass paste-jar) to make quite an acceptable feast.

Strawberries and raspberries did not do well in our garden, probably because they need attention and my father was no gardener. He had a very good alibi as being a " gentleman's gentleman " his hands must be perfect. My mother had hers full with the house and her chickens, so the garden was hardly well kept. The lawn was mown and trimmed however, and it seemed that in due season most fruits and flowers appeared to bless our domain.

The gooseberry bushes had grown together in one solid phalanx of prickly green, but how they bore! I have never seen such crops since. We were able to make jams and jellies and still supply half the neighbourhood with this fruit. There was a particularly delicious hairy-type of desert gooseberry of whose flavour I have the pleasantest recollections.

On the side of our garden away from the neighbours was a field of waste land known as "the wilderness". I believe it has since been built over.

There are two memorable exceptions to those memories of eternal summer in the garden. The first is when my father paused on his way to work, to throw a handful of walnuts up to my bedroom window. The sense of smell has great power to evoke memories, and today the tang of the green walnut-husk, far more than the sight, feel or taste of the nut, brings back those early autumn mornings, the dewy frost on the garden and the rich dead shades of the fallen leaves.

After the autumns, the memory of my first snow which, thickly plastered against the bole of the great tree before my window, showed up the vivid colours of the blue-tits nesting in the hollow. They had passed unnoticed in the summer time, but now I was fascinated by their acrobatics above the snowladen box-hedges. Mother helped me to put out scraps for them. She believed in kindness to all animals—or if, as in the case of mice, kindness was embarrassing, then as speedy and painless a death as possible.

Mother was almost forty when I can first remember her, and I never knew her as being "young". She was not grey, on the contrary the youthful sheen of her dark hair and her excellent carriage made her appear ageless, but she never played with me as other girls' mothers seemed to. Her play ended at reading to me. She could not ride a bicycle or swim, and I never once saw her in a short-sleeved dress or blouse, let alone a bathing-costume.

Until I attended school I seldom had a companion. My only sister was always one phase beyond me. When I was a baby, she was at school, by the time I was at school, she was working for the Automobile Association, before I had left school, she was married.

By the time I was five she was "courting" but took sufficient time off from this delightful occupation to teach me my alphabet, and how to knit. She also, with the aid of an orange and a pencil, demonstrated that the world was round.

Before I had lived many years I discovered that both Kathleen and my mother were not always truthful to me—they " fobbed me off " (particularly in the matter of sex-education)," pulled my leg ", told me " white lies " and fairy-stories. All these I dimly resented, and after finding out the very first untruth began to take all they told me with a " grain of salt ".

This being the case I found it exceedingly difficult to reconcile myself to the world's rotundity. Very much later I began to realise that if one went west across America one came to ports like San Francisco or Vancouver which were termed the gateways to the Orient, and that in fact, if one continued west long enough, Japan was reached. Love of music completed my conversion as I discovered that Tschaikowsky and Rimsky-Korsakov, truly Russian nationalistic composers, revealed unmistakable elements of the East in their work.

When, during the last war, the Alaska Highway was opened to facilitate defence against Japan, I ceased to be in doubt altogether about the shape of the world not to mention its size.

If I learned slowly, I also made as sure of my facts as humanly possible before accepting them.

One of my earliest memories is of crying literally over spilt milk. My earliest companions were a Persian cat Fluffy, and a Sealyham bitch, Peggy. I had been sent to fetch the milk from the dairy at the end of Albany Road (not more than a few yards away) when Peggy in an excess of zeal jumped up at me, knocking the full can from my hands.

I dashed up and down the pavements calling, " Pusseees! Pusseees! " until mother came out to see what I was about. Then I tearfully explained that somewhere there were cats who would be glad of this milk. She said that if I went back for some more they would doubtless find it.

I was very upset, no cats appeared. Spilling the milk was bad enough but for it to run to waste was absolutely awful.

Before I was six, mother had a most severe operation. Since girlhood she had suffered from stomach trouble and now the climax had come. She was convalescent for the better part of a year, but the experiment was a success. During her absence I was left in my sister's charge. She largely solved the problem by packing up our meals and taking me on Roath Park Lake. Here I learned to row, two hands to one oar, and here we spent many peaceful hours moored to one of the islands. From Pen-y-Lan Hill above the Park I caught my first sight of the mountains and soon found that I was deeply affected by natural scenery—that I would sooner look at lakes and mountains than listen to the Band in the Park, sooner follow a flock of sheep than the Corpus Christi procession.

Both Peggy and Fluffy went the way of most pets, the cat had come to our family soon after they came to Cardiff, sixteen years before. We never replaced her, but Peggy's place was taken by a mongrel Yorkshire terrier called Mack. Mother instilled into me that pets had rights of their own and did not exist merely for our pleasure and amusement, but should be treated with kindness and respect. This seemed perfectly reasonable to me as I enjoyed their company even if we did not speak exactly the same language.

Apart from the cat and the dog, a few birds and insects, I saw little other wild life in our city-bounded garden and must make the best of what I had. Butterflies particularly enchanted me, they would shake out their wings from the tall grasses of " the Wilderness ", and I would tie a table napkin to my shoulders and try to imitate them. I was well provided with toys as mother always had a large circle of friends who were most generous to me at Christmas and birthdays, but I preferred the motion of the butterflies to any of them. I would lie in the long grasses and watch the delicate wings hover and then settle on the stems above me.

One day I saw something larger than bird or butterfly in the blue-sky above me. After excitedly calling mother into conference I was told it was an aeroplane. It looked far away, high and insignificant, but I was assured that it was " huge " when seen on the ground, and that there would never be another war because of *them*. " You see, Monica," mother explained, " they would bring the war right to the people at home—the people who were not fighting at all—and that has made war so terrible that there will never be another one again."

I later learned that much the same thing had been said over the discovery of dynamite—and with as much effect.

The war was still a very fresh memory in our household. My father had been a despatch rider in the Hussars (then cavalry) and had been awarded the Belgian Croix de Guerre.

An aunt of mine had married the son of a Belgian refugee family, who had eventually taken her to live near Waterloo.

When I was about seven we visited her, saw Brussels, Ypres and the battlefields. The barbed wire was still in evidence, not all the shell-holes had been filled-in. I saw the Cloth Hall at Ypres, the ruins of Ghent, the cemeteries of Poperinghe. Child though I was I understood the meaning of war.

There were stacks of magazines in our cottage bearing titles like *The War* and *Gallant Little Belgium*. There were accounts of Kitchener's disappearance and souvenirs of Sturdee in the Falklands. The pictures did not appeal to me greatly (except for the one of Tim A'Dair winning the V.C.) and I turned with relief to picture books of birds and animals, to *Comical Doings*, an amazingly clever book about animals, birds and fairies, full of both wit and wisdom, to *Struwwelpeter* or to the tattered copy of *Cinderella* which was all a Cinderella should be. This particular edition was so tastefully illustrated, that years later, when I produced a children's ballet on the same subject I sent to my mother for the book, so that I might model the costumes and scenery on it.

Perhaps best of all I loved Maurice Baring's *The Glass-Mender*. Here again the illustrations were tasteful and colours exquisite. No hard lines or shades, nothing " horrific " or cheap. The stories, set amid Alpine flowers, by lakes and " Silver Mountains ", told of pastoral life, or the ways of fisher-lads when " the sun was shining on the sea and a fresh breeze was blowing."

At first I had to be read to by my mother chiefly, though my sister, who was musically inclined, did read me the story of " Vox Angelica and Lieblich Gedacht " which was the longest in *The Glass-Mender*.

Mother taught me to recite by the simple process of repeating the words after her. I soon memorised quite long pieces and was able to recite them at " Church Concerts " and the like, although I could not read and there was no sign of me starting school. I believe this way of learning poetry helped my memorising which more than one teacher later stated was above average.

One kind of public appearance led to another. And for a short period I joined a dancing class. I was both smallest and youngest of the pupils and was used largely as a mascot by the others. I remember being held aloft, supported on other girls' shoulders, and made to pose as this or that when I really wanted to be doing " The Dying Swan " to St. Saëns' haunting music, which had been allotted to the eldest pupil, a girl of about fourteen.

Meanwhile I danced on my own about the garden, or indoors when my sister was in obliging frame of mind and would play the piano for

me. My favourite pieces were " In a Persian Market" and Coleridge-
Taylor's " Characteristic Dances", until I discovered the music from
Carmen. From that day onwards I was a Spanish gypsy in all my
waking hours.

I visited my father at Roath Court (still probably clinging to my
tambourine) when a film company were using the old house as a
setting for a costume picture.

Some of them saw me, and upon the Cook telling them that I
" Danced like a fairy" insisted upon me joining the proceedings.
They wanted to " sign me up ", but after a conference with mother, I
remained at home. I might add that shortly after their rash offer to a
little dancing gypsy, the company went bankrupt.

My sister appeared increasingly alien to me. I began to be afraid of
her tongue. It appeared she took nothing seriously, least of all music,
which was the one common ground upon which we met. She would
turn from " strumming " a little of Beethoven's Moonlight Sonata to
" Rag-time," which hurt me dreadfully. I could not stand the noise
which even then I considered ugly and somewhat degrading.

She said " In a Persian Market" was "hackneyed" and *Carmen*
overdone, so that I gradually became afraid to confide my tastes
in her.

I thought of course that she was wonderful. She was my sister, she
was very handsome and I admired her tremendously, but oh, what
power she had to hurt me. I was very proud of her, and very afraid of
her at one and the same time.

Her friends who frequented the house were all much the same to me,
clever, rather noisy, bright and smart and one must *never* be a mamby-
pamby before them whatever happened!

Not long ago my good friend our local Librarian and Curator
introduced me to that unusual and neglected writer, Frederick Rolfe,
Baron Corvo.

After reading Symons's *The Quest for Corvo* I read *The Desire and
Pursuit of the Whole* which he had particularly recommended among
Rolfe's books. The author shared my birth-date and this is what he
says of those born on July 3rd:

" Under his shell the crab is as soft as butter, and just one labyrin-
thine mass of the most sensitive of nerves. You should learn to be
as merciful as God to all poor sinners born between the twenty-first

24

of June and the twenty-fourth of July, for they are born under the constellation Cancer; and their nature is the nature of the crab—hard without, soft within."

If I was indeed born with this tendency, as I am sure many people besides those born under Cancer must be, then my treatment at home served to strengthen it.

Both my mother and sister were strong " no nonsense " personalities and one of the first things they made clear to me was that it was disgraceful to be afraid of the dark. So I never revealed that I was, though this came rather hard, particularly in the wintertime, when it was dark long before I went to bed.

Mr. H. E. Balch, explorer of Wookey Hole and many other caves, has declared that our fear of the dark is a legacy of our cave-dwelling days when the setting of the sun brought terrors unimaginable. As the light failed, the hunter would hasten homewards, his mate watching anxiously for his return. After dark, the unknown terrors of forest and gorge, swamp and mountain, held sway.

If Mr. Balch's theory is at all correct, I have inherited my fair share. My sojourn at Romany Cottage where I lived alone in my early twenties did much to eventually cure me, but right up to that time I was afraid of the dark.

If as a child, I had been able to show my fear, it might have been easier, but when I heard my mother stoutly declaring to all and sundry that I was a " sensible child " and " no trouble to put to bed " I knew it must be kept to myself, it would have hurt both of us too much to have told her!

So I grew, even as Corvo has since suggested to me, " Hard without, soft within ". Some of it was perhaps a kind of vanity, there are those who will doubtless say so, but mainly, in my very young days at least it was because I felt a lack in myself—that my mother and sister were right and I was therefore wrong, which drove me to present at least a hard outside.

So and so was disgraceful—therefore if I could not help it, prevent it, or cure myself of it, I must keep it to myself and pray I never be found out. I tried very hard to conform.

My mother and sister " knew all the answers."

It was the early days of the wireless and we had a crystal set. Mother and I would sit on either side of the fire with an ear-phone apiece clapped against our heads. So it was we listened to a broadcast of Masefield's *Reynard the Fox*.

It nearly broke my heart.

Some days later when I felt equal to broaching the subject without letting myself down, I asked the question " Why? " of my mother. " Why was it necessary for the fox to go through all that? Why did grown-ups HAVE to find pleasure in such unequal contest? Why did such things go on? "

My mother tried to explain that though she thought hunting cruel, it was the sport of the " gentry " who thought themselves above criticism—at the moment it was an accepted thing—like war had been, and there was little one could do about it.

Over twenty years later I was stunned by a " badger-hunt " where the victim (who is much harder to kill than any fox) was worried and beaten to a slow, fighting death in the name of " sport ".

It had taken me every one of those intervening years to realise that war and cruelty are BY NO MEANS INEVITABLE. The dignity and decency of man will one day establish itself when he has ceased to be afraid to *think*, when he has ceased to be afraid to face himself.

That still, small voice within which says things like:—

" This isn't quite ' cricket ' there is no sense in this, these people are not very different from me, this man is not my enemy ', etc., etc." is silent when in crowds and masses, is drowned in the heat of battle or hunt, is swamped by ' expediency ' and terms like ' Patriotism '.

Alyse Gregory has put it clearly when she says:

" —the ordinary man would rather be asked to throw away his life in a useless war—than to dig out the real secrets of his own deceitful heart."*

---

* *Wheels on Gravel.*

III

School-days, Cardiff City

WHEN I was six I was sent to school, and now the odour of plasticene immediately brings back the large, sunny classroom at Marlborough Road Girls' School. It was a new, well-appointed elementary school of the best type. Here I played with children from the shopping centre of Albany Road, from the new villas about Pen-y-Lan, and from the very poor localities behind Walnut Tree Cottage. I made many friends from all these varieties of schoolmates, and my birthday parties on the lawn, with strawberry teas and ice-cream, and my Christmas parties in the Nursery with their tree and games, were always strongly attended.

I tended to make friends more with girls older than myself, one of whom I remember, had developed a taste for *The Lady of Shalott*. This was my first glimpse of real poetry, and eventually I learned it from her, saying it verse by verse, but always leaving her to come out with the dramatic, " The CURSE has come upon me! "

My sister hurt my feelings deeply as usual, by suggesting that shallots had something to do with onions. And in return, with one of my rare flashes of aggression, I called her an " asset " (a mere ass hardly seemed strong enough).

Needless to say mother and Kathleen made great capital out of my mistake, and I can hear my sister now chanting, " So I'm an asset to you, am I, dear child? "

While I grew red with mortification declaring, " You know very well what I mean if I *have* got the wrong word."

When I discovered that the fruit of the ash had one wing and the sycamore two, I began to make a collection of fruits of the wild. My sister reinstated herself in my opinion by producing a box with sections, and neatly labelling each one for me. Beech-nuts, acorns and conkers were added to hazel-nut and blackberry (which soon grew mouldy) and then ears of corn, hips and haws. I kept the box until it fell to pieces.

Even before I had started school I had begun to visualise the real country as an ideal place in which to live. When we picnicked on the

27

mountains I prayed that I might be left behind, deciding I could exist on blackberries, nuts and mushrooms, or the raw grain from the harvest fields, for ever and ever. Once at school these sentiments and opinions were more than confirmed.

On Saturdays when I was not playing in the garden with my new schoolfriends I was taken further afield by mother's help and my nurse-maid, Ethel Field. She helped us for several years and is now a respected member of the nursing profession. Now, when I look at some modern " nurse-maids " I give thanks for this friend of my childhood.

She walked me beyond Pen-y-Lan Hill to the real country which was not then built upon, as I believe it now is. Here there were mushrooms, rabbits, pheasants and other wonders, at such time the idea of a home in the country was a heaven on earth to me.

Sometimes we went toward the Docks instead, seeing all colours and nationalities in the drab doorways, and then reaching the shining, heaving expanse of sea would watch the noisy gulls and gaze across to the shores of Somerset.

Sometimes we took tea to Roath Park, boiling a kettle on the penny-in-the-slot gas-rings provided by the Corporation. In the winter we took a tram up the City Road, looked at the Castle and then ended up in the National Museum of Wales.

I know of no other city whose municipal buildings are so well designed or placed in such a fine setting as those in Cardiff. Nor, for its size and commerce do I know of a cleaner city. The idea, held by so many who have never visited it, that Cardiff is a dirty colliery town is laughable. It is not dirty even to the extent of its neighbour, Bristol. Apart from the docks, which, as most water-fronts, contain a little of everything including squalor, the city is amazingly clean and well run. Thinking my attitude to the place might spring from a childhood prejudice in its favour I revisited it after this last war, only to have my early impressions confirmed. Shortly afterwards I met a gentleman from Denmark who told me that the municipal buildings of Cardiff struck him as being only second to the buildings of Paris, in their cleanliness and tasteful arrangement. I consider this high praise from a much-travelled Continental.

For myself, I had to come to truly rural Somerset before I saw a pit-head, and the idea of Cardiff as a mining town is absurd. The only betrayal of Cardiff's connection with the coal-industry is the weekly descent of The Valley (as the inhabitants of the Rhondda Valley are called) for their weekly shopping, entertainment or football matches. Welsh is rarely spoken in Cardiff which on the whole is as cosmopolitan as most sea-ports.

I was now becoming more and more impressed by the wonders and beauties of nature. The reflected glory of a winter sunset in the little stream at Rumney, would have Ethel tugging at me to be home in time for tea. Horses, cows, sheep, pigs, all interested me, signs of farming, like haymaking and harvest, held me spell-bound—I would rather watch them than a circus. I thought the countryside a wonderful treasure-trove of beauty and pleasure to be enjoyed whenever I was permitted.

The colours of autumn always had (and still have) a peculiar attraction for me, spring, which is supposed to be the festival of youth, has never held the same power.

The first poem I wrote, two years after I started school, was about the autumn and began:

> " When the red leaves are on the ground
>   And the plovers flocking round,
>   Hark the rooks call loud and clear
>   Autumn's here, Autumn's here! "

The great force latent in natural beauty now had me fairly and squarely in its grip, and I thought of little but the countryside. I planned to live in a stone hut up on the mountains, in a cabin in a forest clearing, in a shack beside the river, in a tent upon the beach.

I egged on equally adventurous friends to be up at dawn with me and walk to the mountains or find the source of the Rumney stream. That we never reached the one nor found the other, makes little difference, we were outside in the dew and the sunlight. Although we knew little of what we saw, we knew that it was all good and wholly ours. We picked the nuts and blackberries and rubbed the ears of corn between our hands to taste the " flour."

Now that I was bigger I accompanied mother on train trips to the nearby beauty spots such as Cefn-On and The Garth, where we would wander among the ash-thickets and bracken, torrents and boulders until we came out on some wide, turfy upland commanding wide and beatiful vistas.

Often did I turn over in my mind the possibilities of my hiding in some glen so that the family returned without me. For often these excursions included my sister, her young man and some of his large family of brothers and sisters.

I longed to be left alone with the ragged thorn trees of the mountains, though I was not so certain what I should do when darkness fell.

Mother's chant of:

> " Up the airy mountain
> Down the rushy glen,
> We dare not go ahunting
> For fear of little men."

only increased the glamour of these places for me. I wished with all my heart that the " little men " would take me to live with them. Many years later I put some of these early aspirations on paper in my book for children, *The Magic Moor*.

I did not enjoy the visits to the seaside quite so much. Barry Island, Cold Knapp and Penarth lack wilderness, and in the season are flooded with large crowds. I did, however, enjoy the trips across the Bristol Channel to Weston-super-Mare, where I first set foot on English soil—in the county of Somerset, which later was to have my whole heart.

My sister, on one of these visits to Weston, took me up the pre-historic battle hill of Worlebury, and long it stayed in my memory— the glittering town below, the sandy coast, the dark nose of Brean jutting into the sea, and the coasts of Wales across the shining water.

" Look! That is Cardiff—There's the smoke from the Dowlais Works on the way to Newport—Look! Further down there's Penarth."

When I asked Kathleen who had lived on Worlebury, building the stone walls and digging the ditches, she replied quite briefly that it was " Giants."

I was deeply awed by this possibility, even if unsure whether to believe her.

Well, perhaps there were giants in the west in those days, who could tear Worlebury, Dolebury and the rest from the soil and rock of Somerset with antler-picks so that they should remain two thousand years for us to see.

During this last war gun emplacements were set within the ramparts of Worlebury, which once commanded the routes to the Roman lead-mines on Mendip, and to half the roads across Somerset.

This business of believing my sister, was a little bit of a trial to me. I knew very well that I ought to, she was very clever, had not mother told me so, even had I been unable to see for myself? She was also both " level-headed " and " business-like ", two phrases of mother's which I did not think likely she would ever apply to me. It was natural for me to accept everything that Kathleen told me and not argue about it, but just occasionally I permitted myself the high treason of wondering if she was always perfectly right.

I was enjoying my first experience of school and welcomed all I could learn, taking Welsh, though it was not a compulsory subject. Although I cannot speak the language with anything like fluency, I have never regretted those lessons, in the first place they won me my first essay-prize (the subject was Howell Dda) and secondly I have always since been able to pronounce those holiday resorts beginning with double L's!

Although I was learning fast at school, could read and write with ease, and knew all about the Ancient Britons, Boadicea and Caractacus, I had not learned to develop a harder " interior ".

Very occasionally Ethel Field was allowed to take me to the cinema. On one of these occasions we saw the then " Idol of Millions," Rudolph Valentino, in *The Four Horsemen of the Apocalypse*. I can remember little of this old silent picture beyond one flaming caption which stated that the hero was going " Into the jaws of hell on earth—WAR! "

The impact of this caption set my thoughts on the dreaded subject again, only again to be reassured by my mother, " There will never be another."

All through the years I have remembered that fire-dripping dragon's head drooling the letters to form that searing message. I thought of it in 1939 and again when I saw the newsreels, when I was bombed myself, and when I saw the miserable refugees. Why had not mankind taken heed after that other war—the people who had realised the truth about war so that they had called it " hell on earth " where were they? why had they not come forward to point the truth. Or were they dead and silent? Had every generation to learn the truth of this afresh?

Next to war and cruelty, mother's occasional stories of her childhood touched me most deeply. There was one in particular, called " The Plain Piece Story ", which touched me to the heart and which I can still hear her telling as if it were only yesterday. The Plain Piece had nothing to do with cake with no fruit in it, as you may be imagining.

On the contrary it was the name given to a piece of ground used for sports and picnics. It was a general rendezvous for the affairs of the rural locality of Worksop. How far it was from my mother's crowded cottage home I have no way of telling, her memory, or the short legs of childhood may have exaggerated the distance, but it was certainly a place devoted to high days and holidays and should have held first place in the happy memories of my mother's childhood, instead of it being one of the saddest among many that were sad.

Sixty years ago the children of the poor had few treats and pleasures other than those of the field and byway. " Pictures ", cheap books, organised holidays were not theirs, but there was, aye, there always was " The Whitsun Treat ". On that favoured Monday, all those who had attended Sunday School were transported in waggons to the scene of the festivities, to the Plain Piece.

Alas, my mother and her young brother whom she was " minding ", were late leaving home, punctuality was not one of my maternal grandmother's failings. When one has thirteen children and scarcely as many shillings a week upon which to feed and clothe them, time is not so very important.

When mother and her brother arrived at the rendezvous for departure, behold the waggons had left sometime—without them. As I listened to the tale I saw again the clean faces, the starched pinafores awaiting there in the Whitsun sunlight, while the dire fact smote home to the palpitating little hearts—" They have gone without us."

My mother stemmed her tears to grasp Georgie by the hand and set out grimly for the Plain Piece. Every now and then they would break into a run, but Georgie's legs were short and chubby, the day was hot and the road dusty, besides which they were extraordinarily hungry. When they eventually reached the Plain Piece, the festivities were over, the waggons loading up once more, and all the food gone.

A teacher found them some nuts—all that was left of the spread, and they rode home.

It is worth noting that my mother always saw *her* two children were in good time for any event. For myself I try never to be late for anything—the lesson of the Plain Piece went home. When it was first told me it made me exceedingly unhappy so that I wanted to turn back the clock and meet those two struggling children hastening after the departed waggons—wanted to meet them and take them aboard my gig, or pony-cart, and bear them to the Plain Piece as the feast was set, and give them sixpence each (at *least* sixpence) and a whole orange each, and—and——

How passionately did I want to make it " all come right " for them, and how little do we change fundamentally as we get older.

At five or six hearing the epic of Plain Piece, to right it was my wish. Twenty years afterwards, looking for a publisher for my first country book I glanced along our bookcase. I saw the name of Walter Raymond and remembered that he was a Yeovilian, the publishers were Hodder and Stoughton, so to them I sent the *Chronicles of Church Farm*. The Raymond book that had suggested a publisher for me was *The Book of Simple Delights*. In it is the tale of an old woman of Withypool on Exmoor who had a son at London Station. He was a porter, and as she grew older and lonelier, she longed to see him again. One day she went to London and expected to see her son at the Station. Instead she saw " a pack of people ", and at length having the temerity to ask one of them for her boy Benjamin who was " a porter to London Station ", was informed there were many stations. She could not read or write so she sat on a seat under the dome of Paddington, while the flowers she had brought for her unmet daughter-in-law wilted to hay in her hand, and the lollipops she had bought for her grandchildren ran in her pocket and stuck to her handkerchief so that she must needs mop her brow with her sleeve.

When night fell she took her return seat to the west and it was growing dawn on such another misty-hot morning as the one in which she had left, when she put the key in her cottage door once more. But she could not turn the key, she just " Sot upon step and cried ".

As I read that story, *A Landscape with Figures*, at the highly mature age of twenty-six I could have leapt up, got my car out and been in Withypool within an hour or so, saying, " You shall see your Benjamin, today—" But, the old woman was gone, as Raymond who reported her story was gone, and the tragedy of that journey to London was buried along with the story of Plain Piece, or Howard Spring's Massacre of Peterloo in his book *Fame is the Spur*. Dead, long past things, but how they still have power to move to compassion and regret, to make us say, " If only these things could have been made right."

But if sadness touched me deeply, joy did likewise, and on the mountains, straying down to the ruins of Caerphilly's castle, or lying hidden from the rest of the picnic-party in some ferny-dell I knew more than happiness. The grey outcropping of rocks amid the sage-green turf, the wide wheel of clouds above the mountain tops, the torrents accompanying the narrow roadways before the cottage doors all transformed the world for me. I saw wonder in the sheep dotting the smooth hills with a mushroom-white gleam of newly-shorn fleece, the wide vistas of the valley, the light and shade of the ash groves and oak thickets, in the sight of squirrel or rabbit, hare or buzzard. I began to know the ash by her slender fingers, and that the oak was more gold than green. One day I suggested this latter fact to mother, but she failed to agree. Shortly afterwards, at a painting-lesson I learned that yellow and blue make green, which only proved that there must be more yellow or more blue in some of the greens of trees, which accounted for the fact that oaks looked more gold than green. I felt this discovery to be somehow momentous, but my sister called me a " Funny kid " and went back to playing of " rag-time " on our old piano.

She had the passing ambition to play at the local cinema, but mother had forbade it because of the hours and because cinema work in general was considered " not quite nice ".

Silent pictures were still the rule and a piano accompaniment was necessary to render " Hearts and Flowers " when the heroine was turned out into the snow, or " Egmont ", when the hero was spurring to the rescue.

My sister abandoned the cinema idea and concentrated on accompanying her new young man who had a fine tenor voice. He was so good that he was commissioned to sing on the wireless in the old Savoy Hill days and we all listened through our headphones to " Kathleen ", " Nirvana ", " Macushla " and " The Song of Songs ". We were all very proud. My favourite was " Nirvana ". I liked the weird romantic element, the " tremolo " in the base and the idea of the " dumb gods " being " shattered ".

The rag-time was rather departing from Walnut Tree Cottage, and " The Little Irish Girl " and " Take a Pair of Sparkling Eyes " replacing it.

I found that some music, not particularly songs, gave me something of the same sort of sensations which I experienced in the open country. I began to love music and find my way about.

I did not early learn to love Chopin nor Beethoven (apart from " Egmont " and " Leonora "), the former was too thin and fine for me, the latter too imposing and heavy. But the " in between " merchants like Mendelssohn and Dvorak I could appreciate easily.

As I left Cardiff when I was ten, all I did there is in a separate pigeon-hole of my memory which helps me to date it. After my tenth birthday I never stood by the old concert-pitch piano in the narrow dining-room at Walnut Tree Cottage, nor listened to my sister play, nor sat with headphones glued to my ears. After that date I have to visualise other rooms, modern wirelesses and more often than not, no sister.

In the Cardiff days I had come to know and like what would today be called " tea-time " music—the kind heard on the " Palm-Court of Grand Hotel." Strauss and Lehar, " One Fine Day " and the " Barcarolle " from the *Tales of Hoffman*, " Because " and " Valse Triste." Before I could pronounce " Hirondelle " I could trill in something like tune, " If I had the wings of a swallow ", while I soared high on the swing at the bottom of the garden.

I could hum the enchanting melody of " Where the Woods are Green ", while I played in my elder-bush wigwam, or sing most of the words of Woodeforde Finden's *Indian Love Lyrics*. The Strauss waltzes I knew by name and had most of their tunes sorted out in my mind, but the most splendid waltz of them all, the waltz to which it was impossible NOT to dance, was not composed by the " Gay Vienna " man at all. It came from the mind and heart of the dreamy, introspective, brave, hard-working Piotr Ilyitch Tschaikowsky. The waltz from *Eugene Onegin* set my feet singing. I could never resist its lilt and used to pray that they would play it on the " wireless " as a real treat from having only myself to hum it.

Similarly " Chanson Triste " set my heart weeping, and the words " I am but a simple maid " kindly supplied by my sister did nothing to lessen its appeal for me.

I did not then know that they were both products of the same composer, nor had I then met " The Nutcracker Suite " or " Eighteen-Twelve ", or any of the other best-known works of Tschaikowsky. But I gave a great welcome to the first two ambassadors he sent to the stronghold of my musical taste.

Growing close upon ten years old, loving every daisy upon the lawn, and every hour spent on the mountains, delighting impartially in birds, blackberries, Tennyson and *Eugene Onegin*, it would seem that house and playmates had but a small part in my scheme of things. This is both true and untrue.

When I found anything good, be it tune, apple or *Ivanhoe*, I imme-

diately wished to share it and thereby double, nay treble the joy of it.
But I was also anxious not to share the things with the wrong person,
I soon found, as I was to discover even more in after life, that one may
share one thing with one person, another with another, but very rarely
indeed, everything with one and the same.

My experiences of snubbing from my sister taught me that much
early in life. If I was properly humble and ready to learn I might talk
to her of music, but *not* of dancing or poetry. She ridiculed both; I
could, on the other hand talk of poetry to her young man, Montie.
He had an ear for rhymes and rhythm and could quote whole chunks of
Tennyson's "Revenge", beginning: "At Flores in the Azores Sir
Richard Grenville Lay," following this up with "The Pied Piper of
Hamelin", which always held me awestruck. He had a prodigious
memory and although I felt he hardly took his poetry seriously, it was
something to meet a person who knew anything of the subject at all.

My friends were many and varied and always inclined to be much
older than myself (as they still are). What will happen if I ever grow
to be an old, old lady I wonder, will I have no friends at all, or will I
revert to the other extreme and make friends of the very young—if
they will have me, which is of course doubtful!

My friends in Cardiff ranged from those who shared my " wigwam " at the bottom of the garden, to the elderly Major with whom I
would discuss animals and the state of things in general. There was
also an old gentleman of the name of Cronin who gave me two pet
pigeons christened by my sister "Flotsam and Jetsam." His elderly
daughters were keen on handicrafts and taught me to make raffia hats
and to manufacture cardboard dolls with cardboard clothes complete
from hat to shoes that hooked on to the model.

When the weather compelled me to be indoors I played long and
intricate floor games with my friends or by myself with the assistance
of the dog Mack. We made puppets and staged a show (never very
successful) with a clown named " Boko ". After this initial excursion
into the puppet world my admiration goes out to those who master
them professionally.

We made farmyards with ponds made of looking-glass and cottages
of corks and matchboxes. There were villages with silver-paper church
towers and forests of fir cones and acorns. We marshalled, arranged
and organised ; the dog was served from our model shop for which we
had been half the afternoon writing out price-tickets.

In spite of these absorbing afternoons often spent in the company of friends I never minded being alone. The hours spent in the wide window-sills reading G. A. Henty, or Arthur Mee's *My Magazine* were some of the most satisfying and most dearly remembered. I can recall reading a book called, *The Honour of the School*, one hot summer lying among the grasses of the Wilderness, and another called, *A Girl's Loyalty*, sitting behind the window curtains when fog shrouded the Albany Road.

Two ladies who kept a drapery shop just down the road were always very kind to me and often gave me little items of display cards, etc., for my shop-games. One of them is now dead but the other is still as much a friend as ever and we write to each other regularly and occasionally meet. She came originally from Bridport in Dorset and I was primed by her, even in those early days, with some real West-Country sayings. Nearly all the tradespeople were our friends, many of them had received their custom at the " Big House " on the recommendation of my father. All were very kind to me, and have afforded me many happy memories of Cardiff.

In the April before my tenth birthday my mother announced that we were leaving the city. She was inclined to be tearful herself, all her friends and ties were there, it had been her home for almost two decades.

My father had " thrown up his job ", a habit that was to become increasingly frequent.

At ten I was eager for adventure, I did not mind the thought of moving at all. I could write to Eira and Beryl, Jessie and Glennis, Doreen and Lorna. Of course I was sorry to leave my school and teachers with whom I had been extremely happy, but there was no reason why my reception should not be as warm in the next school. I was fairly good at lessons, properly brought up, a good mixer and ready to learn.

Now " Where to? " was all I asked.

The answer was some time forthcoming. My mother bitterly bemoaned taking me from the Marlborough Road Girls' School where there were over 400 pupils in the lower school alone, she bemoaned taking me from the Church House concerts where I did so well singing " Burlington Bertie ", in a proper evening-dress suit made for the purpose. She bemoaned leaving my sister to go into lodgings and above all was she sorry to part with her large, warm circle of friends

37

and acquaintances. Her address book still contains many Cardiff entries—indeed neither of us have shed our friends how ever often we moved.

" Where are we going? " I kept asking, and at length I was told. " A little country town in Wiltshire (my sister had obtained all the particulars from the A.A. handbook). A place with markets instead of good schools—a little tuppenny-halfpenny place—called Warminster."

" Is it in the country? " I asked.

" Oh RIGHT in the country," answered my mother with what I now take to be something like misgiving.

That was *all* I needed to know. " Rabbits, Mack! Rabbits!" I cried, to see the dog prick up his velvet brown ears intelligently. " We are going to the country and you will see Rabbits! "

IV

Warminster in Wiltshire

FROM out of the dark mouth of the Severn Tunnel we burst forth into England. It was April and a time of violent rainstorms and equally violent sunshine. We arrived at Warminster's tiny station (so odd to me after the Termini of Cardiff) to the accompaniment of a rainbow. I was more than delighted at this phenomenon.

Sniffing the clean, rain-washed air of this downland countryside I observed the exciting white scars of old chalk-pits on the line of hills above the railway, and the crouching shape of copse and wood. What a fine, clean, open country it looked.

A taxi bore us through a tidy little town and up a great hill crowned by a lofty church. Then we turned off and ran along the crest of the hill for some way, the golden rods of rain beginning to fall once more, and the rainbow bravely striving to shine through them. The celandines that starred the hedgebank either side of us, shone and glistened as if newly varnished.

"What a lot of buttercups!" exclaimed my mother. I was too excited to think of correcting her. I could see a shaggy mass of woodland marching over a bright green hillside to halt by the banks of a shining stream. Our hill-road overlooked a wide expanse of watermeadow intersected with sparkling water-ways.

On the very edge of the hillside the taxi pulled up and we were deposited before a veritable doll's house perched on the side of a sloping garden.

The newness of the tiny bungalow, its paint scarcely dry, the rawness of the half-made garden, the freshness of the rainwashed day in the opening month of the year were all symbolic of the fine new life awaiting me here.

I found the woods full of primroses, the banks fragrant with the wild white violet, the tender bracken fronds unfurling, the marsh busy with trout. I found the evening air wild with curlew cries and the rides lit by chestnut tapers. For the first time I heard the mocking, inviting notes of the cuckoo, the serenade of the nightingale, the mournful hoot of the barn owl. I gathered bluebells and then armsful of marsh-marigolds as foils to the blue flowers.

Where our lane descended to the marsh lands, there began a walk known locally as " Up the Leg and Down the Stocking ", or more briefly as " Up the Leg ". This walk, as the Americans would put it, " had everything ".

First of all it bordered the water-meadows and all the teeming life they supported. Here, the aerobatics of the black and white lapwings were breathtaking to watch, and their calling strange, wild and full of yearning. Here, the fat trout, facing upstream, waggled with the current, almost invisible in the claret-coloured water, or dreamed away in the shadow of the luxuriant growth on the river banks. Here, bloomed fine wild flowers, king-cups and lady-smocks, cuckoo-pints and water-plants that were nameless to me.

Then two streams had to be crossed by two rustic bridges, and a diving water-rat might be seen, and almost always a busy moor-hen and her bobbing brood where the willows trailed their feathery tresses in the clear swirling waters.

After the bridges, the track branched off through a field by a hunting gate, climbing slowly past fine hawthorn trees towards the inviting woodland. Here was a happy mixture of old and new. There were opulent rhododendrons and sear, ancient oaks, majestic beeches and newly planted larches, all mingled happily above a perfect sea of bluebells.

The walk led through the heart of this woodland, frequently breaking into open glades and clearings, dappled with wood anemones and startled with pigeons' wings. Brightly coloured fungi blossomed above last year's fallen leaves. Here were fir-cones, pine-needles, beech-mast, hazel-nuts and acorns. Here were foxes and rabbits and sometimes a busy, flashing squirrel.

The birds of the woodland were legion—they were indeed the vocal expression of this lovely place. Their wood-notes were its music and its background, their voices such enchantment that they became part of the air one breathed and they would have only been noticed had they suddenly ceased. I did not know their names, nor their individual voices, except the outstanding soloists like jay and cuckoo, but I was yet aware that they added immeasurably to the beauty of primrose bank or mossy glade, and my cup of beauty and happiness threatened to overflow.

The path left the wood and turned down a steep-banked lane, crowned with ash trees and bramble and loud with the voices of nearby flocks. Down, down went the lane, twisting through wood-shaded hollows, and so back to the river-bridges and home again.

This walk was just one of the many with which the little town of Warminster is blessed. There are others, many others, not all have escaped the ravages of time, war and " progress ", but they are not greatly altered from the days I knew them as a child.

There were walks by the Folly stream, by Crockerton Mill, by The Deverills, through the woods of Longleat, by the lakes of Shearwater, among the glades and beeches of Heavensgate, or over the rolling immemorial downs that linked the woods with the town, and the lakes with the water-meadows, that joined and divided, that beckoned and repelled in all this wide and generous landscape.

My school did nothing to mar the beauty or spoil the new-found joy for me. I had long wished for a friend or parent who knew and cared about the things that mattered to me. If only I could have gone walks with someone who would have told me the names of things, pointed out their habits and peculiarities, so that I might learn and know! My new schoolmistress went a little way towards reme-dying this lack. Not nearly enough of course, for she could be with me little, in or out of school hours, but at least she did make a start.

Mrs. Wyer was kind, firm, and full of a proper recognition of the part natural study should play in the world. She was always willing to name any flower or herb I might bring to her for identification. She encouraged me to write and was always ready to lend me books. As the first summer drew on she took me with her to Salisbury, and on the way, taught me the difference between oats, wheat and barley. Years later, I was astounded at the number of adults, including my sister, who could not distinguish one cereal from another.

Here of course, one might say, well why should your sister know one from the other any more than you should know the numbers and destinations of the London buses? My only answer to that is one given me by a member of my publishing house.

" It seems to me personally, that there are certain things every living person *ought* to know—natural things, that if our civilisation crashed, would still remain to us—things like how to milk a cow or ride a horse —just as one automatically grows up these days to drive a car or use the telephone."

I loved Salisbury with its magnificent spire, its secluded greens, old buildings and busy market. I thought it a fine place and was no less thrilled to find that this matchless spire in the Avon Valley was on the same level as the Town-Hall steps of our own little town. Twenty-one miles to the north-west I was living as high as the top of that Cathedral—higher in fact, for the dwellers beyond Christchurch Hill were above the Town Hall.

This drive to Salisbury took us pass Battlesbury, Scratchbury and Middle-Hill, all hill-forts of great strength and impressiveness. I was awed by them. Further along, on some of the gentler slopes, service men of the last war had emulated the men who carved out our West Country White Horses, and left their regimental badges and mottoes in the clean chalk of the hillside, but already, some were growing faint.

The little school at Warminster was a mixed one, and for some time I sat next to a tow-haired boy whose compositions were plentifully sprinkled with terms like mangel-wurzels and muck-spreading. He was knowledgeable about farming matters but little else. He read in a jerky, halting voice with much prompting from his desk-mate. Each afternoon, a battered motor-bus bore him and his companions from other classes, away from the school, down the hill, out of the town and up the climbing, winding white road to Imber.

" Imber on the down
Six miles from any town."

As the spring blossoms disappeared in the blaze of full summer, when mushrooms took the place of cowslips in the meadows, and the wild gypsy-rose was succeeded by the honeysuckle, I decided to investigate this magic place called Imber.

I was joined in the expedition by a school friend living in the nearby village of Bishopstrow. She was the daughter of the Master and Matron of the local workhouse, or " Union " as it was called, and was fortunate enough to live in a charming thatched house by a river that was complete with a mill.

To get to her house I must go " Up the Leg ", across some water-meadows and along by the river. This was a fine start to our expedition. Leaving Bishopstrow we climbed steeply by the great entrenchments of Battlesbury and, panting and warm, came out in the fresh breezes of Salisbury Plain.

The downs were lovely that summer. I was much taken by the blue cushioned heads of the scabious, by the magic of the dew-pond (the mechanics of which my friend Ruth tried rather unsuccessfully to explain to me). We saw the flying clouds reflected in its calm surface, we saw the woolly flocks coming down to drink, and talked awhile with the shepherd and fondled his shaggy flea-bitten dog. The cloud-shadows chased across the hills before us. We were grown-up, we could talk to strange people—we were pioneers, explorers, adventurers. There was no such thing as home, parents or school today. It was a holiday and we were ourselves. We had set out to find the promised land of Imber, where the boys knew all about mangel-wurzels!

At length our road wound gently down from the high ground, revealing a comfortable sort of village, well-sheltered by trees and watered by a bright brook. We found a cache of hen's eggs in the long grasses beside the road and thought it would be fun to try them. But the first one we cracked was badly addled, so we left the rest alone.

We meandered about Imber, gazing up at the venerable church, tip-toeing inside to stare at the Crusaders' supine on their tombs, conscious all the time that we were seeing how " the other half lives ".

We would tell the Imber children when they came back to school that we had seen their village, meanwhile we saw no one we knew, and so we footed it back again, running wild over the sweet turf, and nibbling the apples and sweets we had brought to fortify ourselves on this epic journey.

I went to Imber again in 1939 when the village had just been re-conditioned by the local Council. It looked trim and thriving, and the signs of harvest in the fields were more than promising.

Two years after this last war had finished I went again, and so grieved and shocked was I, that I said it would be for the last time.

Creeper had met entirely across the face of one good farmhouse, so that it turned sightless windows to the broken road. All about was neglect, waste and decay, and only hordes of rabbits used the village street. I was reminded of Tennyson's " Mariana in the Moated Grange " :

" With blackest moss the flower-pots
Where thickly crusted, one and all;
The rusted nails fell from the knots
That held the pear to the gable wall.
The broken sheds looked sad and strange,
Unlifted was the clinking latch;
Weeded and worn the ancient thatch,"

I looked about me and saw a village dying, though not yet beyond hope of recovery for many of the buildings were still sound, and the new houses were hardly affected.

As I write this, Imber is quite dead, its fate sealed by a War Office statement beginning: " Owing to the increased size and range of modern weapons—it was decided that the village would have to be evacuated——"

I can remember Imber as a thriving village, whose people were of an independent turn of mind, and whose acres produced good food for the nation.

Now the great wrinkled folds of the Downs, their generous sweep and breadth were beginning to exert the attraction they still hold for me. I felt free, happy, and immensely adult, when roaming their open, cloud-shadowed spaces. I was grown-up, with a mind of my own, thinking great thoughts which were entirely my own property and no longer subject to the criticisms of my elders. I had indeed immortal longings in me, to which I could lay no name, but which momentarily could make me as wise, gracious and bold as the landscape which surrounded me.

I took a 'bus to the next town, Westbury, and walked out to the famous White Horse, Wiltshire's oldest. Here I sat in the monster's eye, sufficiently large, so the guide-book told me, to accommodate eight persons. The folds of the Downs beneath this prehistoric monument, were fluid as water, and their pattern delighted and awed me. I began to wish I could paint, or even draw successfully. But alas ! I was good at none of these things, I seemed good only at looking and observing, at watching and beholding, at knowing and admiring.

But the Downs had not my whole heart. I divided my allegiance between them and the fragrant woods whose spires were reflected in the waters of the lakes. Here wavelets lapped a shore carpeted with pine needles and embossed with gnarled roots and bronzed mosses.

Once again the sense of smell comes to evoke recollection, and the tang of sun-warmed fir-bark, damp after rain, the pungent earthy smell of the woods in autumn, or the fresh green odour of growth in the springtime when the larches are a living green fire, can transport me back to Warminster, and I am ten years old again.

At Cardiff I had seen dead pheasants, strung out in the game larders of the " Big House " after a " shoot", but now I saw the live bird in all his Chinaman's glory, and heard his unexpected note. For the first time I saw the spooky bullet-headed white owl at close quarters, shuffling uneasily upon the limb of gnarled oak, regarding me balefully the while.

I found my first magpie's nest, lidded and wonderfully made, saw my first congregation of swallows meeting for their farewell flight. When the exotic rhododendrons had fallen, and the azaleas burned themselves out I found the woods bright with berries and glorious with turning leaves. Just to walk alone in them was joy enough. It was living.

At Warminster I found my first scarlet pimpernel at the same time as I first read the book of that name, and as I came to discover Shelley, watched for myself the lark flinging himself into the blue sky, such a tiny scrap of life to outpour so much music.

> "Higher still and higher,
> From the earth thou springest,
> Like a cloud of fire,
> The blue deep thou wingest,
> And singing still doth soar, And soaring ever singest."

There was so much, so many things contributing all at once to the beauty and joy of living that sometimes I seemed in danger of being overwhelmed. The loveliness and the happiness sometimes went too deep for any form of self-expression beyond weeping and I had been brought up to despise tears.

This intense happiness and appreciation I found much easier to bear and take lightly if I had a companion. The friends I made in these Warminster days went deeper and lasted longer than any others so far. At first there would seem to be wide differences between us. They took their heritage very much for granted, while it was all new to me. But I for one, felt I was with my own kind of people, and any gulf between Cardiff City and the Wiltshire countryside was easily bridged.

My mother, on the other hand, made no real friends here and certainly none to replace her city ones. So many country people were " not quite refined ", while country housing was definitely " primitive ". However, she was well pleased with all scenes of natural beauty, and set about making the best of things, as was her habit.

Her fortitude was soon to be required of her as my father " threw up his job " again and we were threatened with another move which would make heavy inroads into the family savings.

The immediate danger was averted by a compromise. My father

went off to London on " supply " work, and mother and I moved into an unpretentious bungalow near the marsh.

The fact that we had to come down from our high hill I found amply compensated by the fact that we had the unparalleled attraction of a real brook flowing through our garden. Moreover, it was a very proper brook, crossed by a plain wooden bridge and with all the attendant wonders of mills, hatches, and water-wheels.

The Folly brook was flanked by mushroom fields and cowslip meadows and was busy with minnows and fresh-water shrimps, its course was exciting and varied. In places, as in our garden, it ran deeply between high banks, presumably to avoid the risk of flood, in other places it sparkled over pebbly shallows or spread out into muddy drinking bays for the cattle. There were sharpish meanders resulting in gravelly shallows on one side and overhanging banks on the other, there were little stony, muddy islands left at low water. Overgrown hedges, running down field boundaries, met across the course of the brook, trapping sticks and debris and making a natural dam sometimes resulting in deep pools and miniature waterfalls.

One of the first games I played in our new home was to map the course of our little " river ". There was " Half-Moon Bay " where the three old shorthorns, Nancy, Dolly and Granny, came to slake their thirst; there was " Willow Bridge " where a venerable old withy leaned so far across the stream that it was possible to climb into it and then jump down on the further bank, dry shod (well almost!); there was the Leaning Fir, Tadpole Corner, and Wopsie Beach. This last was the place where we found a wasp's nest in the grassy bank, a thing of frightening wonder and intricacy, eventually dug out by my father on one of his visits home. This same beach was a certain place to catch a glimpse of a whiskered water-vole.

The Folly was an ideal playground, it afforded such a variety of pursuits and pastimes that one hardly knew what might turn up next. Boredom was unknown, and toys, beyond an occasional toy boat were unnecessary. Sometimes we would bring these boats, purchased for a few pence, and set them over a given course, with a prize for those who arrived first. Many never arrived at all, or only did so after frantic poking and pushing made by the skipper with the aid of a long stick. Sometimes they would meet with disaster, sink, or drift broadside on over some minor rapid, or drift under some overhanging bank and defy all our efforts to dislodge them, or sometimes, even *find* them.

Sunny day after sunny day would find us taking our tea out and eating it beside Half Moon Bay or Willow Bridge, or with bread and jam in one hand and our " daps " in the other, kicking up the bright water all the way down Wopsie Beach.

The fields on either side of the Folly varied from pastures complete with cattle, to a rather stony arable, and from open marsh land, to meadows laid up for hay. Thus we found a variety of scenery and employment merely by paddling down the brook.

One day my friends and I set out to trace the Folly to its source. That we were progressing *downstream,* never seemed to occur to any of us. How often have I smiled at that since! Armed with a day's provisions, and our shoes knotted over our shoulders, we boldly set out. We had not gone far from home when the brook went to earth in a culvert leaving us completely baulked. That it appeared again only a few yards away on the other side of the highway never entered our heads, so we abandoned the expedition and gave ourselves up to playing leap-frog over stooked corn.

In return for the hospitality given by my brook, one of my friends who lived " just down the road " offered to take me to one of her favourite picnic places, called, above all things " The Isle of Man ".

Off we trudged along the road to Maiden Bradley, I could see no sea, no lake, no river even, so how there could be any island defeated me. Presently we burst through the hedge of a ploughed field, and there was our destination before us, and I was forced to exclaim, " Why it is just LIKE an island."

The " sea " was an expanse of ploughed furrows, and from it rose the " island " of what I have since taken to be a large round barrow, or artificial burial mound of some kind. It was crowned with a group of pines, honeycombed with rabbit-holes and plentifully decorated with brambles and pine-cones. It was exactly the right kind of place for a picnic.

We scrambled up its sides out of the stormy sea, pretending we were shipwrecked sailors. The furrows of the field were the waves, the banks below us were the sea-cliffs, and the woods across the flat field were " the mainland ". From this shore came the peculiar " Cok-Cok " of the pheasant, and occasionally we could see the vivid plumage at the " water's edge ". We said they were parrots in the jungle. Beyond were the whalebacked Downs like the bluffs of some distant islands. We returned to this spot again and again.

I have heard it called " The Life of Man " and I am not sure that this name does not give added credence to the barrow suggestion. Perhaps some Bronze Age chieftain was buried there, and the name " Life of Man " is a relic of legend concerning the place, such matters have a habit of dying hard.

I was learning, learning all the time but never could any knowledge have been reached by more pleasant and natural paths.

The curriculum at Sambourne Elementary, Mixed, Church of England School was sufficient and most happily balanced. The Three R's, games, sport, art, literature were all blended into one useful whole which makes Sambourne stand out in my mind, after half a dozen other schools, as what an elementary school should be.

We learned the words of hymns by writing them out during the first period of each week, thereby fixing the words in our minds more firmly, and practising our handwriting at the same time. The boys were taught gardening and the girls sewing (no highfalutin terms like " needle-work " in those days). I was not too good at this subject and Mrs. Wyer would patiently show me how to stroke gathers, to draw threads and to hem-stitch handkerchiefs, and how to darn properly, so that the hole was not drawn up.

Tuesday was composition day and there I came into my own. Once a composition of mine was read aloud to the class, but Mrs. Wyer hastened to deflate my pride by explaining to me in camera that my country-bred class-mates had been brought up with a greater concern for material things and were not encouraged at home in any gift for words. Therefore it was to be expected that if I went again to a city school I should hardly shine so brightly. Lack of that kind of competition here must not encourage me to be lazy. No! I must work well and work hard, and practise my handwriting which was VERY BAD INDEED!

All was going well, my fair-haired, freckled, sunny-tempered friend Ethel, was made Captain of the House, Ruth from Bishopstrow had the advantage of a brother and sister at college and was forging ahead with all subjects and my first " boy-friend " was doing very well indeed.

At fourteen, Norman Gilbert had become organist of Norton Bavant church, a downland village just outside Warminster. He could play the Moonlight Sonata so that I was carried away on a tide of notes, or thump out " Finlandia " until the ornaments must be removed from the piano. We knew him for a prodigy and a genius but he was also a very nice person in his own right, but more fond of the indoors than the outdoors, so my friendship with him was kept very much in one pigeon-hole, and the real adventures were reserved to be shared with Ruth and Ethel, or Dorothy and Margery from the local orphanage.

I practised hard enough to be able to play a very simple duet with Norman at a school concert, but thereafter I lapsed sadly, finding music altogether beyond me in the role of performer.

In the company of Ruth and Ethel I practised the high-jump and hurdling, and managed to do very well at the local sports day.

Yes, things were going well, and then scholarship time came along. Ethel did not compete, but Norman, Ruth and myself won the coveted awards, and went our separate ways. Norman to the Boys' School, and Ruth to a lower form than myself as she was a year younger. But at least our destinations were roughly the same, for we were all bound for Trowbridge High School, nine miles away.

I was loath to leave the hymn-singing, and sewing classes of Sambourne, and the painting sessions when we could bring a bright feather, a bunch of cherries or a spray of flowers for our " live " model. I did not want to stop singing the good old songs like " Old John Braddelum " and " Shenandoah ", nor miss the gusto with which the boys demanded " *What* shall we do with a drunken sailor? "

I was in no hurry to leave those Shakespeare readings, when as Helena I had been given some very saucy lines to deliver:

" Oh spite, Oh Hell, I see you all are bent
    To set against me for your merriment."

while Margery Tanner from the orphanage did a dignified job of Hermia, and her soul-mate Dorothy Burrows limped over the thankless part of Lysander.

It is more than twenty years since I left Sambourne School, but the same master and mistress are there, unchanged to my eyes except for a few grey hairs. On a recent visit I found the same atmosphere still obtained, although the school had been altered structurally, and innovations like school-meals were to be encountered. While I engaged Mrs. Wyer in conversation, her class, as might be expected, attempted to take advantage. The buzz of talking rose.

" Children, you read with your EYES not with your Tongues! " came the sharp reminder.

Then my old schoolmistress permitted the severity of her countenance to soften.

" Used I to speak to you like that when you were Monica Scott? "

Did she? I can see her now, severely regarding a row of " cat's-teeth " stitching, and hear her declare:

" Your instrument is a needle, Monica, NOT a hedge-stake—use it as such."

V

School-days, Trowbridge

WITH a great leap my horizon had now widened to take in a daily train journey, new scenery, new knowledge and the companionship of children living in other places.

Fortunately I was utterly unselfconscious, there was no room in my mind for fear or strangeness, there were only the feelings of exploration and adventure, of being free and yet more free, which seemed to have laid hold of me on the day I first beheld the high, wide, handsome Wiltshire Downs.

In those days the junior forms of the Trowbridge High School for Girls were housed in Ex-Army Huts. This greatly added to the attraction of my new school-life, giving me something of the impression that we were permanently " camping out ". The buildings were airy, warm and well constructed and, I should say, superior to the Nissen Hut type of to-day. At the foot of the wooden steps leading from the long buildings, stretched our playing fields, a generous acreage; and beyond them were the fields and hedge-rows of the true countryside, as yet unbuilt upon. So my new town-school was still in the country. Here we studied nature with an enthusiastic, happy-tempered biology mistress, and more was learned out of doors, in the proper environment for natural and botanical study, than in the " labs ".

An added zest to schooldays were the periodic visits to the senior school within the town. Here were folk-dance festivals, prize-givings and school parties, and here we rubbed shoulders with impressive looking seniors. Should we be like that one day? Ruth and I enquired of each other, even while we made fun of them.

The hopping on and off trains twice daily, and the changes and waits at Westbury, made us all feel extremely self-reliant and grown-up. If there were a hockey-match or other important event, we might even have to stay till a later train and not get home until after seven p.m. It was all most adventurous. From the carriage windows we could see wintry sunsets over the elm-studded Vale of the White Horse. For us the fields of home blazed with buttercups, the sallows and bul-rushes waved above Westbury ponds, the autumn beeches burned on

Bratton Downs.   Happy are the children who have a ten mile railway journey every day!

Our landscape-watching was varied by views on each other's prep, by discussions on this and that, or by exchange of plans for the coming " hols ".   If no adults were present in the carriage, somersaults might be indulged in from the luggage-rack, or other acrobatics practised on the upholstered seats.

As for the school hours themselves, they passed pleasantly enough. I had now been introduced to both French and hockey and became ready recruits to both.   A peculiar second-hand hockey-stick was found for a few shillings.   It was so much longer than the modern type that to save me giving " sticks " too often, the top had to be sawn off and a rubber pad put on to save my hands.   But it served me excellently and against modern and expensive sticks made me many a resounding goal.

I continued to be as bad as a human being can over mathematics, but the fact did not trouble me unduly, nor was it allowed to make the rest of my school life a misery, as it did at a later establishment.   My Maths mistress also taught history and was inclined to take a lenient view of my short-comings as I happened to be good at her other subject.

Most of all I loved ancient history and learning about the Hyksos, the Shepherd Kings, and Ur of the Chaldees.   In my mind's eye I watched the Pyramids being built and saw the activities on the banks of the Nile and Euphrates.   I dwelt with the Hanging Gardens of Babylon, the Medes and Persians, Hector, Alexander and Hannibal. Even now my half-baked, experimental interest in archæology can be traced to those early hours in the airy classroom overlooking the playing fields.

Then came the much loved French lessons, with the knowledge that I had an Uncle and Aunt in Belgium spurring me on to pronounce my phonetics with a fine abandon.

The language served to remind me of the roof-top restaurant in Brussels, of my glimpse of King Albert, of Waterloo and Quatre Bras, and the bright shells on the beach at La Panne.   As I mouthed my verbs and memorised my genders I could see Ghent and Ypres and feel a link with the people whose language this was.   It made it all most interesting—and easy.

These excursions into a new language brought an increased interest in my own.   I soon discovered that some words had common roots in more than one language. There was *fenester*—a window in Welsh, for the French *fenêtre*, with similar words in both German and Latin so the French mistress told me after I had voiced my discovery.

Then there was *uscol,* the Welsh for school, the equivalent was the French *école*. The link between French and Welsh was strengthened by a link between Welsh and English with words like avon—a river. I began to take delight in words for their own sake and was recommended R. L. S.'s *Travels with a Donkey in the Cevennes*.

How greatly I enjoyed, what many of the class deemed to be a dull book. Today I still carry a picture in my mind of Robert Louis Stevenson curled up in a sleeping-bag in the howling blackness of a wood, taking bite by bite of the doubtful mixture of chocolate and Bologna sausage, while nearby the exasperating Modestine browsed in the darkness.

The school badge of Trowbridge was a daffodil, conventionally styled. We could draw the flower, full-faced to its trumpet, with the aid of a compass. It seemed to me a lucky and a fitting emblem. Green had become my favourite colour, perhaps because it was the predominating shade of growing things. Trowbridge's green and yellow badge seemed to express the spirit of the time and place. Green for the leaves, yellow for the spring flowers—not just the daffodil, but all those clean new spring flowers, celandines, and crocuses, primroses and buttercups and marsh-marigolds.

I possessed a new and heightened consciousness which made me at one with the rest of the world, however different it might be from my own corner of it. When Robert Louis Stevenson came upon the ring of playing children, at nightfall on the marshes, and they broke up and fled, or when he followed in the tracks of the Wolf of Gévauden, I could identify not only myself with the author, but my surroundings with his. The marshes would be a composite picture of the Wiltshire water-meadows, with the Welsh mountains beyond, and the Beast of Gévauden would have lurked in Southey Woods beyond Crockerton Mill.

I was taking in a great deal, but as yet I felt no desire to be giving out again. At Sambourne I had wished so hard I could paint, or even express myself by playing the piano as well as Norman, but both these accomplishments were obviously quite beyond me. I felt now no wish to write poetry as I had done three years ago at Cardiff. I did my best in my essays, particularly when the subject was in any way connected with my countryside, but there was so much to take in and absorb that it was all sufficient for the time being. If poetry is emotion recollected in tranquillity, how much more so is appreciation of the wonders of nature. At the moment of the sunset, or the bee swarm, the snowfall or the autumn tapestry there is a kind of mental indigestion at so much rich fare. It is only when digested in peace and quiet we can really savour what we have experienced.

I could write about " Romany Cottage ", only after I had left it, about Church Farm only when the stress of battle for cultivations was over, and of the countryside in summer only when winter had cut it off for me.

Similarly I had no wish to be giving out the impressions I was taking in, this would not follow until I was in a city once more, and *recollecting in tranquillity* the teeming life I had known before!

My first Christmas at Trowbridge drew near and a school fancy-dress party was held. I went as Anne Hathaway to a class-mate's Shakespeare, roping in one of the juniors as our offspring in home-made doublet and hose. Our headmistress arrived as a Welsh woman in tall black hat and wimple, and my much admired English mistress, with her smooth honey-coloured coronet of plaits, swept in as something out of classical Greece.

Soon after the party, came my first country snowfall. It was holiday time and there followed tobogganning on the hillside above the marsh. Ethel and Ruth and I were joined together once more as we had been in summer pastimes before the scholarship.

I began to notice a difference between the children who had been left behind at Warminster and those who had gone on to Trowbridge. The boys were going to work on farms and many of them already helped after school and in holiday times, while the girls were going into service. None of them seemed to want learning for learning's sake, as Ruth, Norman and I did. *They* looked forward to leaving school. While the end of our learning days was by no means in sight. Norman was looking ahead to a musical career, Ruth was working towards a college education, but what for me? I knew that what happened to me depended largely on my father's employment, but I did resolve to make the best of whatever came my way. Life seemed full of possibilities, there was so much to it.

I began to notice that although the Sambourne children spoke well enough while in school, when out of it they said things like " I *seen* " and " Are you coming home with I " or " Who done it? ", which my mother assured me were most disgraceful lapses. Before long however I began to notice that she was not entirely blameless, that she pronounced boulders as "boolders" and photograph as "fortagraphs ", and that unless I watched myself I was inclined to do the same, having always followed her example. She would refer to the dog Mack going into " ecstasies of joy " at being taken for a walk, or describe some girl's eyes as being " genetian " blue. All of which I had to unlearn.

Then would come my sister, home on one of her frequent visits, clinging perilously to the back of her fiancé's motor-bike, with a new set of slang expressions on her lips each time. How the fashions changed! I would hear them and then fight them out of my consciousness. I have always hated slang, and yet language can never be entirely free of it, the slang of yesterday is accepted tomorrow, and I am often forced to admit some of the expressions, particularly when they are Americanisms, are forceful word-painting and meet the situation exactly.

But of more recent years I have come to resent the infiltration by means of reputable concerns like the B.B.C. and the better newspapers, terms like " soften up ", " open up," and " check up ", when soften, check, and open, are all that are required. I also resent the term " in years " in place of " for years ", and a word like " cages " being permitted for a place that houses human prisoners of war.

In the Trowbridge days I endeavoured to keep my sister's slang out of my compositions, but I found that the Bible offered no help in the matter of correct language either. To my young way of thinking it seemed entirely reprehensible to meet with phrases like " Our Father *which* art in Heaven " when plainly it should be " who ", or to encounter, in the Book of Common Prayer phrases such as:—
" To acknowledge and confess our manifold sins and wickedness " or—" That we should not dissemble nor cloak them ". This all seemed to be repetition for repetition's sake, and therefore bad English. I also criticised the ambiguity of the following:—

" Give peace in our time, oh Lord, for there is none other that fighteth for us." Now I considered that an insult to the Almighty, yet when I tried to tell others about it, no one could see my point and agree with me.

If God was such a good fighter, and as the God of Israel he was supposed to render his people well-nigh invincible, why ask for peace in that craven manner? If He was really fighting for us, then that should be all that mattered, instead of that we were craving peace because He was the only one who would fight for us. The only one! Surely He was enough?

I began to decide neither Prayer Book nor Bible should be taken too seriously. It was a type of ancient history compiled by some not too scholarly historians whose grammar was on occasions as bad, if not worse, than the children of Warminster's less favoured homes.

The winter season was the time for hockey and now I developed a talent for the game. I might not be able to "slog" as hard as some of the bigger girls, but I was quicker on my feet, and my redoubtable old stick held the ball well in a dribble and tackle. Because of my fleetness of foot I was put on the wing or inner. Though I was very small for my age, and in those days quite painfully thin, the body began to mean more to me than the brain. Gym I loved and I began to long for the day when I could go to the upper school and use all their apparatus. I again competed in the high-jump at the county school sports, and though the youngest in my class was very well placed. I was conscious I was good at games and sports, I was also conscious that I was not pretty, but as yet it troubled me not at all.

In those days I was not the only girl in the form whose long, straight hair was confined in "pig-tails", so I was in no way conspicuous. I realised I was not pretty like Ethel from Sambourne, nor Ruth of the fine eyes, nor had I her long, slim legs, but I could not see that it mattered. Being small and wiry I could "nip" in and out of the hockey field. I had not yet to worry about "carrying" clothes well.

That I was plain, freckled, with not one good feature, and the suspicion of a receding chin, bothered me not at all. People were very civil to me and someone had once remarked that I had nice shaped hands and a very good speaking voice, that seemed quite a bit to be going on with.

My mother did not refer to the subject at all, but always spoke of my sister as being "a very striking girl". I thought she was more than that myself, I thought she was beautiful. Her face was so alive, animated, expressive. Her teeth were white and even, which made her smile dazzling, her skin was good, her hair always waved and shining. Her candid grey eyes were set wide apart beneath nicely arching brows (my own beetled and met in the middle), and her clear-cut aquiline features seemed the perfect complement of her rather tall, tailored figure.

During those Trowbridge years I had begun to realise that there was slight hope of me taking after my sister, but I prepared quite cheerfully to make the best of it. She was wonderful and I'd never grow up like her, but I would develop other things—I'd manage somehow, things wouldn't be too bad!

I read *Ivanhoe* and imagined myself like the Lady Rowena. I did not look in the mirror to verify the difference which I well knew existed. I was all the things that mattered in my own imagination.

Trowbridge High School for Girls knew me for about eighteen months. During this time I continued to explore my own corner of South West Wiltshire in my spare time. My favourite haunts were still " Up the Leg " and Crockerton Mill, the Marsh, The Isle of Man and Southey Woods, but I went further afield, along the high ridge of Downs behind the town station, in the directions of both Bratton and Imber. Once, my Mother and I, walking through the woods by Heavensgate in rhododendron time, attached ourselves to a party being shown over the great mansion of Longleat. I was amazed and delighted at the rich interior of this imposing house, and henceforward, the phrase " stately homes of England " ceased to be hackneyed, it really meant something to me. I stared at lacquered cabinets, at tapestries and oil-paintings, at gilded ceilings and magnificent fireplaces framed in plaster and decorated with heraldry. I pored over Sheraton and Chippendale and warmed to the happy blend of so many ages and fashions within one English home. Later I was to come across Oscar Wilde's *Pen, Pencil and Poison*, an extract from which fitted well the happy profusion of art and wealth that was Longleat:

" —the very keynote of aesthetic eclecticism, I mean the true harmony of all really beautiful things irrespective of age or place, of school or manner. He saw that in decorating a room, which is to be, not a room for show, but a room to live in, we should never aim at any archæological reconstruction of the past, nor burden ourselves with any fanciful necessity for historical accuracy. In this artistic perception he was perfectly right. All beautiful things belong to the same age."

Although I never again went as far as the house, one of my favourite haunts was Heavensgate, with its beautiful beechen frame for Longleat, its lake, deer and backcloth of hills.

Sometimes after supper, it became a habit for Ethel and one or more of her brothers together with myself to run up the Bradley road, through the Heavensgate woods and back by Shearwater. Our running soon deteriorated into a jog-trot, which in turn subsided into a rather breathless walk, but we kept up the movement all the time, padding along in our gym-shoes.

We were quiet enough to encounter much of the natural life of the woods at night. We went always at the time of a full or nearly full moon, so that we had light enough to follow our chosen route easily. But even so there would be patches of inky shadow beneath the great oaks and beeches, or along the thick coniferous plantations. The clearings and glades however were soft and lovely with silvery light, soft bodied moths would blunder into us, cockchafers zoom by, and glowworms sparkle out from between the greenery of the hedge-banks. White-scutted rabbits would whisk away down moonlit tracks, while occasionally a ghostly owl would screech or hoot from close at hand, causing us to momentarily stiffen in our tracks and glance apprehensively about us.

How daring we considered ourselves, the memory of those fresh-dewy, nocturnal runs will long remain with me as a symbol of those happy, Warminster days.

My last love in Warminster was perhaps my greatest and it was very near home. It was a farm (since become a Guest House), set at the edge of water-meadows, which in turn were framed in a crescent of wooded hills. Here was everything which to my young mind rendered life worth living. It became the Chosen Spot. Here would I live and build my house and stay for ever when I was quite grown up!

In early spring there grew upon the banks here, the largest prim-roses, and later the finest bluebells, almost like cultivated flowers. Here the may grew the sweetest and the cuckoo could be heard and even seen more often. Here the spring came earliest, and the autumn brought more beauty. There were chickens, ducks, clean cows, pink, bright-eyed pigs and one fine golden retriever dog. There were blackberries and mushrooms as fine if not finer than any to be dis-covered further afield, and there were apples and plums from which it was possible to gather windfalls in due season. One of the pastures boasted two felled tree-trunks that made a fine playground, for the end of one felled giant soared high above the ground and by a hazardous balancing effort one could stand on the farthest extremity and enjoy a superiority over the surrounding country. If the cows came grazing too near, we could pretend we were treed by savage wild animals, and plan our escape for when baulked hunger should eventually drive them away.

Connecting the farm with an upper pasture on the summit of a hill overlooking the water-meadows, was a delightful little lane edged with fallen chestnuts. It now led to a fine field of clover, rich with the scent of the honey-sweet flowers. Here I searched for a seven leaf clover, but always in vain, but I liked to feel the dewy leaves against my bare legs.

It was to this field I came when I had to say " good-bye " to Warminster. I ran unsteadily up the Deverill road, that takes its name from the Deverill villages which, with Crockerton, were known locally as " the seven devils and a crocodile ", and there found myself looking down on the farm of my choice.

It seemed as if I were the pebble dropped into the centre of a pond. The first ring of ripples round me was the clover field, the next were the green pastures, round them again were the marshes, and beyond the shaggy fringe of woodland, beyond that again was the outermost ripple-ring of all, the rounded ranges of the Downs with their slopes turning a golden-green in the evening sunlight.

I was too deeply moved for coherent thinking. This was the first real parting of my life and I hated it. It was the first time I had to leave part of myself anywhere. Why could I not stay here always, with my friends and my happy school, the mistresses I had grown to know and like, and all the beauty that had become part of me—my stream, my battle-scarred Downs, my woods and meadows? Oh how dreadful to have to say good-bye to it all. What was there left?

I spoke to the white scars of Warminster Down, to the crouching shadow of Cop Heap Wood above the Station, to all the things and places visible and invisible which I had come to hold so dear. What is there for me? I asked them agonisedly. Why should I have to go to London—are there woods and downs there? Are there owls and squirrels and picnic places?

So I stood and looked and knew for the first time that adults know nothing when they say childhood has no troubles or problems. Then it came to me, a resolve that was a ray of hope, a resolve that made the parting bearable.

I would go to London, I would look into that great city, I would explore its art galleries and libraries, I would visit the Tower and Buckingham Palace, no one hereafter should accuse me of being a country-bumpkin, but when I'd served my enforced apprenticeship I would COME BACK.

Perhaps I must wait until I was sixteen, eighteen, twenty, but I would come back. I made my chosen field a solemn promise, plucking a clover-head and pulling its petals apart one by one as if in some ritual. Then, dropping the petals among their magic leaves, I swore,

" I will come back to you some day. I will, I will, I will." The rain came down and drove my petals with goblin feet into the soft soil of the meadow. I went home slowly. It was my last night in Warminster.

VI

The Tree of Knowledge

" We should now clearly recognise the fact that the wealth and the
knowledge and the culture of the few do not constitute civilisation
and do not of themselves advance us towards a ' perfect social
state '. Our vast manufacturing system, our gigantic commerce,
our crowded towns and cities, support and continually renew a
mass of human misery and crime absolutely greater than has ever
existed before—This is the lesson I have been taught by my observations of uncivilised man."

A. R. WALLACE. *The Malay Archipelago.*

AT Reading station, the uniformed boys on the platform offered
" T'ppney haypney bars of plyne choclit " and I began to
realise we were in foreign parts. Up to this point I had still felt
at home. The tongues of porters and passengers alike were vaguely
familiar, and the landscape was but a renewal and variation of those to
which I was accustomed.

But Reading began a new world, from thence onwards, the farms
and cottages began to disappear, to be replaced by drab villas, tatty-
looking shacks and bungalows decorated with hen-runs or a few
tethered goats. The very trees and soil took on a poorer aspect. The
bridges were ugly, the streams without character, the hills shorn of
majesty. The land became steadily flatter and steadily more swamped
by a fungus growth of ugly building. In vain I looked for the age-old
repeated Mary of farm, manor and church. Yes, we were come to
foreign parts.

The last few miles running into Paddington were bad indeed. My
mother, who spent all her days trying to " keep things nice ", turned
away in horror and disgust. The squalor and ugliness of that approach
to Paddington was my first glimpse of Dick Whittington's city, whose
streets were paved with gold. They are also the first glimpse that
travellers up from the West must receive of the Capital of the world.
Well, well! A rural slum may be picturesque and at least it has the
merit of good clean air all round it, and fine fields in which the children
can play—but these! Now where was my Mother's jibe about the

" primitive " housing conditions of Warminster? She said little. She had been to London before, had indeed lived in Oxford Street for some time. She remembered the fine centre of the city (finer still before some of the alterations of the past 30 years) and had told me nothing of this sordid frame.

The gloomy roar of Paddington enveloped us. It was summer and the sun was trying to penetrate the murk. I stared aghast at Praed Street and the Edgware Road, I had never imagined anything like this—how did all those dingy little shops keep open? Where were the people they served? Did they live in rabbit-warrens at the back somewhere?

And then, past Baker Street and the Marylebone Road, the taxi turned into a new world, a pleasant and serene country. Here, the sun shone clearly enough, here was peace and beauty again.

The broad highway was flanked by gracious trees, and beyond were the far stretching realms of Regent's Park—flower-beds, trees and shrubs and acres of grass where there were actually sheep.

Through the other window could be glimpsed tall houses fronted by formal gardens with classical stone balustrades—the kind seen on biscuit tin lids with Harlequin and Columbine disporting in the moonlight. The farther we went the better were the houses, until sweeping round to Cumberland Terrace it seemed as if the architect had excelled himself.

Here plainness and austerity vanished. Here were columns and porticos and pillars, decorated fanlights and an array of fine statuary along the Parthenon-like roof tops.

I grasped Mack's lead firmly while my Mother supervised the unloading of our luggage. I gazed upwards over the well-proportioned Regency houses, deciding this was " Quality Street " or that at any moment Jane Austen might arrive with sweeping skirts and a parasol, escorted perhaps by a pair of brightly uniformed officers.

It was the place for a Carriage and Pair, but instead I could only see a car with a large studded bonnet, which I later discovered to be a Rolls-Royce, and a " Nannie " shepherding her charges to their wellbred games in the ornamental gardens, while beyond, the children of Camden Town disported themselves amid the yellowing grass of the Park.

Mack had discovered an ageing spaniel who apparently lived at our new home and I had to drag the little terrier " below-stairs " to save him making mincemeat of the elder dog. It was " below-stairs " we were going to live. The basement was all ours, the rest of the house belonged to my father's employers. My bedroom was at the front of the building facing the Park, and by getting close to the windows and peering between the iron bars I could just glimpse part of a beech tree and a small remnant of sky. All the other windows or skylights looked out on a tiny " area " or the cobbled Mews, where over the spiked wall could be seen the Albany Street Barracks.

My mother considered the " Albany " part a good omen, even if it were suffixed with " street ". I had been born at Albany Road, Cardiff. I was soon sent out into the street to find suitable shops and purchase a few necessities such as bread and milk, while mother unpacked. Albany Street was rather exciting, the ample Cockney woman who served me was ingratiating and intimidating, all in a breath. As I turned the corner by the Terrace, some dirty, wild-looking children on their way to the Park ran after me shouting :

" Anna Mye Wong! Anna Mye Wong! "

My dark plaits and straight fringe seemed to suggest to them some resemblance between myself and the Chinese film-star. I ignored them, as I knew mother would have me do, and made my way to our new home clutching the loaf and the bottle.

After safely delivering my shopping, the next thing to do was to take Mack for a run in the Park. I dodged cruising taxis and opulent looking cars, and slipped the leash undone as soon as we touched the grass. The air seemed good in the Park after Albany Street. Mothers were shepherding excited children towards the South Gate of the Zoo. I could hear the solitary roar of a lion and the staccato barking of the seals. It seemed a big park, quite a tidy bit of country to explore when I had the opportunity. As it was, I had been told not to go far nor be away long, so I turned my back on the old gentleman feeding the pigeons and sparrows, and the student earnestly consulting the pages of a text-book, as he sat hunched up on one of the Broadwalk benches. Coming home across the Outer Circle highway, I looped the lead through Mack's collar, instead of clipping it in properly. A lady with a yapping Peke was passing on the other side of the road. Mack incensed, suddenly made a dart, the lead slipped from my hand, ran through his collar, caught with a jerk by the handle end, and the clip fastened in the fleshy part of the third finger of my left hand.

A Taxi-man, crawling by, on the look-out for fares, saw what happened, saw the blood run down my hand as I tried to take the dog's pull with my other.

I gained the pavement. The lady with the Peke held Mack by his collar while her own charge attempted to tie her into knots. How I admired her fearlessness. The Taxi-driver manœuvred the clasp out of my hand. It was something like removing a fish-hook, but presently it was out and I was able to suck the wound clean. It did not seem too bad, though it stung a little. I can still see the faint scar, after all this time.

Well, that was my welcome to London—slums and a fair park, " Anna Mye Wong " and the kindness of two strangers to a little girl with an oriental " hair-do ".

That evening, the " family upstairs " being away, I explored the rest of the house. On the ground floor was a fine dining-room, all shining mahogany, like some still dark waters, with silverware gleaming against heavy curtains, and a carpet that muffled the tread. The well-proportioned windows gave on to the formal terrace and gardens. It was a very different world from Warminster.

There were five floors altogether, and on the next was a sumptuous green-and-gold brocaded drawing-room with the largest settee I have ever seen. It was JUST the place for turning somersaults, better even than the padded seats of the Warminster-Trowbridge railway-carriages. I practised acrobatics on it (having first taken the precaution to remove my shoes) until I was exhausted. Then I strolled across to the tall french windows that opened on to an iron balcony. They commanded the Park which was now flooding with the westering sun. The sounds from the Park were too far distant to intrude on the silence that filled the tall house.

It was so quiet, filled with pools of shadow and bars of sunlight, that it was almost like being in some silent wood—" And no birds sing ". The nursery, which was the next room to be explored, was on the other side of the house and no sun reached it. It was too dark to look well in the toy cupboard and I hesitated to switch on the electric light, so I mounted still higher, following the sun.

Now I came to bedrooms, the like of which I had never seen before unless it be in pictures. They were all flashing satin quilts and hangings, and cut-glass toilet fitments, and shining silver-articles.

Nearby were the bathrooms, all marble and glass with many tall

Cumberland Terrace, Regents Park

Whitestaunton Lodge, Church and Manor gateway

flasks of highly scented bath salts. I tried the chromium taps tentatively and wondered what it would be like to bath in such a place. I even tried the queer little foot-bath and investigated talcums and bath-essences before proceeding to the floor above.

And now the richly carpeted stairs ceased and cold linoleum led me to the servants' quarters high under the roof. These were drab, comfortless and lacking in interest. But from the topmost landing an iron-runged step-ladder led to the roof. I climbed it and pushed open the trap-door. I had come out on the roof at the front of the house. Before me, the slope of the tiles and the crowning line of statuary hid the road and park from me. I turned round. Behind me the roof line was level and London lay spread out like a map.

The dome and twin towers of St. Paul's were easily recognisable from illustrations. For the rest, the City was a mass of roofs, of great blocks of masonry that soared above their neighbours, of spires and towers, steeples and chimneys, softened with evening wisps of smoke-haze and domed by the evening sky of summer, pricked out with the first stars.

From the barracks over the way, lonely notes floated up to me beyond the hum of traffic from Albany Street. It was like being on top of the world, up there in the gathering darkness, looking across London. Cities have their moments of beauty and this was one of them.

On my way down I found one of the landing-windows opened on to a small roof-garden, furnished with hydrangeas in tubs, and chairs and tables made from barrels, gaily painted. Pausing to examine this original method of furnishing I heard a perfect cascade of piano music issuing from a skylight a little further along the terrace.

" Da, diddle dee, diddle dee, diddle dee, diddle dee, diddle dee."

I listened until the last note died away, and then I scuttled down to our realms in the basement.

" Someone up the road can't half play the piano! " I exclaimed to my father, who was helping mother to put the house in order. They were playing a scale-sort of thing that goes on and on ' Da-diddle Dee ' until it runs downhill and finishes *beautifully*."

" You hardly surprise me," answered my father drily. " Mark Hambourg lives there. It may have been he or his daughter Michal."

I had heard of Mark Hambourg from Norman. I had an idea

he played mostly Beethoven. But Beethoven had never sounded like that. The notes chased each other through my brain and I hung on to the fluttering little tune until one day, much later, I eventually learned its title. It was the Chopin Etude in G Flat—the " Butterfly ".

Such was my introduction to Chopin. Before I had finished with London I was to learn much more about music and about many other matters which I had not even considered before. It was to be a time of growing (without the pains) both mentally and physically.

The fourth school which my mother now had to set about finding for me was the Camden School for Girls, a sister school to the North London Collegiate. Though unremarkable in its situation, Prince of Wales Road, Kentish Town, it stands out for me as the model of what every good Girls' School should be. My scholarship, together with a substantial grant to cover books, etc., had been transferred from Trowbridge, but I was not accepted without a personal interview.

My new Headmistress was tall, grey-haired and severe, so that I quailed while I admired. After this initial interview we returned home with a list of compulsory uniform and a formidable array of unbreakable rules and regulations. First of all, everything appertaining to clothing must be bought through the school tailors, everything from shoe-bags to gym-knickers. For " best " in the summer, we wore tussore silk dresses of a kind shade of green trimmed with natural tussore collars and cuffs. These dresses averaged about thirty shillings each, according to size, which seemed a huge sum for a girl's dress in those days. For every-day summer wear, there were green-and-white striped cotton tennis-dresses, and panama hats with the school band, in colours green and blue.

(Green for the grass, blue for sky, said I, well content with this extension of the green and yellow colour scheme of Trowbridge.)

During the winter term green gym-tunics and square necked blouses were worn, with a special high-necked silk blouse for " functions ". In addition there were hat-bands, ties, blazers, name-tapes, rain-coats, top-coats, stockings and swimming-costumes to be bought— all strictly uniform. There was absolutely no fear of the varied income-groups who attended the school, dressing differently from each other in *any* respect, thereby inviting odious comparison among each other.

Some of the unbreakable rules were:—

> Watches will not be worn except by prefects.
> Fountain Pens will not be used except by prefects.
> No jewellery will be permitted in any form.
> Gloves will always be worn in the street.
> Eating in the streets, public vehicles, etc., is on no
>   account permitted.
>   And so on——

After the helter-skelter rough and tumble of my Trowbridge days, I fell in with these rules better than might have been anticipated. The motto of my new school was " Onwards and Upwards ", and it was onwards and upwards I desired most to go, so sacrificing a few odd bits of freedom on the way hardly seemed to matter. Manfully did I determine to be worthy of this fine new school.

And now, lest the reader, in these days of makeshift, lowering of qualities and slackening of discipline, think that undue stress was laid upon the outward and visible signs of this school's culture, let me hasten to add, the inward and spiritual were equally well cared for. The standard was high in every department. No phase of education for life was neglected. I have often wondered how different my own future would have been had I been able to stay at the Camden as long as I wished. Its old girls have distinguished themselves in so many walks of life, because there was always a real attempt, quite early in school-life, to ascertain the special trends and talents of each pupil. There was a " mass-grounding " in the things that matter, but no mass-production beyond that. The individual counted at The Camden. In the later forms, every period spent was intended to further the learning and personality of each girl to the top of her bent.

Each form had three divisions—bright, medium and not so bright. In the main, it was the scholarship girls who occupied the top section, while the paying pupils were divided between the other two, but quite often, as in my own case, it was found necessary to spend some periods in one division and some in another.

My main position was the middle or medium division, but for English and history I was elevated to the top class, while for maths and science I had to go below. In this way, the pace of most members of each class was nearly the same, and the most forward pupils were not held back for the backward ones.

Each new period found me moving from classroom to classroom, with my books secured by a strap, enjoying my upper-class subjects immensely, muddling through the middle periods, and floundering hopelessly at maths and science as usual.

Presently my case was reviewed, and I asked to be allowed to try cookery, but eventually decided in favour of a ballad class instead. I did however have one cookery lesson, at which I was armed with the school-cookery book, which I still possess and often use; and where I learned to make a very proper sponge-cake, using eggs, flour and sugar only, and no fat. During these times of rationing my one cookery lesson has come into its own, and I have been able to make a speciality of my fatless-sponges. I never forgot how we were shown to prepare the tin, dusting it with a firm coating of mingled flour and castor sugar, so the cake would turn out purposely, beating the eggs with the sugar until the great air bubbles broke on the surface. Many, many people have asked me for the secret of my sponges and as I try to explain the technique, they usually finish by saying, " Oh, I could never have the patience for all *that*."

Yes, the Camden taught us how to do things the right way, even to making sponge cakes.

The ballad classes, which fitted in with my one free period each week better than the cookery ones, were a great source of delight to me. The ballads may not have been great poetry, but there was something stirring and very English. I thrilled to the tale of Sir Patrick Spens:—
" The King's daughter of Norroway, 'tis thou must bring her hame."
I was moved by the fate of Lord Ullin's daughter and the great hunting in Chevy Chase. I do not consider those ballad hours were wasted. It brought the heather and the burns, the bracken and the forest glade, the deer, the mountains and the sea-coast into that little top class-room in Prince of Wales Road, Kentish Town.

At the same time, in the course of the more orthodox English lessons, I was learning to appreciate Keats, Shelley and Tennyson, and the matchless sonnets of Shakespeare.

" Can I compare thee to a summer's day?
Thou art more lovely and more temperate."

There followed Browning and Mathew Arnold, Milton and Byron, and all the singing poets, Herrick and Sidney and Lovelace, who adorn the pages of Palgrave's *Golden Treasury*.

In the matter of appreciation of literature I was at one with the city scholars, but when it came to physical culture I found, in spite of my healthy country upbringing, I was far behind. I had never worked with horizontal bars, climbed the ropes, or used a vaulting-horse— nor, more important than all the rest, had I learned how to swim !

My long hours of hockey had kept me fit and vigorous, and I had soon mastered the apparatus and found a keen delight in the gym-periods, but swimming did not come so easily.

I learned all the strokes, but it seemed to take more confidence than I possessed to take both feet from the bottom of the baths while I practised them. My problem was soon solved however. I had grown to like the water well enough, even though I could not swim, so that when Mother took me on an outing to Runnymede, I must needs bathe in the Thames. The wash from a passing launch soon had me off my feet and I found myself swimming several strokes in order to reach the shore again. After that, everything came easily and I spent as much time in the swimming baths as I could.

At school, living in the memories of past beauties in Wiltshire, I again began to write poetry, some of it was published in the school magazine. My mind was alive to every impression and I became interested in people as I had been interested in trees and flowers.

My friends were of widely different types and races. Among them was Morita M. who came from the shores of the Black Sea, and Hertha B. who was pure German and adored Adolf Hitler and all he was beginning to do for her countrymen; there was Anne Marie O. who was a French Swiss and who could recite the metric tables with an authentic accent; there was Ivy H. whose mother was Lancashire and father was Chinese (she was a scholarship girl) and there was Henrietta D., a heavy handsome Jewess.

They all brought something to their friendships, beyond an un-questioning friendliness—some spirit of discovery and comradeship I have valued to this day. The actor's daughter, the assistant-editor's daughter, the retired business man's daughter made no fuss at all about me living in a basement, or my father being an indoor servant. They were broadminded and tolerant. One friend, who was a brilliant girl, had a mother who kept a stall in the Caledonian Market, and who wore tiny gold rings in her ears, like any gypsy. But we liked and admired Kathleen for herself, not for her parents or environment. The test was: " Was she a good sort—could she swim, was she good at games, did she excel at English or some other subject? was she a sport and a decent friend, an asset to the form? Well then, what did anything else matter. We all looked alike in our uniforms didn't we? "

Class distinction had no cause to worry me at this school, and I found the memory of the Camden tradition dying hard with me in later years.

In spite of the prevalence of uniform, the Camden girls were fashion conscious. They persuaded me to have my plaits cut off and my hair waved, and to manicure my nails (though coloured polish was forbidden). It was also considered the correct thing to wear silk stockings with holiday clothes and not socks or gym stockings as I had always done. Fashion was losing the cloche hat and the low-waisted shapeless look of the twenties. Waists were coming high again, skirts were flowing fully, colours were coming back from the beiges and fawns and khakis of the " aftermath ". Film stars and actresses were studied, and there was a proper consciousness of the part dress and grooming can play in a woman's life—we were now commencing on our " teens ". And although the word " teen-ager " had not yet been coined, we were all more or less resolved to make the best of ourselves. We were no longer children, we were beginning to have " shapes ". Henrietta, who was fourteen, even laid claims to sex-appeal. I felt very gauche and immature against some of them, but it hardly bothered me, there was a sprinkling of tom-boys in my form as well, and we all seemed to get on very well together.

At the school Christmas Party, some of them turned up in real long, grown-up party dresses. I was one of the two or three who had not left their childhood sufficiently, or whose parents had not been able to find the wherewithal, to be so becomingly attired. I wore my " function " school-dress and my enjoyment was in no way impaired— a year more and it might have been, I do not know. I still think uniform is a good idea!

When in the following spring, my sister was married, I had to play bridesmaid in the same school-dress, although I understood that a long flowing affair and a wreath of flowers would have been " the thing ". I did feel that a little, but after all, it was my sister's wedding—wait until mine came along, I'd make up for it—I'd look like a dream in white, with veiling and orange blossom and a sheaf of lilies, and pearls in my hair—and everything. It did not really matter, I could wait.

The Camden had little more than a yard for a playground, though it was beautified by a large mulberry tree, under whose shade we drank our " elevenses " milk and nibbled our biscuits. Our tennis courts were away at Parliament Hill, and our hockey-pitches at Burnt Oak. Visits to these (made two or three times a week) involved tube, bus or tram journeys. We returned to our homes unsupervised and I soon found myself plunging about London's transport system like a native. The Trowbridge-Warminster line possessed no escalators!

I was not very keen about tennis, but I did very well at hockey, having practised so hard at Trowbridge, and was soon in the junior eleven.

Life was very good and very full in those days. My schoolhours could scarcely have been happier, nor better spent. At home, it was less happy. Never before had we lived so much with my father's work. Always before we had been in a house of our own some distance away. I for one, must neither be seen nor heard, our dog must be kept out of the way of the " family's " dog, and our bathwater must not be drawn off until " upstairs " had had their sufficiency.

Meanwhile our kitchen living-room was a right-of-way from the garage in the Mews to " upstairs ", our tiny scullery was stacked with dinner party washing-up and our premises thickened with the sulphuric fumes of the central-heating boiler.

My mother hated to hear me having to call our employer's eight year old daughter " Miss Betty ", or to have to " Sir " or " Madam " anyone who came through our kitchen on the way to those upper regions. " Miss Betty " sometimes broke away from her dreary governess and came to play with me. She was old for her eight years and I quickly detected that she envied me my school and my degree of freedom. She was poised and self-assured and vaguely resembling Heather Thatcher to whom she was distantly related.

At Christmas she gave me a present I still use and shall always treasure—a Reeves paint-box which I used all my schooldays. Also being a member of the Zoological Society she gave me a season ticket to the Zoo.

I spent many half-days roaming the Gardens. I loved the penguins, the bears of the Mappin Terrace, the little active lemurs, the pacing slinking wolves, but above all did I like the Bird House.

The rapture with which I watched those myriad flitting feathered bodies, of tits and finches, weaving beautiful, delicate symphonies of sound and colour in their high cages, reminded me of the best of my days in the woods at Warminster. At such times I was back there in spirit, but never with a shadow of unhappiness. I had perfect faith that when this apprenticeship was over I would go back there, even as I had promised My Field. I would take back with me all this new-found knowledge and experience to an even greater appreciation and understanding of all that beauty and goodness which just waited for me.

I never visualised building on my field, nor the army desecrating Imber, nor the ribbon-development nor the jerry-building that can assail and despoil. Warminster would wait the same as ever, untouched and perfect as I had always known it. This was more than a hope, this was a faith, and I am happy to say, as *real faith*, it did not go unrewarded.

Ruth and Ethel both came to spend holidays with me in London, and I wrote occasional letters to Norman, though I did not see him again for some years. When Ruth came to stay, we daringly conducted a midnight feast, on the roof-top, and without being detected. One of the ingredients of the feast was a tin of sardines, from which the opener broke off rather prematurely so that we had to fish out the contents with the aid of a hair-grip.

Now my sister had a home of her own and a proper cabinet gramophone, she gave us her little portable machine and " Miss Betty " brought down a whole pile of records which she said were not wanted any more.

Most of them were pre-electrical recordings, and some were so old that they were recorded on one side only, but there was some good stuff among them. I now possessed the whole of the " Casse Noisette Suite", Irene Scharrer playing studies and nocturnes of Chopin, and suites like the Caucasian Sketches of Ivanov Ippolitov and the " Karelia " of Sibelius. There were pieces like " Dubinushka ", "La Mariposa " and " Valse Triste ". Mother called it all " heavy, weird music", but I liked it very much, and the Tschaikowsky especially brought back a keen desire to dance. Dancing lessons at the Camden were however an "extra " and therefore beyond my reach. When at a school concert, some of the pupils gave a display, I longed and longed to possess their prowess. Here was no precocity, no ill-bred, untalented " showing-off". The dancing class were taught by the gym-mistress, and they reflected her admirable technique and craftsmanship in their every movement. This was dancing as it *should* be. I did not know I was really getting my first taste of " ballet ".

At home I tried to memorise their steps and copy their arm and hand movements which were obviously part of one correlated whole.

I wrote to Norman of my interest and ambition in this new art. He was now fifteen years old and a fully-fledged organist, he dabbled in local pantomime and concert party—he was expressing himself in ways denied me. But his advice came back :

" Practise that dancing—borrow books on Ballet, do backbends and ' splits ' and ' high-kicks ' and all the exercises, and don't go in for this tap-dancing which isn't real dancing at all."

" This tap dancing " was sweeping the entertainment world, fostered by the influx of American films with sound tracks. Now as I walked from Regent's Park to Kentish Town I saw the flaunting hoardings advertising " Great 100% all-talking Film-Show "—the stars were Bebe Daniels, Eddie Cantor and Ronald Colman. Ann Harding and Frederick March were " coming up ", Clark Gable had yet to be discovered, but Richard Dix, Tom Mix and Jack Holt were there, so were Marie Dressler and Wallace Beery. The Silent Era had passed.

Occasionally Mother and I would vary our visits to the Tower, Madame Tussaud's, Richmond, Epping or Hampstead, by visits to the Polytechnic Cinema in Regent Street. We saw *Africa Speaks, Rango* and Frank Buck and Cherry Kearton travelogues.

The world was opening wider and wider. I was beginning to know London and more than London. My sister, living first in Staffordshire and then at Leeds, invited me to spend short holidays with her. The long train-journeys, undertaken alone, were full of interest for me. I saw Chesterfield's crooked spire and the slag-heaps of Etruria, I climbed the Yorkshire Moors and took the " Transporter " from Widnes to Runcorn.

I was always glad to return to the South. For one thing I had developed a very strong friendship for a girl whose father was a chauffeur, living a little further along the Terrace. He drove a fine Packard for his employer and an old Clyno himself. The car had a dickey-seat and occasionally on a Sunday we fared forth to Box Hill and Staines, to Reigate and St. Albans, and once, even as far afield as Brighton. It was my first experience of the delights of motoring, and sitting in the open dickey-seat I soon learned that although almost every part of London looks alike, with a Woolworths, a " Co-op " and a " Fifty Shilling Tailors ", the countryside has each place a character of its own, so that Essex is not like Surrey, nor Hertfordshire like Kent.

Daphne attended the Burlington School for Girls off Regent Street, she seemed more in the heart of London than I was, and she was a confirmed film-fan.

With her I saw *Trader Horn* and was left speechless by the gripping adventure of this amazing film. Although I have seen Harry Carey (the Trader) and Duncan Renaldo (Peru) a few times since, I have never been able to find the champion blonde screamer Edwina Booth again. I heard she contracted some kind of jungle fever after the filming of that great picture. I remember her tiger temper and her lovely limbs and wonder again and again whatever became of such undoubted " star-material ".

Another memorable film which we saw together was *City Lights*. Mother had told me that I should not like Charlie Chaplin, that I should find him " too silly to laugh at ". How wrong she was. She had not taken into consideration that " hard outside—soft-inside " that was my birthright. At the spectacle of this gallant little man fighting a world single-handed I could not prevent the tears from flowing. Daphne was quite surprised, so I sat it round again just to prove that I could control myself. I can remember the effort of will that involved, the chewing of my handkerchief, and the concentrating on the head in the row in front of me.

Virginia Cherrill as the blind flower seller, added immeasurably to the film's effect on me. I never saw her again either, but later learned that she had married into the English nobility. She was *very* beautiful, with a roses and cream beauty. Sylvia Sidney in *Madame Butterfly* also made the tears flow. I believe these are the only two pictures that have ever had this effect, and I was surprised at myself. I was however " growing up ", and I was beginning to think more about things in general, and the world in particular and not just myself and my own small share of it.

The effect engendered by the touching tale of Mother's " Plain Piece " or the harrowing account of *Reynard the Fox* was now equalled by my feelings on contemplating Man versus the City. I was beginning to *know* for a certainty, that which I had been suspecting for some time as I viewed the crowds of Camden Town and the Caledonian Market, of the Potteries and the Back to Backs at Leeds—that when Man received a raw deal from the City, it was very raw *indeed*, with no mitigation. Besides his misery and privation, his squalor and poverty, the lot of the poor *countryman* was a happy one.

I found too, that the financially better off people spent all their spare time trying to get out of London. Everyone went to the sea and the country whenever they could. The wealthier the people the more often they " got out ". The " family upstairs " went for months at a time during the summer, the very poor of Camden Town seemed to manage about one day—at Southend, enlivened by a few Sundays on " The Heath ".

It seemed strange to me—By these standards our remote ancestors were better off. The cave-dwellers, the hunters and food-gatherers, could have picnics any day they wanted to, they could always enjoy the sea, and the woods and hills. *They* were in the midst of them already, but modern man, had to save and scrape and plot and plan to see his own countryside or sea-coast for a few hours each year.

It was a funny state of affairs to be called by the name of " Progress ". Here, when I was thirteen years old, the film *City Lights* brought home to me the truth contained in a book I was not to discover until I was thirty :

" Humanity has reached a point in the evolution of our race when we know for certain it is a simple life alone that brings to human beings that desirable condition known as happiness. We have reached a point where the fallacy has been exposed, that the increase of social intercourse and the apparatus of social pleasure, does anything but murder real happiness—these rocks and stones have now in their new shapes of master-slave machines, begun to dominate our lives from quite a new angle; and modern men and women who give no thought to the elements, find themselves compelled all day long to wait on iron, to serve steel, to obey the commands of stone. Never since it built the pyramids has Humanity lived so closely to the inanimate; and when we walk through the iron and stone canyons of a modern city—a feeling comes over us as if the mountain we have fled from, and the rocky fastnesses we have desecrated, have risen up again, like vast overpowering Frankensteins—to reduce us to appalling insignificance."*

Charlie Chaplin walked away into the sunset—the unknown—clutching the hand of his little waif. The City receded, the clouds welcomed him.

*John Cowper Powys, *The Philosophy of Solitude*.

VII

Enchantment

IT was a hot summer and the Camden School for Girls was closed for nine long weeks. The building was being redecorated which accounted for what was an even longer summer break than usual. On the last day of term we chanted:—

> "No more Latin, nor more French,
> No more sitting on the fifth form bench."

And we ate for the last time for nine weeks the school-dinners at the long tables in the dining-hall. Here the excited conversations buzzed into life, and for once the prefects made no attempt to quell them. My friend Mavis was off to Paignton for a few weeks. Delyse F., the Italian girl with the blue-black hair and exquisite colouring, was bound for Switzerland. There were talks of Continental Expresses, ships and sailings, of launches on the Norfolk Broads or cars bound for the Highlands of Scotland. I envied none of them. I was going to Warminster—alone.

How brightly the sun beamed down on Regent's Park that end of term. The trees and grass were golden, the pavements hot under the sultry July sky. There were rivers at Warminster and cool woods, and a tiny open air swimming-pool in the little park.

"Change at Westbury," said the Ticket Inspector. I nodded happily. Had I not been changing at Westbury for two years? Did I not know *ALL* about this particular line of the Great Western Railway?

The White Horse came into sight. I blinked, and there were the Downs again, rolling shoulder on shoulder and crest on crest. Then there was Cop Heap, that well-shaped crouching mass of wood above the little station, there were the gleam of assembled milk-churns, and Ethel's mother waiting to meet me.

I stayed in Warminster a fortnight. During the first week I went over all the familiar much loved ground in Ethel's company. There was Shearwater and Heavensgate, the Isle of Man and "Up the Leg" to be visited. Then Ethel went to stay for a prearranged week with

76

some cousins the other side of the county and I was left to my own devices.

The first thing to do was to visit The Place again. Once more I stood on the spot where I had shed the sacramental clover petals. Around me the woods were in their full summer glory, dome, spire and minaret, standing out or blending in almost every conceivable shade of green, from the near-black of the Wellingtonias to the emerald of the larches.

I knew, even without plunging into them, all the magical teeming life of those sunny woods. I knew the jewelled mosses, the gnarled roots, the shreds of sky between the spires of green. I knew the chiding of a squirrel from his fastness in an oak limb, the little bright birds darting among the equally bright leaves. I knew the musky scent of fungus, the fragrance of fir-bark, and the lacquered leaves of laurel and rhododendron.

Looking down from my hill field I saw the water-meadows nearer at hand, with the shaggy fringe of the woodland behind them, and the Downs behind that again. I knew the lush growth of those meadows, the gnats sarabanding above the shallows, the trout lurking in the shadow of the many bridges, the weeds that streamed on the current like a mermaid's hair. I knew where the curlew wheeled in mournful flight, and where the brown-velvet headed rushes grew in serried ranks.

And those Downs that rose whalebacked between myself and the slender spire of Salisbury, the Downs that hid Imber and wore wreaths of beech-trees, whose badge was the horse and the dragon carved from the ancient chalk, these awesome yet friendly Downs, old battlefields, children's playgrounds—how I knew and loved them too.

I suppose I loved Warminster as one may love a person—completely, wholly, with all their moods, features, mannerisms and their many incongruities which makes up a whole personality. With me I had brought Palgrave's *Golden Treasury*, and just as all topics seem to lead to the loved one, so I found praise of the place I loved on almost every page from Shakespeare to Rossetti.

Certainly none of these poets mentioned Warminster by name, but Shelley might have been lying on his back amongst the downland hare-bells and the restless grasses when he saw his Skylark leaping into the clear air. Keats might have been in the Southey, Longleat or Heavensgate Woods when he listened to his Nightingale, while surely Gray, when he wrote that long, quotable Elegy had somewhere like

Christchurch in mind. So all the nature poets of the *Golden Treasury* came to life for me that summer—they were more than a collection of dead words on a well-thumbed page, they were Warminster partaking of immortality.

My holiday ended on a strange note, leaving with me a lost, if happy feeling, for on my last night there, I fell in love. He was tall, dark and handsome, with kind eyes and a winning smile, and a very beautiful singing voice. He had notes to woo the nightingale out of the woodland or the lark from the heavens. His broken English was like the broken moonlight on a woodland pool, he could sing like a troubadour and dance like a gypsy. His name was Ramòn Samaniegos. He was better known to the majority of people as Ramon Novarro.

On my last evening in Warminster, Ethel's mother had, by way of a small celebration, taken me to the " pictures ". The film was a sadly sweet confection starring the demure Dorothy Jordan and this singing Mexican, who had been named a successor to the late Rudolf Valentino. It was entitled *The Call of the Flesh*, and in my own case aptly enough. It was certainly the first time I had ever heard the flesh calling, and even now it was a very ethereal flesh.

Ethel's mother sensed my abstraction as we climbed Weymouth Street hill on the way back from the cinema, and suggested I had lost my heart. She was more right than she could have known! The whole affair had made a very deep impression upon me. I had always a good memory for names, and now my thoughts had gone back to those Cardiff days, and one of the first films I ever saw, *Ben Hur*, Ramon Novarro had played in that too, and a very noble part, long had I remembered him as the Son of Hur, and for long that film had been the very epitome of all wonders for me.

In that story however the Star had been rather overshadowed by the Cross, and had left me admiring and impressed but still with my heart my own; and then of course I had only been eight or nine. Now, here was Señor Novarro become all close and friendly, and I myself was thirteen, which made all the difference. The addition of this new fangled " sound-track " business also contrived to bring him much nearer than he had been in *Ben Hur*. He could sing, he could dance, he could act, he had such a nice face—in the words of the moderns he " had everything ". Yes, I had lost my heart, Ethel's mother was only too right.

I returned to London the next morning and Daphne was only too ready to assist me to the information I wanted so badly. Of course I had to ask for it in a roundabout way, I could not " let her know ", I was no " bobby-soxer " to push and shove with an autograph book in my hand over some matinée idol. Daphne loaned me some kind of a Screen Handbook or Year-book which told me almost all I wanted to know. My hero's real name was Samaniegos, he was born in Durango, Mexico, and had a musical sister Carmen (how very picturesque!) and was fifteen years my senior. This last gave me some little pause for thought, but presently I rallied, deciding the difference inconsiderable and what was to be, was to be.

I was more than gratified to find that my love was a good sort of person. No scandal attached to his name, there were no marriages and no divorces. He was described in some quarters as a misogynist, but I knew that was doing him a grave injustice. He was very fond of his mother of course, and was just waiting for the right girl to come along, which of course she would do—now—when she was old enough! Hollywood is far from Warminster and Mexico from London. The title of my favourite's next effort was *The Impossible Lover*, again with Dorothy Jordan. Did I lose heart at such an unpropitious title? No, in spite of the great gaps in age and distance, and of the difficulties which even thirteen sought in no way to minimise, all would undoubtedly come right in the end. Meanwhile I had some growing up to do in order to be ready for my destiny when I was at last face to face with it.

I had been back from Warminster but a few days (and how close and small London seemed after it) when the Family Upstairs packed up and departed for the coast taking their butler and his family with them. Our employers had taken an old Manor-house near Fairlight Cove in Sussex. There was a room there for my father and mother, but I had to be boarded out. A bedroom was found for the dog Mack and me in a farmhouse close by the sea. I had most of my meals with my parents, but at night returned to my solitary eyrie up the steep wooden " backstairs " of the old farm. My luggage consisted entirely of dog-biscuits, my school bathing-costume, the *Golden Treasury*, and a picture of Ramòn filched from Daphne's *Film Weekly* (she much preferred Ronald Colman herself).

The farm was kept by a widow and her three daughters. The mother and Ivy looked after the farmhouse, the second daughter, Violet, specialised in horses, and May, with the aid of one farm-labourer, attended to the cows and the prize bull, " Sir Alan Cobham." This farm was a wonderland to me. It was almost as good as Warminster, for though there was not the same variety of scenery, there was always the proximity of the sea to make up for it. I had not had much to do with the sea since I left Cardiff, and there it was a very different kind of sea to the eyes of a child. Here I saw barley growing right to the cliff's edge, and here I wandered along lanes festooned with honeysuckles and banked high with shining bracken. The perfect freedom of those unexpected, unplanned-for weeks at the sea will long remain with me. Almost always, my only companion was the dog Mack. I made one friend of a girl a little younger than myself who lived in a summer châlet near the cliffs. We bathed together, and all went well for awhile, and then she asked me home to tea, but I never got that far. Her people seemed to have ascertained that I was a daughter of one of the " servants " at the Manor-house, and the invitation was withdrawn. When her people were present she was distant to me, pretending she had not heard my " Hullo ", but when left alone she would speak to me as usual and join me in getting Mack into the sea for a swim. Her name has long since passed from my memory, but I can see her now in an orange swim-suit, such a contrast to my navy-blue regulation school affair, and her bangles which she never removed before entering the water.

This incident had no power as yet to hurt me. I took it as a matter of course, and it so happened that although I liked the girl well enough I did not care for her people any more than they cared for me, their opulence repelled rather than awed me and I was just as happy to be alone.

Not before, nor since (to date) have I been fortunate enough to be able to spend a holiday of more than a few hours by the sea. Now I swam two, three and four times a day. Had I possessed any money I would have taken a boat out to test my prowess there; after all, I *had* learned oarsmanship on the lake at Roath Park.

There were apples and blackberries in plenty within the precincts of the farm, and a drink of milk to be had when I asked for one, so pocket-money was hardly a necessity. My amusements cost me nothing. In addition to bathing and the wonderful rabbited walks with Mack, there were explorations to be taken further afield to Rye and Winchelsea or to Battle where our English Harold lost his eye and the day, before Norman William. There were the rockpools of the seashore, the

Somerset Harvest Field

Monacute House, Yeovil

vegetation of the crumbling cliffs, the bracken-edged paths between the trees, the glimpse of an oast-house and the entertaining round of the farm. When all these palled, or the thickly falling rain marred their enjoyment, there was still the *Golden Treasury*. And now I became discontented with reading it only, my feeling for beauty and happiness spilled over, so that I wrote on the fly leaf and every other blank space in the much treasured volume such of my thoughts as I could shape into words.

One of the entries reads:—

" An old sea wall, a seagull's call,
　The fragrant tread of the heather,
The twisted thorn tree, leaning out to the sea,
　They will live in my heart for ever.

A window that glows, when the West turns to rose,
　The hills where we wandered together,
To each simple thing will my memory cling,
　Cling to them fondly for ever."

If I had met my love in Cardiff, been introduced to him in Warminster, I now did my " courting " at Fairlight. Between that and the *Golden Treasury* the late summer had me fairly enchanted.

When in the early hours of one morning, a very severe thunderstorm broke above my head, the enchantment did not permit me being afraid. Holding Mack closely I sat in the wide window-seat of my little bedroom. Two electric storms seemed to be fighting it out just above the sea. How the thunder rolled and reverberated and the lightning blinded again and again with forked flashes. It was as if two giants were locked in mortal combat. Then came the rain, and a bathing-costume under a macintosh seeming the most sensible attire I went down into the farmyard. May was in the stalls, soothing the bull who was showing signs of getting restive under this continuous bombardment. At last the storms raged away out to sea, and for long we could hear the muffled thunder rolling away toward France as the dawn came up over our streaming landscape.

I went with May to bring the cows in for milking. How sweet hedge and lane and byre smelled after the rain, and how good the bread and butter and hot tea tasted which Ivy found for us when the milking was over. We sat in the stone-floored back kitchen, with Mack asleep on the hearthrug (their own dog was kept chained to a barrel), while our saturated shoes steamed before a fire that never seemed to be out. After that I was an accepted member of the farm-household, and when it rained I was invited to leave the fastness of my back-stairs bedroom and sit in the green-plush parlour and look at the books in the ornately carved bookcase. Their bindings were often mouldy, and the paper on the parlour walls, limp and discoloured by the damp, for this room was only used at Christmas and great festivals. But the old-fashioned casement window looked out on colourful if untidy flower-beds, and on cornfields, now being harvested, and the sweep of cliffs above the sea.

I grew into the habit of awakening with the dawn that usually came with peace and sunshine. I went less and less to the Manor, and would beg bread and cheese or a piece of cake from the Cook and a few coppers from my mother and be gone all day. It was impossible to be lonely with the life of the farm round me, it was impossible to be lonely with the company of such an ecstatically happy dog as Mack, or with the *Golden Treasury* in my blazer pocket and the thought of Ramòn in my heart. My cup was indeed full.

But my holiday was not without its clouds. When I told my mother how much I should like to live on a farm, she said I wouldn't really. They were nasty, rough, dirty places, with a good many ignorant, loutish people about. May, Ivy and Violet for instance, were down at heel and untidy, the mother always seemed to be in a muddle. There were hens in and out of the back-kitchen, and swarms of flies everywhere from the dung-heaps. There was ugliness and cruelty on a farm, trapped-rabbits and chained savage-dogs and pig-killing. She knew, after all, she had been brought up in a rural cottage, even though her father had not been a farm-worker. Her aim ever since had been to get as far away from that pig-killing atmosphere as possible. I but dimly understood my mother's point of view. I felt drawn and attracted by farm-life, even as I had done in Warminster. Mother was a lot older than myself, a lot older indeed than most girls' mothers, because (it had been explained to me) I had come to her " late in life ". Now my sister was a little nearer to me perhaps she would understand better—perhaps she would. I MUST share my new-found knowledge and happiness with someone. Daphne was out of reach.

My sister was now living at Brighton, and presently I had my opportunity when she came over to spend the day with mother. Proudly I dragged her away to meet my farming friends.

Her only comments were:—

" What a dreary house, and what a damfool girl that Ivy is." I was shocked. Quite apart from the swear-word which seemed so uncalled for—almost as if she hated the girl, Ivy was not a fool. She was a little simple perhaps. As a matter of fact she had fits at every full of the moon, when she would foam at the mouth. I had seen her, but for the rest of the time she was as normal as the rest of us, albeit a trifle quiet. She could cook beautifully—and she was good— and well, I liked her, and what was more I am sure she liked me, and she *did* work terribly hard in that farmhouse, looking after the others.

Farm-people were obviously not my sister's " type " and I must try to placate her with something else. Now what for instance did she think—and I had difficulty in getting his name to pass my lips— of Ramòn Novarro?

" What, that Dago? Don't tell me you've got a pash on him! " Dago? Dago? I hunted frantically through my mind for some explanation of this term, meant I knew to be derogatory. I brought out *Ben Hur* which she had seen and apparently forgotten, I suggested Mr. Novarro had his talents.

" Poo, he looks like a Welsh Shawnie on a day off from the Rhondda Valley. He's only a piffling little actor."

It seemed that unless I wished to be hurt, I must never ask my sister's opinion of my friends. It was a lesson learned the hard way and which if ever ignored always brought me unhappiness.

I tried now to mind too much. Perhaps there was something a little wrong with me. I was obviously not smart like my sister physically, so perhaps I was lacking mentally, as well. It seemed I liked the wrong kind of people and would never be the credit to my family that my sister was. It seemed my judgment was in some way at fault. Both my mother and sister seemed the enemies of my natural inclination (not so my father), therefore if they were right, and I supposed they must be, more especially as father was something lacking, my inclinations must be naturally wrong.

These guardians of my taste made " snap-judgments ", dismissing people and places with a few well-chosen words, which in my opinion did not apply at all, only revealing in fact that they knew nothing of the subject under review. Now if I wished neither to be hurt nor laughed at, I must be careful what I shared with them. If I could not change, then I should dissemble. But should I make a real attempt to change? Was I wrong? Was I wrong?

Why did I prefer Ramòn Novarro to Ronald Colman and Clive Brook? or the *Golden Treasury* to Ethel M. Dell? Was there something the matter with my sense of values? I knew I HAD a sense of values, for at the Camden we were taught to think for ourselves, we were treated as people in our own right. Why did I prefer horses to motor-cars and farms to flats in Brighton? Why did I love the sea and the sky as much as I did my father and mother? What was the answer to this riddle that was beginning to frighten me? Was I not the same as other people?

Then there was this question of sex and love. I was in my teens now, and had had to face that. My girl-friends at the Camden did not seem very interested in boys and when they spoke of them it was as if they were an inferior species. Quite rightly so, they didn't seem much good for anything and were perfectly horrible until they were grown up. All except Norman, who had been born grown up, it seemed to me, and Ethel's brothers who were just Ethel's brothers, editions of her in trousers and who ran through the woods with us as if they were of the same kind and species.

Boys were obviously, in the main, no good until they were grown-up and sensible. Then they became poets and actors and musicians and very worth-while people—more worth-while than women in fact. But at the moment they were hardly to be considered. I was fortunate. I did not need to consider them, I had Ramòn, and if he had ever been a boy, I preferred not to think about it.

Sex was also as easily dismissed. I knew all about it. On the face of things it looked preposterous and resulted in an extraordinary complicated and messy way of bringing new life into the world. Had not Shakespeare said so in fact?

My mother had not explained " the facts of life to me ", I had picked them up from reading as I went along, never at any time had I dis-cussed them with any living person. It was not " done " and it was not necessary.

I knew certain changes had taken place in my own body and in those of my friends, but it was part of a scheme of which we could not see the end. Sex was such a monstrous, inexplicable, unreasonable thing, it was too weird of God to have invented it, BUT I withheld a complete and ultimate judgment on it because the poets assured me that there was one alchemy that brought sex into line, that transmuted it, that made it both understandable and indispensable. The alchemy was called Love.

Therefore I sensibly shelved the spectre and problems of sex until the poets should be vindicated. Once, and only once my mother in some fit of communicativeness declared that there were many " nasty things " in married life, and sex was sordid and ugly.

I said nothing, I preferred the judgment of Byron and Shelley, the evidence of Shakespeare and Keats. It was not for nothing Man and Woman were called each other's " better half ". My reading assured me, that one without the other was incomplete, love and sex were the " desire and pursuit of the whole ". How incomplete had I been before I had " met " Ramòn, and how " whole " I should be one day.

I came back from Fairlight to London, bronzed and healthy in body, but a little troubled and shaken in mind. These differences of opinion with my mother and sister might only be " growing-pains " but they were having an effect on the normal tranquillity of my outlook, they had in fact, shaken my faith in myself and the road I had chosen, yet I decided to stick to it, in spite of them.

When I had returned to school, all seemed normal again. The faith was regained, and the enchantment though not entirely lost, was held in check by the round of activity and the presence of so many friends. I found myself winning the high-jump again and shooting most of the goals in the hockey-matches. I was a respected member of my form, neither too clever nor too dull, too forward nor too backward. The girls of Lower Four, ten, had all " gone up ". Most of us were fourteen years of age or a little older. We had come to the stage of using make-up discreetly when no one was looking. (I still rather despised *that*.) We paid more attention to our hair and our hands, and dressed in an almost grown-up fashion out of school (I only had my uniform to wear, so there was not much choice there). Some of the prefects in the forms above us were eighteen and more, the head-girl was twenty, they were absolutely adults, and set us an example we were not loath to follow.

My mother had put her signature to a form stating I would stay at school until I was eighteen, and there was some talk of college after that. I supposed I would teach—perhaps English and History. I could look ahead at a long vista of learning and self-improvement. There was plenty of time, there was also plenty of room for me to grow

more worthy of my destiny. There was so much in the world and
" Onwards and Upwards " was such a good motto.

It was Chalmers who said:—

" The Happiness of life consists in having something to do, some
one to love and something to look forward to."

By this standard I was indeed happy.

But that applied only to my school life. At home matters were less
happy. My mother was nervy and irritable, and even Daphne was
moved to comment on the fact. Her own mother was happy and
easy going, she was also young and very good looking.

I liked my father well enough, we had a great deal in common. He
loved horses and country pastimes, he was keen on sport, especially
cricket, but I was forced to realise that he was being a bit of a trial,
not sticking to his jobs better. What I did not realise then as I do
now, was that he was a perfect example of the square peg in the
round hole.

Brought up on the Yorkshire moors, he had gone out to South Africa
while yet in his teens. He had skirmished and scouted and known
Bloemfontein and the Paardeberg Laager. He had slept in Kaffir
kraals, and eaten under the shadow of Spion Kop. And when it was
all over he had returned to England in the service of one of the officers
with whom he had campaigned. Modes of life changed, horses
vanished and my father stayed on as a " gentleman's gentleman ",
thereby, no doubt, taking the line of least resistance. But there was
still a little outdoor life to be had. On a country estate there were
shooting parties and fishing parties and trips to the deer-forests of the
Highlands. There were hours off-duty in the company of game-
keepers, or with rod and gun alone among the meadows. At first
it was not such a bad life and the livelihood was steady.

There was always the best house on the estate for the butler's wife.
It was always a house by itself, and never one of a row. One was
always sure of pleasant surroundings and a good table and the respect
of the local tradespeople.

After the Nineteen Fourteen war, the situation deteriorated somewhat, a butler became less the major-domo and more the general
factotum, parlourmaids were less expensive and footmen almost
extinct.

My father had served through that first World War. He was back
in the saddle, delivering despatches for which he was decorated with

the Croix de Guerre. His South African training was not lost and he was several times mentioned in despatches.

But when he returned home there was a new restlessness. To use his own phrase, his work made him feel " chained like a dog to a kennel ". Drink became his only refuge. In other respects he remained a good husband and father. He loved his children deeply, and no father could have been kinder or more generous. Mother was still all women to him. He was chivalrous and thoughtful towards her, but his love was not stronger than his weakness.

After we left Cardiff the weaknesses became more frequent, and the consideration for family ties less and less. My mother, while being sensible of his love for his home and children and of his faithfulness always to herself, must have had her nerves worn to shreds by constant shadows on the security, without which no home can be run successfully.

When my father's temptations gained the upper hand, those dependent on him were threatened with two catastrophes—first that he would be caught in an unfortunate condition and dismissed, possibly instantly, or, that primed by alcohol to rebel against an unnatural existence, he would " throw up his job ", as mother always put it.

As we could afford neither such contingencies, whatever my father's own inclinations might dictate, one or the other of us had to keep constant watch that he never appeared " Upstairs " in an unsafe condition. As his lapses became more and more frequent, life at the Terrace became more and more hazardous.

There could be one end to all this, and shortly after our return from Fairlight the worst happened.

I received the news with equanimity, almost anything was better than the nagging atmosphere and the suspense of our household as it was. After a long session between my mother and " Upstairs ", a compromise was reached. It was impossible for my father to remain after the way he had treated his employers, but he would be given a reference to enable him to obtain another post. Without one, the situation would, of course, be absolutely hopeless.

There were still a few families who desired a butler of the " old-school " type, and after all he was superlatively good at his job, whether he liked it or not. A new post was quite speedily forthcoming. It was to take us to Somerset.

I had no regrets. So far I had been happy everywhere, and especially in the country, and I knew well enough that ALL Somerset was in the country. There was the Island Vale of Avilion, there was Glastonbury and Wells, and Holy Grail, the Flowering Thorn and Camelot. There was both Arthur and Alfred. It was a land of promise.

I was very sorry to leave the Camden, but there was sure to be another " Camden " whither we were bound, and there I could pursue my studies. It was obviously no use crying over spilt milk, I was becoming almost hardened to moving, if move we must. Mack would be very happy in the country—my father would like it better too. Mother was pretty well the same anywhere, she always tried to make the best of things. I could always write to Mavis and Kathleen and Daphne.

Of course it was good-bye to the Zoo and the Tower, to Undergrounds and Old Mother Redcap of Camden Town. It was good bye to rides in the Clyno and films with Daphne, and the mulberry tree in the school garden and hockey in the shadow of Hendon's Air Pageants, but there would be other things waiting for me. Somehow, thus early I had discovered the law of compensation at work, and the fact that one door opens as another closes.

At the last moment my mother and father went down to Somerset without me, as I decided to stay with Daphne while I played in a very important hockey match. There had been a loud outcry at the thought of my departing before this event. I was glad I stayed, for I shot the only goal of the match, winning it for the Camden.

Thus it was I departed in a blaze of glory as well as an aura of regret.

My form-mistress seemed very concerned about my educational future and I could hardly appreciate why—then. Had not every move my father had so far caused us to make proved to be for the better?

It was just after half-term and I was thirteen years and four months old when I came into Somerset, all by myself. . . . Once again did I see the White Horse of Westbury, greeting it like an old friend. Quite a large share of my heart was still at the Camden and Regent's Park, but I instinctively knew that I should remember *them*, long after they had forgotten me. Someone else would sit at my desk in Upper Fourth, someone else would take my place as right inner with the team. My place would be taken, so I had to find a new one for myself whither I was going. After all I was not travelling alone, Mack and the *Golden Treasury* and Mr. Novarro were going with me.

It had been spring when we arrived in Warminster, summer when we came to London. Now it was autumn. No primroses and celandines, only a wan sunlight and the falling leaf. From Chard station, the taxi bore us over Snowdon Hill, along an upland road, until it turned right-handed by a plantation of beeches and dropped down between high banks into the hamlet of Whitestaunton. As we turned the corner by a leafless orchard I was confronted with the filtered sunlight falling on the group of Church, School, Lodge and Manor gateway. I almost hugged myself with glee. " What a lovely, lovely place! "

I saw swans and the church tower mirrored in the still surface of a lake, I saw copper-beeches drooping over a velvet lawn.

" It is a nice little house," said my mother. " With electric light and everything, and such a nice outlook—don't you think? "

My father beamed at us both. " This is better than London now, isn't it? "

I do not believe my mother replied, she was probably thinking of the twenty odd pounds she had had to pay the removal people for bringing the Scott home half-way across England again.

VIII

Catastrophe

I AM not in the happy position of the old man who, when congratu-
lated by his Vicar on the announcement that he had not an enemy
in the world, added, " I have outlived them all! "

It will now be seen that writing an autobiography at an early age
has its drawbacks as well as its advantages. In deference to those living
we must curb our pens, where the choice may lie between doing so
and being dishonest by avoiding some subject altogether.

I have called this book an autobiography of kindness, and certain it is
that I have believed in the virtue of kindness and of tolerance above all
others. Yet where cruelty exists, tolerance is difficult, even dishonest.

Here, I may not leave a gap, even when I would, it would be dishonest and representing my life other than it was, painting it all one
shade—rose-coloured.

The names of my school and schoolmates can be changed, and I
can take some of the blame for what happened upon myself for being
unduly sensitive (if indeed I was), and leave it at that.

Up to now I had enjoyed all my school life to the full, ever since
at the age of six I had taken my first lessons in " modelling " and " twice-
times-two ". And although I had enjoyed my holidays to the full,
there had never been any reluctance about my return to my lessons.

The tiny school at Whitestaunton which houses sixteen scholars
of all ages from four to fourteen did not cater for a scholarship girl.
I had to look farther afield. There was no vacancy at the nearest
county school, so we had to look elsewhere. This would mean a
" boarding school ". Eventually one was decided upon. They would
not take me in the middle of the term, I must wait until after Christmas.
I promised myself I would " swot " at home, in order to keep up-to-
date. The school governors having discussed my case and that of my
family's finances, allotted me a boarding-grant, so this school should
cost no more than the Camden. It all seemed very satisfactory, and
the idea of a " boarding-school " was indeed a new experience. Daphne
was thrilled and envious when she received my letter. How I wished
she might be coming with me.

I spent the remainder of the half a term running errands for my mother to nearby Chard or the little village of Combe St. Nicholas, under the Blackdowns.

The woods and hills about Whitestaunton were enchanting. It was a very different countryside from Warminster's, less open, less bracing, it was close, lush and secret, but full of beauty.

Our hamlet was very isolated, there was no Post Office closer than two and a half miles. Parcels for posting might be given to the postman when he made his daily collection, and stamps could be purchased in the same way. To let us know his whereabouts and to save us waiting, often in bad weather, to catch him, he would blow a whistle when he arrived at the little letter-box.

The Norman church was one of the smallest I have seen, but there was a fine view to be had for the climbing of its old squat tower. It looked down on the group of farm, manor-house, cottage, lodge and rectory, and the overgrown remains of a Roman villa.

There had once been lead-mines on the hill, and the owner of this Roman dwelling-house may have been an overseer to the industry. Its foundations and broken pillars were only a few yards from our lodge. We had a good house as usual. It was small but very pleasant inside. We shared the private electric light supply from the manor, the rest of the village including the church was lit by oil-lamps. On one side of our house was the lane and orchard, on the other the lake and the Roman villa. Above the manor gardens and the ferny traces of the villa brooded a Bronze Age earthwork, known as Whitestaunton Camp.

The little river Yarty which lends its name to Yarcombe across the Devonshire border, flowed down a fair valley from these manor gardens. Truly we found ourselves in a sylvan setting, and although it was winter time I was in no hurry to leave it for my new school, though I told myself it would be a great adventure.

One bleak January morning I caught the 'bus. Already I had had to cycle several miles to do so. Beside me and all about me were boys and girls bound for the same destination. Apart from the school colours displayed in the boys' caps and the girls queer shaped hats, there was no attempt at uniform. I am afraid I found myself rather disappointed and disapproving. My own, long, thick hair had looked well enough beneath a decently brimmed hat of velour or panama, but sticking out from this woollen monstrosity I felt very queer indeed.

They were becoming to no one, and on myself must look like the proverbial "pimple on a hay-stack".

No one spoke to me and I thought it better not to start a conversation. We arrived at an unremarkable little township and the boys and girls divided and went their several ways.

I found myself following a crowd until I stood before a pleasing, elegantly old building.

How much nicer than the Camden's was its exterior. I felt a little glow of pride that this was to be my school. I knew it had a history and I was happy to see that history written on its face.

I was told to leave my case in the hall until lunch-time when I should go up and unpack. Lessons went a bit hard, I found I was half a term behind with my French, and giggles met my "phonetic" accent, while even the mistress looked at me in distrust. I had been used to a French mistress who *was* French, and insisted on the real thing. Here, my efforts were viewed with suspicion. Too bad!

The morning wore on somehow. At break I read a film magazine over a day-girl's shoulder. She was a pleasant girl and there seemed nothing else to do as I did not know where the playground was, and it was raining anyway.

At lunch-time I found my way to the dining-hall, seated myself in a vacant place and was promptly moved by a form-mate to a site she considered more suitable. Here, the mistresses dined with the girls and so the conversation lacked all naturalness. I missed the friendly atmosphere of school-dinners at the Camden, but I told myself it would wear off. True I had never felt strange at Marlborough Road, at Warminster, Trowbridge or Kentish Town, but then I was getting older and was noticing things more—that was all it was. I should be "one of them" in no time.

After lunch my house-mistress conducted me to my dormitory, waved me to a bed and a chest of drawers and left me to unpack. My bed was surrounded by other beds, as it was set in the middle of the room. The one window opened on to a brick wall. There were no signs of the occupants of the other four beds apart from an occasional suit-case or dressing-gown. My sense of adventure received a check. It was bitterly cold in the dormitory.

The afternoon dragged on. At three-thirty, the bus girls departed. I discovered then that most of them were day-girls living in the neighbouring town, and that they stayed only for school-dinners, even as day-girls had done at the Camden. I began to envy them as I watched them dressing for departure. If I were going with them I could be back home in time for a late tea. I too was assuming my outdoor things for I had been given to understand we were going for a walk before tea. With memories of my country walks fresh in my mind, I took heart. It was too soon, however.

A mistress appeared and marched us off in a " crocodile " through dreary wintry streets. Because she had little imagination we were walked for about twenty minutes and then turned round and made to retrace our steps for another twenty minutes.

As a " crocodile " is composed according to size, with the tallest at the front and the " tail " diminishing, and as I was small for my age, I found myself almost at the back and walking with children from the junior forms. The faces with which I had at least grown vaguely familiar during the day, were almost out of sight at the top of the saurian monster, while I was stuck with a vacant little girl with never a word to say for herself.

At tea conversation was rather pointedly directed to the subject of girls who had their hair waved. Several of the girls agreed it was " ridiculous ", heads were nodded and giggles rippled down the length of the table. As far as I could make out, I was the only one to whom this remark applied. Had I been in any real doubt, the looks cast at my head would have resolved it. I found my tea very hard to swallow. Was this what was meant by " ragging? " At the Camden we had only done it when we knew each other VERY well. This method of attack seemed rather unfair to me. After all I did not know even the names of my antagonists—I had to learn about them all, while I was the only new girl at the table, so they only had to master the character of one.

After tea we were hustled into a large form room to do our " Prep ". At the end of an hour the Juniors departed—to bed. We had yet a further period to do. No speaking was allowed, we were still " in school ", though the time was close on 7 p.m. Remembering the homework attacked in the train coming back from Trowbridge (or going to school in the mornings) and the peaceful hours swotting in Regent's Park, or by the fire at home, I applied myself regretfully to the work before me.

At last the bell went and we were free to please ourselves for half an hour before supper. At least that was the principle, in practice it was a little different. One did what certain self-appointed leaders wanted to do. There was no sitting at a desk reading by oneself, even writing home was frowned upon. " You'll see 'em at the week-end anyway! "

If one girl wanted the raucous gramophone that played the latest jazz hits, you had it, and liked it. For this half-hour we had returned to our original form-room, after all there was nowhere else to go. Our prep. had been done in a junior room, possibly because the lighting was better. I do not know. Our own form-room (and the majority of the senior boarders came from this one form), was not a good room at all. I dared not compare it with the Camden. Strange that a school could look so well outside and be so disappointing within.

That first evening, there was no gramophone, only holidays and topics of mutual interest to discuss. I squatted quietly, pretending an intelligent interest which I did not feel. Suddenly someone said, pointing at me:

" Just look at her terrible hair." There was a murmur of assent. The girl came up to me with a particularly terrifying smile.

" What does your father do? " She asked uncompromisingly.

" He buttles," said I brightly. Had I said that to a Camden girl I could have expected laughter—appreciative laughter.

Instead there was a scandalised silence.

" He WHAT? " cried my questioner.

" He's a butler," I explained happily, relieved that at least they were including me in their conversation at last.

I can see that form-room as I write, can almost smell the scorching smell that came from the little stove. It seemed that none of them had ever considered there was such a thing in real life as a butler, let alone that he should have a daughter—and a daughter moreover who would think of going to the same school as themselves.

Then I made my fatal mistake, for brightly returning the compliment I asked " What does *your* father do? "

For a moment, I was stared at and I did not think I was going to get a reply. Then, " He farms, of course," was thrown at me.

The schoolroom returns to me, the glow of the stove, the poor light, one of my form-mates with her high almost purplish colour, another leaning against the mantelpiece, and a third smiling all over her pretty, vacant face. I was soon to know them better, and realise that among my companions one was a moral coward though the only girl with any pretence to real culture in the form, that another was a bully and an unmitigated snob, that a third was not a bad sort though she swore like a man, had a filthy mind and was never above cheating, while yet another, languid and good-looking, would do anything rather than use her brains. The only other scholarship girl in the room was brilliant at both maths and games, and so well able to take care of herself that no one tried to bully *her*. Now she regarded me with shrewd, bright eyes.

" Come on, better wash your hands, the bell will go for supper in a minute."

I followed her to the icy cloak-room. The buzz of voices rose behind us, before we heard the footsteps following.

" What did I say that was so awful? I can't see anything in what I said." My companion did not answer.

" If a man is a farmer, it only means he waits on animals, while if he is a butler he waits on human beings—I don't see anything in it."

" Shut up," I was told. " Some of these girls' people are big land-owners, and it looked like awful cheek you answering back like that! "

I learned my lesson quickly and left them alone, with the exception of my fellow scholar and some of the day-girls who were quite decent. But they did not leave me alone.

Even the day-girls began to realise there must be something wrong with me. In class nothing ever went right for me. At " break " I was something of an outcast. Mealtimes were a torture, and I began to suffer from nervous indigestion, which I have had more or less ever since.

The strange thing was that I repeatedly told myself that things would get better. They did not. I encouraged myself by saying I should get used to them and they would get used to me. But it did not work out that way. The longer I stayed the worse things became, and certainly it seemed that no passage of time would ever effect any improvement.

Where was the happy companionship of my other schools? Here there was only one girl whom I could say remotely resembled a friend, and she was a day-girl, so that when she had caught her bus I was left to the tender mercies of my bullying form-mates.

No, they did not leave me alone—*that* would have been bearable, since I had never been afraid of solitude. In London I learned to grow and shape my nails, and although I never used polish I took a pride in my manicure. One night after prep. some of the girls caught me and held me down while one of them cut my nails. It was a long and difficult job as I struggled like blazes. One or two stood aside and said nothing, but the remainder cheered on the operation. The nails were eventually all cut (or rather hacked) down to the quick. It was difficult for me to use my fingers to fasten buttons or any similar job, as their tips were unduly sensitive having been long protected by the growth of nail. Their sensitivity was agony for many days and nights.

One girl did declare, " It was a bit thick," and even suggested I " took it pretty well ".

As far as I could see I had little choice, the odds being about ten to one.

We went to bed at eight-thirty after a supper that was almost a " late-dinner ". Now I very much wanted to like my mistresses. I had always done so at my previous schools. The benevolent head of Marlborough Road girls' school, the shrewd Mrs. Wyer, the firm intelligent Miss Moore of Trowbridge, and the gracious justly-minded Miss Wright of the Camden. All, in their several ways, had won my admiration and trust, even affection. Then why not these last?

Well, it was difficult to like people who had obviously taken what one could not help feeling was an unreasoning dislike to oneself. Worst of all when it came to the teaching of English, which was my best subject. It was early decided I was no good at the subject, so any source of happiness or consolation there, was denied me.

So that instead of looking forward to English lessons as I had done for so many years and at so many schools, I began to dread them. I saw these periods marked on my timetable with a sinking feeling of dread at my heart.

To this day, if I ever have a nightmare, it is not that I am being chased by wild beasts, or falling through space, or walking without my clothes through some busy thoroughfare. No, my nightmares are always on the same theme—that I am back at my last school, and an English lesson is about to begin. Under my breath I am praying as hard as ever I can:

" Oh God, get me out of here, Oh God, let me run away." But I know in my nightmare that I am trapped for ever and ever in my class-room, that there is no running away, and I wake up sweating and distressed. Then I hear the familiar sounds of home—the bull rattling his chain, the mare stamping in the stable, perhaps the early cock-crow, I see the shape of tree and sky through my window and relief comes flooding over me. I DID escape from that school, I must have done, for I am not still there. I remember how I did eventually get out, convinced I knew nothing, that I would never amount to anything. And I remember how, after many years, my mind slowly recovered so that eventually I started to write again—but only after many years.

Then I try to forget, until the next nightmare. For the business of these English lessons was the worst of all. I could have borne the boarding-school part of the life, the loss of the easy comradeship to which I had been used, if only I could have been happy at my work. But in the first place, so far as I could determine, no single girl, with the possible exception of the other scholarship girl, seemed remotely interested in learning for learning's sake.

Education was "pi" and "cissy". The girls planned to leave school at the earliest possible moment and either stay at home and do nothing but "help" mother, or take up cheesemaking, or parochial duties of some sort. Few, if any, seemed seriously to consider earning their own living, or taking up some individual career.

As for staying at school until one was eighteen, as I had signed to do at the Camden, why that was absolutely laughable.

Certainly it seemed that I alone of the girls I knew were remotely interested in the subjects of English, History and Geography.

As for the majority of the mistresses, "hostile" is the word that best sums up their attitude to the new scholarship girl. Though I must be fair and add that two of them were tolerably kind to me, and my only passably happy moments were spent in their classes.

Now although I had begun to realise that for some reason or other I was not approved of, I never suspected that there would be any kind of unfairness. If a mistress disliked me, she had her own private reasons for that, of which I knew nothing. I could not expect to go all through my entire life and have everyone I met like me! It was just unfortunate if she happened to be the gate-way to my favourite subject.

So I searched my own heart. Now the dislike was mutual, was it not? I did not like her, now did I? I tried to be scrupulously fair in discovering possible reasons why. First of all, there was the fact that she did not like me, but that should not be entirely reason enough. Yes, I tried to be fair. I did not like her nicotine-stained fingers, didn't I rather secretly despise her for smoking so much—and in class too?

Of course, I despised all women who smoked, they looked so silly and somehow " unsuitable " with little bits of white stuff in their mouths.

Now perhaps I did not really consider her a suitable figure to teach a particular subject, she was not up to the standard of the others, wasn't that it?

Well, yes, that was about it, but that she would be unfair, well, that was of course unthinkable. Yet, as the weeks went by, even that heresy became entertainable to my troubled mind.

This worried me so much that I thought I would put it to the test.

We were set to write an essay with a choice of subjects, one of which was " colour ". Remembering Richard Jefferies, " Pure colour is rest of heart ", I chose as my subject, colour in nature. " The rich blue of the unattainable flower of the sky drew my soul towards it, and there it rested," wrote Jefferies. And I wrote of the blue of the sky, the gold of the oak, the green fire of the meadows, the crimson of the sunset. I put my very best into that essay. I can remember much of it now, though the actual wording has escaped me. I had introduced life into it, in the form of a milk-maid, with plump brown arms and shining curls. I forgot the lack of encouragement, the frequent ridicule and censure, I took heart, made a great effort and put my best into the work.

At the end it was read out to the class—even as my essay on Howell Dda had been at Cardiff, even as my essay on the Marsh had been at Warminster. But this time it was held up as an example of how NOT to work.

It was false, pretentious, and unbalanced. It was rubbish.

I was astounded, and for perhaps the first time in my young life, I was unable to sleep that night. Here, when I tried to write of the loveliness I knew, I found myself being rebuked and made a laughing-stock before the other girls.

I did, however, have one friend, who was fond of English herself and who had often stated that she much admired my style.

She was quite heated over the treatment of my essay. After I had considered the matter for a few days I asked her assistance with a plan I had in mind.

The next time essays were written I would do hers and she would do mine. She agreed with some alacrity.

When they were finished, we had the job of copying out each

others' version, and I only just completed it in time. The essay had been set as " prep ", and how I scribbled !

My friend's essay (which was mine really) received very high marking, coming next to that of the girl who was the English favourite. Mine (actually written by my friend) was marked down and scored with criticism.

There was no need of further convincing. So soon, rightly or wrongly, I ceased to try, and in spite of my friend's protestations abandoned all thoughts of serious writing. Often in the privacy of " prep " I had composed poems which I had shown her. Now even these ceased. I admitted I was beaten. No mistress could be that far wrong.

Nor was I any luckier with games, for I, who had shown fair prowess at Trowbridge and London, was not even tested for my fitness to be included in the hockey team. The team which was largely picked by the Games Captain, was made up before my advent. True I was put down as a reserve, but there were several others, and I never received the chance to play. There was no proper games mistress, and playing periods were supervised in turn by any mistress who happened to be free, but in the main they lacked the keenness and encouragement of " specialised " games mistresses.

I slid down my class. On my mother's anxious enquiry at my deteriorating reports, she was told that there was little point in me continuing my education beyond the usual school-leaving age. It was suggested that perhaps I had more aptitude for domestic work.

My mother was indignant at this. When I came home at week-ends, she barely offered me a duster, I always had so much homework to do, or else I was out with Mack in the woods. Domesticated, pah! And what was meant by that one word against " Conduct "—UNSATIS-FACTORY. My mother looked at me sadly, gone was the promise of the other schools. I knew I was a disappointment to her.

I never asked why the other schools had been unanimous, why I had done well up to now. If I thought about that side of things at all, I was too miserable to draw deductions from them. No, it must be I who was to blame.

Three weeks after my fifteenth birthday I left school for ever, having added little to my previous store of knowledge except that members of my sex can be hurtful to each other, but having lost a lot of ground in the matter of faith in my fellow creatures. The crab's hard crust was a little harder than it had been before, but the inside was raw and bleeding. Yet had I not met with kindness even here? There was my friend who had shown interest in my writing and the maid who had found me crying in the dormitory, had not she been the soul of goodness to me? I remember the incident so well. One of my tormentors had been extraordinarily beastly to me, my stomach was hurting me and there had been no letter from home. Suddenly I had to get away from them if only for a few minutes. At the foot of the stairs I almost cannoned into a mistress.

" Where are you going, you KNOW it is forbidden to go upstairs in the daytime."

I gazed at her blankly. This was the last straw. Then I told a lie, I had to—or I felt I had to.

" Please, I asked if I could go up and get a hanky, I forgot one," I said, and went on past her before I should burst into tears. Was that what was meant by the word " Unsatisfactory " on my report, did she know it was a lie and I had a handkerchief all the time?

Once in the dormitory I let my tears go. Not for long, I dare not. I must not let them see I had been crying, besides, " Break " was almost over.

Then the maid came in. I do not remember what she said or what she did, but she put her arm across my shoulders, gave me a drink of water, and spoke a few sympathetic words.

She told me her name. I was to meet another of the same name who worked in another school later. They were both made of the same kind of material—starched on the outside, but kind enough inside.

Yes, of course it was not all bad, there is kindness to be found everywhere, but mostly where it is not expected.

IX

The Compensation

AT this school there had been no girl's gymnasium. We were allowed to " borrow " the boys' in another part of the town, but the loan did not appear to extend to the use of apparatus. Here again I was disappointed. Swedish drill was a poor substitute for rope climbing, vaulting and acrobatics on the " horse ". Perhaps that was not considered " quite nice " for young ladies. I only know I missed this physical expression very badly. Hockey was virtually denied me, unless I liked to knock a ball about by myself, tennis was the only substitute (and that only in the season). Partners at tennis were already made up, and when I did have a chance to play it was with a junior. There were no dancing classes and no swimming. I do not know if the town boasted baths, but if so we were not allowed to use them.

It seemed that almost all culture, physical as well as mental, stopped for me when I entered those lovely ancient portals.

I had been so keen on the Greek ideal of a healthy mind in a healthy body that I ached to see my muscles growing slack and my limbs itching for some kind of employment.

Taking the stairs two and three at a time was some small consolation, but from Monday to Friday athletics seemed virtually written off for me.

At the week-ends I tried to make up for it. First of all there was my bicycle. It was a Hercules, the cheapest model made, costing just over four pounds when new, incredible as it may seem in these days. There must have been good steel in it too, as it is still in use, almost twenty years afterwards, and nothing but the tyres have been replaced. I should like to know how many times over and over again that bicycle has earned its purchase price.

At first, I did not care for my high-framed iron-steed very much. My only experience of it was the ride to catch the bus at week-ends. All the roads around Whitestaunton are high, exposed and exceedingly hilly. It made cycling very hard work, and I usually arrived at the bus with my hair standing on end, my nose running, my eyes watering and my shoes and stockings splashed with mud. In addition, I began to carry a passenger on Monday mornings and Friday evenings. A farm-labourer's child, member of a family of sixteen children who lived in a condemned cottage beside the Yarty, had actually won a scholarship to an intermediate school in the town from which I caught the bus.

This child, before reaching Whitestaunton, had already walked a couple of miles, part of them over sodden fields. Before the day I overtook her on the road to the town, she was walking rather more than five miles each way.

After the first " lift ", when I wobbled precariously into the town, with the child on my carrier, it became the accepted thing for her to call at my back door about eight o'clock of a Monday morning. Often she was wet through to begin with, but she was a cheerful little thing, with a shiny face and two short stiff plaits. Her father did not favour " book-learning ", but the teacher at Whitestaunton school had pre-vailed, and here was Vera heading for learning " beyond her station ".

Ours was a precarious mode of travel, but better and quicker than walking. At every hill I would pedal with all my might, and then when I could go no further, we would both tumble off and begin pushing like mad; Vera's hands on the saddle, mine on the handlebars.

When it came to going down hill, we really travelled. With hands ready on the brakes, in case a rabbit dashed across the road, or a cow suddenly turned out of a gateway, I would yell, " Keep your feet out, Vera—don't get 'em mixed up in the wheel whatever you do—keep 'em well out! " And we'd go faster and faster.

I do not know what happened to Vera after I left school. Like Felix, she just kept on walking, I expect.

The compensation for the purgatory I endured at school was the life I spent at Whitestaunton during the week-ends and holidays. Quite recently a relative told me she remembered my mother writing to her when we were at Whitestaunton and saying,

" Monica is so happy here, Dolly, I believe she loves every blade of grass."

This hamlet on the borders of Devon was different from the other countrysides I had known before. It was another world from the suburban estate-covered Pen-y-Lan and Roath Park, or the châlet dotted coasts of Sussex. It was better even than the trim magnificence of Warminster. Yet one could never come to know it all as one had known them. It withheld itself, in parts it seemed to belong to the wild people of Whitestaunton Camp, or the Romans and their Cymric dependents who had mined the hills and built the villas.

The twentieth century had partly subdued Wiltshire, had defaced much of Sussex, but it seemed to have made no impression on Whitestaunton.

Twenty years ago I visited Whitestaunton for the first time, as the taxi bore me there from Chard station. This year I visited it again. It was unchanged except for some new farm-cottages beside the farm-buildings. There were no pylons, no bungalows, no army camps, no Nissen huts even, no barbed wire, no concrete, no gun-emplacements, no factory chimneys—no progress—apart from the farm-cottages, which in my opinion is progress indeed.

I was able to go to the same spot in the wood where I knew I should find a clump of oxslips—and after twenty years—there they were. And then I hastened to the stretch of turf beside the Yarty—striking it at the right place, and yes—there were the wild daffodils, even as Wordsworth has written of them in the Lake District.

This stretch of Somerset-Devon countryside has suffered less from progress than any I know, yet it is not without its riches, as the Neolithic men and the Romans knew.

I had come to Whitestaunton at the close of autumn, and although I loved the place well enough, it was not until the spring that I truly awoke to its loveliness.

All places have their best season. Give me the coast in high summer, with blue skies and a dazzle on the cliffs, while beyond the waggons are being loaded high with the brown barley. Give me autumn in the wood, whether it be Stourton or Warminster, Cranborne Chase or the New Forest—then are seen splendours undreamed of outside a picture gallery. For winter, give me the Hardy Country of the Dorset Downs, particularly those above Weymouth along to Sutton-Poyntz. Here the landscape is like a picture by Rowland Hilder. The arable fields look as if they have been brushed and combed, the folds of the hills fall in clean shadows, the structure of each clump of trees is austere and beautiful. Here the wintry sunlight gleams upon thatch and chalk stream impartially, the blue smoke rises to the milky sky, and the starlings wheel across the barrowed line of downs. The time to see the real beauty of this landscape is when it is unencumbered with too much growth.

But in the spring, then it is to Whitestaunton I turn, the very essence of the season is in that place. It begins early in the secret hollows by the Yarty. The hazels put out their catkins and every bough carries a bud. The snowdrops come first, but e'er they are gone, the yellow tide of " lent-lilies " breaks beneath the leafless boughs, as if sunshine was spilled over the greensward.

Here I saw my first kingfishers, breathtakingly jewelled in their plumage, hawking alongside the brawling Yarty. How different was this stream from the Folly at Warminsrer. Its torrents and falls, islands and oxbow lakes were in greater variety to those of the Wiltshire brook. It ran wilder and cleaner, unpolluted by any town. Old trees leaned above it, trailing ivy-tendrils into the currents, like the creepers of some jungle river. I was instinctively reminded of *Trader Horn*.

After the daffodils, came the primroses in drifts and clusters of untouched beauty. Their scent was an elixir—such clean freshness, better even than the delicate sweetness of the white violet, soon to follow. With one's nose in a cluster of primroses it was easy to imagine a world entirely re-born each year.

The mossy banks now became sprigged like a chintz with white and purple violets, an occasional cowslip and the early bluebell. Sometimes the mixture of these spring colours would be a result any textile designer would be proud to achieve. There was something Alpine about the colour and freshness of these banks in April and early May.

The tide of bluebells would grow stronger each succeeding day until they overcame the primroses and flowed misty and unchecked between the boughs of oak and hazel. . . . Then the hyacinth blue would be interspersed with the bridal lace of the garlic. One of the loveliest sights in spring is a stretch of garlic, the flowers are so lace-like and beautiful and of such a pure design, and yet when the leaves are crushed underfoot, the pungent odour is unmistakable and long-lingering.

The honeysuckle and the dog-rose followed these ambassadors, and the spring gave way to summer. Then there was less inducement to wander farther afield seeking new treasures, such as oxslips and orchises. It was pleasant to sit on a fallen trunk beside the Yarty and read the *Golden Treasury* to the accompaniment of the water's song. It was a song which altered with the weather and time of year, but which never ceased for a moment. Sometimes I would put aside my book and sit and listen to the music of the stream alone. Babble, babble, gurgle gurgle, tinkle tinkle, plop! It was like a Chopin Etude or a Schumann Sonata, only it had no end. Day and night it flowed on, the same for

the lark as for the nightingale, the same for the robin as the swallow—
day and night, summer and winter. To listen long enough was to be
mesmerised into believing time did not matter. Thus had the Yarty
sung to the Romans, thus would it sing after I was gone. To sing
was all that mattered.

I would gaze upstream where it glittered over very lush meadows,
all bumpy and hillocky (there were no level water-meads here), bab-
bling by the Roman villa before it entered the wood beneath an archway of hazels. Then I would turn downstream where it flowed
through a world of dazzling, sunlit greenery, where wrens and finches
flashed among the leaves as they must have done when the world was
young.

After the Yarty valley and copse-glade, the Manor Wood was my
favourite haunt. This was close by our lodge that I could enter it
without leaving the garden if I wished, simply by ascending the old
steps under the roadway. Before entering the wood, it was always a
joy to linger among the cresses and broken columns of the villa. Tessellated pavements had been removed from the bath and taken to
Taunton Castle Museum and now the hypocausts were choked with
weeds. Tongue ferns sprang from the crannies in the masonry and
a moorhen had her nest where once may have been the kitchen quarters.

Between the villa and the steps into the wood was St. Agnes' Holy
Well, which once had been a Roman shrine. Here I might pause to
make a wish, since the water undoubtedly had magic properties.

After the wishing-well or pagan-shrine according to the ideas of the
time, a narrow track, overgrown with bramble and fern, led into the
heart of the wood.

Here in broad daylight I could hear the nightingale bubbling over
among the voices of chiff-chaff and black-cap, and mocked at by the
distant cuckoo.

If I stayed quietly on the bronzy mosses I could see rabbits resume
their play, a fox lope across the pathway, or a squirrel going about
his business. Here I found my first tit's nest since the Walnut Tree
days; noticing the little bird return again and again to a beech bole, I
investigated and located its home.

A frantic, cat-like mewing soon attracted my attention, and lo!
there were a pair of buzzards wheeling above my head, thinking I
was about to threaten their nest of coarse twigs in the very top of an
ash tree. They were so menacing that I retreated. Their wild mewing

touched the same chord as the lost curlews at twilight down on the marshes. Oh to be a bird—free to leave ugliness and all bondage, and to seek only the beautiful and the good.

From this wood the owls came sailing on soft-feathered pinions to haunt the villa. Sometimes I could see them in the moonlight, crossing above the lake, when I put my head out of my bedroom window. I loved to turn off the light and then stay and watch them before climbing into bed. The sights and sounds and scents of the nights of spring, summer and early autumn made me give thanks for Whitestaunton and the mere fact of being alive, even though the purgatory of Leachester still lay in wait for me.

Such little things had power to please me. I was delighted at the perfect reproduction of the church tower in the lake, or with the procession of a mallard and her brood along the bank. The first discovery of oxslips so much more splendid than their cowslip cousins, a new kind of fern in the stone wall crannies of the lane, the flight of starlings in the twilight, the unexpected appearance of a seagull, or the commotion of the rookery in Manor Wood, all gave me untranslatable pleasure.

One summer afternoon, a girl from my school surprised me sitting in the orchard, reading as usual. I heard her horse's hooves and wondered idly if Ben Hur and his chariot were approaching, but saw instead only the angular form and Eton-cropped head of one of my chief tormentors.

"Well," she hailed me. "So THIS is where you live." She turned in the saddle. "Not a bad place!"

I sat on the edge of the orchard wall and eyed her mount with approval. "It's a nice little house," I said in a fair echo of my mother. "I've always liked it here."

Here, I was on my own ground and my unbidden visitor had no power to hurt me. She must have ridden a good many miles, but showed no sign of it. I fetched her a drink of lemonade.

"This is better than your old bike, isn't it?" she asked patting her horse's flank.

I laughed. "It's the country for horses, I suppose, but you'd be surprised where I get to on my old bike—I guess I take it most places you would take your horse."

"Can it jump?"

"No, but I can, and then I haul it over after me."

We regarded each other for a moment.

" Well, I'm damned," was all she said, then—

" Well, I gotta get back."

" The postman's lane is a nice way—for a horse," I suggested. " No traffic—soft track—short cut to Combe."

She waved her riding-crop at me and was gone.

As I resumed my reading, the handlebars of my bicycle winked at me through the half open back door, and I remembered another girl asking me: " Do you ride? "

And my reply. " Yes, a bicycle."

The following autumn I rode my bicycle all the way to Brighton to see my sister and her husband in an amateur performance of *Les Cloches de Corneville*.

For days my mother had talked of nothing else. As a girl, she had joined an operatic society and appeared in the same musical comedy. Our kitchen was treated to " Just look at that, just look at this! " and " Scandal-monger, gossip gadder ", to prove the excellence of her memory.

If only one of us could have gone—but the fare—right to Brighton, no, it was impossible.

Then I hit upon the idea of cycling. It was half-term and could be done. It was about one hundred and sixty miles, but I could just keep pedalling until I got there.

I had no map, but thought if I went south almost to the coast, and then east long enough I was bound to get there.

It was a drizzly day when I set forth in my school tunic and mackintosh, with my best dress in a box on the carrier. After Chard I was in a strange country and a sense of adventure came to me as I climbed the high ridge of Windwhistle Hill above Crewkerne. After this town noted for sail-cloth and rope-making I found myself entering a new world. At the top of Wynyard's Gap I was in Dorset, and pedalling along a lonely road which traversed the very crest of the Dorset heights.

Years later I was to cross this highway, once used by the Romans, to discover the great fortress of Eggardon Hill. Later still, I was to come here with a film-unit, capturing Dorset for the cinema screen. Even this first time, with a long journey still ahead of me, this stretch of high road impressed me very deeply, and I could often see it in my mind's eye, long after I was back from the ride.

By way of Maiden Newton I entered Dorchester, and from thence I pedalled through the Tess haunted country of Bere Regis, into Bournemouth, where I stayed overnight. (An explanation of this belongs to another part of the story.)

Early the next morning I entered the New Forest, still hung with the tattered flags of autumn, on my way to Southampton. I found the great port a little bewildering, but presently got on the right road to Chichester and Arundel. I was crossing half England!

The seclusion of Whitestaunton had given way to those awe-inspiring hills of Dorset, which in turn had been followed by a land of heath and bracken which terminated in that grand stretch of forest to the very gates of Southampton. From that city onwards, I met with an almost continuous ribbon-development that obscured the true character of the countryside behind it. Nutbourne and Fishbourne, Fareham and Cosham, Bosham and Southsea, linked by every sort of architecture. Here was an old cottage, relic of the days when the built-up areas had been farm-lands; tea-shacks, and petrol-stations, villas and farms and blocks of shops, chicken-runs, and grazing fields, churches and cinemas, all seeking to edge the road, followed each other almost unbrokenly until I came to Portslade and Brighton.

By this time I was getting tired. The sight of Brighton's sea-front revived me, but I was cycling in my school stockings, and one of my suspenders had chafed my leg, I longed to remove them but I did not like to arrive stockingless.

I enquired the way to Preston Park, and at last, at last, came to the very place, the very road, the very house. It was just getting dark (I had averaged about 8 miles per hour) and two figures were seen moving away from the door. It was my sister and her husband, just off to the dress-rehearsal. A few minutes more and I should have been too late.

They were rather more than surprised to see me, saying that it seemed quite a long journey in a car, to them; but on a bicycle, well—Yes, my bicycle proved a good investment, but cycling was still no complete substitute for the athletics and swimming of my Camden days.

I began to practise all the ballet movements I could remember. During the winter, there was only the kitchen, but mother was often out at the Manor helping for hours on end, and I was alone and could please myself. With my sister's old gramophone and " Miss Betty's " records I began to write dances to suit my own requirements. When summer came along, I packed up both gramophone and records and went into the wood where I had more room, and could be in the fresh air as well.

There was a little thatched table-like contraption which may have been used for the artificial feeding of pheasants, and it made an ideal stand for the gramophone. I practised long hours whenever I could, until I could feel my limbs flexible and it was no effort to kick my own height. I even tackled *entrechats* and *fouettés*, with the tattered pages of a ballet-handbook to guide my movements.

A friend from Chard knew of an enterprising young lady who taught dancing for the modest fee of ninepence a lesson, and who sometimes put on concerts for charity.

Soon I was cycling into Chard every Saturday morning for a half-hour lesson. My new teacher seemed pleased with me. In a few weeks I was dancing in a concert with two solos to my credit. One was an Eastern dance to Tschaikowsky's " Danse Arabe ", and the other was a Spanish gypsy dance to the music by Marquina.

For both, with the help of my teacher, I made my own costumes, taking great pains with the details, and copying the Eastern one from the coloured pages of *Peoples of All Nations*. I bought a tin of gold enamel from Woolworths and made a great deal of " barbaric " jewellery. On the night of nights I even gilded my eye-lids and finger nails.

My reviews in the local press were very encouraging. One reporter interviewed me at home and asked if I were going to take up dancing seriously. He suggested Madam Italia Conti's in London. But I knew it was no good, there would never be money enough for that. I went on dancing by myself, and for myself.

It got around at school that I had danced at a concert, and in due course I was mobbed in the form-room between prep. and supper and commanded to dance.

It was useless to expostulate that I could not dance without my proper music. There was a gramophone, wasn't there? Some music could soon be found. It was a " rag " and I could hardly escape it. I offered to look through the records for them. That " tear-jerker " known as " Hearts and Flowers " had a peculiar tune on the reverse side of the disc, called " Hobomoko—an Indian romance ".

I selected this, and with my tongue in my cheek, began to dance. I gave a burlesque of my own " Danse Arabe," making it as " snake-charmy " as I knew how. I slunk and wriggled and made " abracadabra " hands over the girls sitting in a semi-circle on the floor. I rolled my eyes and looked sinister. It made one girl laugh until she wept, another voted it was " bloody good ", while a third not to be moved from her usual antagonism, remarked that it was " just like her to be so damn silly ".

Afterwards one of them said: " You didn't really dance like that at the concert, did you? "

If they had meant to " rag " me I had forestalled them that time. The complete lack of athletics had driven me to dancing, but I still pondered on the unfairness of the hockey situation. I had not changed, I was as good as at my other schools, why was I treated like a " rabbit " here? "

It was not as if I was an " intellectual " and excluded from the sporting category. I did not shine at a single school subject, neither did I swot unduly—there was no encouragement to do so. I did what was required of me and that was all.

Four English mistresses had taken me to their bosoms and suggested I might consider a writing career when I was older. Four games mistresses or captains had let me represent my contemporaries at sport. Surely they could not all have been wrong?

My only release from this endless, hurtful riddle was the peace and beauty of Whitestaunton. There, at the small American church organ I picked out the notes of Bach and Handel while the martins flew in through the open porch, and wheeled above the chancel. I discovered that music was as important as movement, scent or colour, and that symphonies and arias are but an extension of brook music or bird's song. Music could be as harmonious with nature as the grey tower of the Norman church, or the broken column of the Roman villa, or the deep ramparts of nearby Castle Neroche.

Looking down from the parapet of the belfry tower I would try to fathom the pattern of living. Music, poetry, nature, all had some part in the whole; dancing and swimming and sharing things with a friend— oh, there was so much to life. There was so much behind—Whitestaunton went back beyond the Romans; and so much in front—who knew what discoveries? But what were the things that mattered? What were the *abiding* things?

First I put kindness, possibly because my own life was so starved of it at the moment. Kindness had made the people of Warminster take me, a stranger and a city-child, into their homes ; kindness had sweetened the arrival at Trowbridge and given me the happy comradeship of the Camden. There it was a rule that any new girl be given a " friend " to show her her way about, to initiate her into the ways of the new school. They went about in pairs until the newness had worn off and the new girl was no longer new. But I met with little kindness at my last country school, apart from the maid and the day-girl to whom I've referred.

As I descended the spiral staircase, shutting out the vista of Whitestaunton set in its encircling hills, I passed the folded, leathery bats hanging by the bells.

And after kindness and friendship, came those other " good " things. The church tower had taken the place of My Field in Warminster, from each I could survey a loved demesne. The next on my list, was certainly the countryside. Oh, to have had some of those girls from the Camden, here beside me now—to show them and share with them, all this wealth of beauty.

I felt so sorry for the people shut in London, it seemed such hard lines for them, for certainly the next best thing in life to friendship and kindness was to be able to live in a place such as this.

Our crystal-set had now given way to a modern wireless and I began to listen to music more seriously, striving to understand it. My interest in " tea-time " music developed to include Mozart and Haydn and the perplexing, modern, Delius. The further I delved into Tschaikowsky, the more I loved him. He had not yet become " popular ", having his piano works made into " Concerto for Two " and themes from his symphonies and overtures crooned as " Moon-Love ", " Our Love " and " This is the Story of a Starry Night ".

I began to feel I knew what manner of man it was who had created so much beautiful music, music to which one could dance, or sing, or dream. He became like a friend to me, he became almost as close as Mr. Novarro, only Piotr Ilyitch was dead, and my golden voiced one very much alive. He was just making a film with Greta Garbo, called *Mata Hari*. I wondered if I should ever see it.

Interest in the singing Mexican had led me to an interest in the human voice as an instrument of music. My pocket money bought " Lo ! Hear the Gentle Lark ", sung by Galli Curci, and " Solveig's Song " and " She Wandered Down the Mountainside " by the boyish-soprano voice of Dora Labette.

On my fifteenth birthday, I made myself a present of Georges Metaxa singing " Ay, Ay, Ay ". The peasant quality of the melody had an irresistible appeal for me. Having heard it but once on the wireless I had to possess it for myself. I marvelled at the wealth of feeling Metaxa put into the simple Spanish words, no translation was necessary, the expression and the music told all one needed to know.

Many years later this lovely folk-song, robbed of its original words and language, was crooned to the accompaniment of dance bands with the title " Out of the Night ".

When classical composers are used up by the moderns in this way, " Night " seems an indispensable part of the title, even Chopin succumbs under " So Deep is the Night ". I wonder is it because the classical composers seem all darkness to those who find such melodies beyond their own composing?

I still treasure the Metaxa recording, though the singer is alas! dead. The disc has been played many times, but the notes are still true and the old fire is there. Buying the record seemed to bring me momentarily closer to Ramòn. It was the kind of song he would have sung, and Spain was linked with Mexico, it was the next best thing to a recording of his own voice, which was not to be had anywhere.

It was not until this year, that a Danish friend, hearing me praising *Ben Hur* and its star (for yes, I have remained faithful!), produced Novarro's voice singing " The Maids of Alcàla " with " El Relicario " on the other side.

As I played the worn disc I was transported in time back to Whitestaunton, when such a gift would have meant endless happiness for me. Once again I could see myself cycling back from Chard with the substitute Metaxa on my carrier!

But one joy there was in store for me. *Ben Hur* was reissued, with I believe the addition of an " effects " track. As the little cinema at Chard changed its programme bi-weekly, I waited in an agony of apprehension to see if it would be showing during the first or the last three days of the week. I was fortunate, it eventually arrived at a week-end.

I went on the Friday evening, after I had returned from school, thereby missing my tea. I took great pains with my appearance, for after all I was going to see a very great friend. Even at fifteen, no one had replaced the Gentleman from Durango in my scheme of things.

The last time I had seen *Ben Hur* I had been a mere child of eight or nine, taken by my nursemaid Ethel Field, in Cardiff. How I sighed and waited for the credit-titles. I was not disappointed. The production had stood the test of time, and my hero was as fine as ever, even without the help of his golden voice.

Such were the compensations of Whitestaunton.

X

The Maids of Swanswick

WHEN I finally left school I was in a poor state, my spirit all but broken. The midday meals had been just bearable in the presence of the day-girls, but tea and supper were always sheer agony. The meals were quite appetising and well cooked, and I believe the domestic staff was competent enough, but I never seemed to have enough to eat, and unless I was assailed by the nausea which sometimes took away my appetite, was always suffering the pangs of hunger.

For one thing I ate rather more slowly than most of the other girls and consequently missed all chance of second-helpings. At the close-quarters antagonism of tea and supper I dare not ask for the extra slice of bread or a little more honey or jam. I was never ill to the point of being bed-ridden while at school but the tea-table was often enlivened by so-called wit at my expense, when the giggles would ripple round, and my colour would rise. There seems small wonder that I could not digest my meals.

For I was still a child in many ways, and in being hurt by sarcasm most of all. I was small for my age and did not look as big as some of the juniors and yet I lacked the assurance of most of my companions. I had no thought but to go on learning, while they openly boasted that they knew it all and were only marking time until they could start living properly.

True, the majority had a place ready to accept them, while I must make my own. Once, I had looked forward to staying at school until I was eighteen. Now at the age of fifteen I was only too glad at the chance to escape from what seemed to me to be an intolerable tyranny.

Continuing my education was beyond question now. Not only had I no prospect of ever passing any exams (according to my report), but my father had once more " thrown up his job ", and the future outlook for the Scott family was, to say the least of it, unsettled.

Daddy had gone to Bournemouth on a temporary job, which afterwards proved permanent, and that was how I came to stay the night there when I was cycling to see my sister at Brighton. He was butler-manager of a small residential hotel. Mother, declining to remove yet again, was allowed to stay in the lodge rent free, providing she boarded the single butler, engaged in my father's place. She also continued to help at the Manor when she was required, and to clean and look after the little church.

When I left school that July, with my fifteenth birthday only just behind me, I had no certificates, no diplomas, no special training for anything, no money for premiums or apprenticeships, and no experience.

This, moreover, was at a time when a well-known firm of provision merchants were advertising for secondary-school boys to pat up butter behind their counters. Grammar-school type of educations were ten a penny. Such children, with nothing else behind them, were merely looked upon as being slightly educated above their station in life.

The child leaving school at thirteen or fourteen and going straight into a factory or shop had a twelvemonths start of the secondary school child, who with no special qualifications could lay no claims to a better kind of job.

In the year 1933, amid slumps and depressions, when " cut-prices " were the order of the day and goods were " dirt " cheap, I was thrown on what is happily termed " the labour market ".

The question was when, how and where should I earn my living? At Whitestaunton there was nothing. The farm was adequately staffed by the farmer's own family of eleven sons and one daughter, and that was the only industry.

I answered advertisement after advertisement, and cycled miles, considering anything, but with no success. All of them seemed to want money from *me*, for teaching me something!

At Hemyock, whither I cycled in search of laboratory work with the great dairies there, I was offered eighteen shillings a week and a bicycle ride of almost forty miles a day in all weathers.

The job was almost mine, for I said I was quite prepared to cycle, but my mother said it was too far. I thought eighteen shillings a week a princely sum, but it was not sufficient to pay for lodgings in Hemyock if I were not allowed to cycle.

Mother gave me my fare and two pound notes beside and packed me off to London, with injunctions to go round all the registry offices and find if anyone wanted a nursery governess. She implied that the West Country was dead, and that to get a good job I must go to the centre of things. I have since come to resent this implication. London is not and has never been paved with gold for those seeking work, unless they have *made their name elsewhere first.*

It was a hot summer and after the greenery of Whitestaunton, the London pavements scorched my feet. Not very far away, my old colleagues at the Camden were still attending ballad-classes, or taking headers into the swimming baths. I went from one employment agency to another, seeking a post as a nursery governess, as a minder of babies, a washer of dogs, a digger of gardens—as anything!

The questions were always the same—what age? what experience? (Never what education?) And the replies were always variations on same theme, " Sorry nothing suitable—insufficient experience—too young."

I stayed at the Y.W.C.A. in Russell Square, and homesickness descended upon me in full measure. The last morning I was there, I sat confronting fried bacon and tomato and suddenly I wanted to be back at Whitestaunton so much that it paralysed me. I was much ashamed of my difficulty in withholding my tears and felt that perhaps if I might write to my mother, the feeling would pass. A few days later, when I was no longer at the Y.W.C.A. I received her reply. She was not sympathetic. My letter had depressed her, and heaven alone knows she had enough with which to contend in those days.

So I learned another lesson. Afterwards I never wrote in the heat of the moment, and told of my troubles only when they were safely past and I had triumphed!

London crowds are all very well for the visitor, the spectator, or the interested, detached scholar, but to be one of them, and to be job-hunting, well, that is different. London had changed her face for me. The pavements blistered my feet—the same pavements over which I had skipped so blithely on some outing with the Camden. I felt real fatigue, I who had walked mile upon mile in Somerset. I began to hate the stale bread and margarine and the unsweet milk of the tea-shops on which my pocket forced me to subsist. Above all I hated the incongruities and contrasts. In the country everything seemed to have its appointed place, there was some kind of blending. But here was opulence alongside the most degrading poverty—and here, on the grimy walls of a slum tenement was the chalked slogan:

" God is love ".

Who had put it there? Was it a mark of irony or most sincere faith?

One might have expected bawdy comment on such a wall in such a place, but not " God is love "—there was little enough evidence of it here.

The sun shone down on a brick and concrete wilderness. People lived here *all their lives*, they did not just visit here, or go to school here, or come up for the Old Vic season. I began to grow frightened, I did not want London to get me, I would sooner be on a desert island. I was forced to spend a Sunday in London, and I sat in one of the city parks, where the " grass " was like brown paper, and watched an old couple feeding sparrows out of a paper bag.

Were these sooty, drab little birds really the kin of those darting, twittering songsters of the Whitestaunton woods ? By a great mental effort I conjured up visions of the rabbits frolicking in a clearing, the light of the falling sun illuminating their fur and giving them a bright silhouette, as I had often seen them.

The following day, at an employment agency in Oxford Street, I was literally press-ganged into a job no one else seemed to desire. I was ushered into a little cubicle with a brisk, red-haired woman from Kent who needed a dormitory maid for her preparatory school. My lack of experience did not matter. Was I *willing*? Then that was settled. I would receive seven shillings each week (less insurance); oh yes, and I had to find my own uniform—it was nothing very much. I was engaged.

The point was, I should have a home and a few shillings pocket money and no longer be any kind of a burden to my mother.

The next morning I was on my way to Kent, and once I had escaped the dingy tentacles of London, the countryside belonging to the Garden of England looked very fair indeed.

I was met by the red-haired woman at a small country station reminiscent of Warminster's, and then whisked off in a small car (which she had some trouble in starting) into the heart of the country between Crowborough and Tunbridge Wells.

We turned up a drive and came to a stop in front of a large, well-proportioned country house. This was Swanswick Preparatory School, and I arrived there wearing a white-silk tennis dress and sandals, and with my hair tied by a watered-silk bow.

This was the one and only time I was to use the front-door. It was opened to us by a severe looking maid of middle-age, all starched and ironed, and with her hair strained back in thin braids. Behind us, a pleasant garden fell away to a wooded valley, and I caught the glimpse of a graceful church spire, like a tiny replica of Salisbury, in the distance.

My new employer introduced me. " This is the new dormitory maid, Gladys—Monica Scott. Look after her."

" Yes, Madam," said Gladys in a tone to match the starched apron. She led the way " below-stairs " without further words. A baize door closed between the two precincts of the employers and the employed, and I found myself in a servants' hall.

Then the starchy one turned to me.

" Welcome to Swanswick, Kid," she said surprisingly. Then, opening the door into an adjoining kitchen she called,

" Olwen, ower Blod, yere a minnit—yere's the new girl, Monica Scortt."

Olwen and Blodwyn emerged from the shadows of a huge Aga Cooker, where they were toasting tea-cakes. Olwen, thin, pale and almost beautiful, Blodwyn, plump, bucolic and pretty.

" There's pretty 'er 'air is," was Olwen's greeting.

" What d'you say 'er name was? " asked Blodwyn.

Gladys repeated it.

" There's nice now. Poor dab, she must be hungry. Come and have some tea, kid, cook's day out, see—getting it ourselves we are."

" Just going to wet it," put in Olwen.

" You're Welsh, aren't you? " I said.

" Course we are, an' proud of it," they chorused.

" I was born in Wales," I said shyly.

" Wales, Wales, what part? "

I told them.

" Cardiff! Lovely mun! Christmas shopping we used to do in Cardiff—there's nice you wear yer 'air," said Olwen again.

" I've wet the tea, kids."

" All right, ower Glad."

That was my welcome from the three Welsh maids of Swanswick. Why were so many maids Welsh? Because there was nothing left to do in their own valleys—they were dying on their feet, there was no life in them any more. The girls were glad of any kind of a job, providing it just kept them. Employers knew this. A Welsh girl would often accept a job turned down by the others, she was glad of anything. And more often than not they were good workers, taking their little bit of Wales with them, content as long as they could sing their hymns in chapel.

Besides the two dormitory maids, Olwen and Blodwyn, and the head housemaid, Gladys, there was a young Irish butler, a kitchenmaid from Canterbury, called Eadie, and a very fat, very deaf cook. The school term was not due to start for a few days, though I was assured life would be very much less leisurely when it did. At the moment I was glad of the lull while I was initiated into an almost completely new way of life. The end of the holiday was utilised in doing a little late spring-cleaning to the dormitories, the games-room, etc. Meanwhile the usual life of my employers continued. They had late dinner with the Matron (Red-hair had once been a Matron herself before the Headmaster married her, so Gladys informed me), who conformed pretty closely to my idea of what a Matron should be.

I, who had never done any housework before, learned to polish floors and furniture, scour baths, clean windows, and cut bread and butter. The cook fed us fairly well (she was so deaf that she called me " Mona " to the end of her days).

The unaccustomed work tired me and I shared my attic with Eadie without being kept awake by her snores. My appetite and digestion improved. I had to eat to keep working, and I had to work to keep living.

My mother was gratified that I had found employment compara-tively soon after leaving home, and if the pay was hardly excessive she seemed well satisfied. We wrote to each other several times a week.

Eadie, who was cook's assistant, earned rather more than the dor-mitory maids, as she had been at the school a greater length of time. Blodwyn and Olwen and I considered her really well off with twelve and sixpence a week. But then she earned it, a kitchen-maid's job was a hard one, and I for one would not have liked to peel the potatoes and prepare the greens for the staff and sixty or seventy boys.

Blodwyn and Olwen shared the bedroom below Eadie and me, while Gladys, in recognition of her superior status and long service, had a bed-sitting room all to herself. True the only sitting-room was on the bed, but Gladys had imparted to the room touches of " home ". It was unlike our other bedrooms. There was even a gas-ring where she could boil a kettle. On Wednesdays which was her " half-a-day " I was invited into this cabin for the unparalleled luxury of " an egg to my tea ".

These were my only treats at Swanswick, apart from occasional walks in the neighbourhood.

Once the term started, I worked hard indeed. My day began at 6 a.m. when Gladys, that miracle of womanhood, called me, having already " wet a pot of tea " in the kitchen (cook did not stir until after seven).

I cleaned the front stairs and hall and then the headmaster's study which was crowded with books and furniture, typewriters and gun-cases, and several baskets of dogs. While I was thus engaged, Blodwyn was scrubbing the front steps and entrance hall (a cold job on a winter's morning) and Olwen was tackling the drawing-room, which was also used as a reception-room for parents.

A few minutes before eight o'clock, a wild scramble commenced in the dormitories, and as the clock struck the hour there was a stampede for the dining-hall, previously cleaned by Eadie before she helped cook to get the breakfasts.

The butler and I dispensed the meal and then went to our own below stairs. He was a good-tempered man, fond of a smoke and read. He was easy to work with, but not very content with the conditions at Swanswick. He was always talking of leaving to improve himself, and before long he did.

After breakfast I helped the butler to wash up the glass and cutlery and the small plates, all the rest went below to the kitchen. There were unbreakable rules about the division of work in such matters.

When this job was completed I had to scurry upstairs to " do " the dormitories. Olwen and I shared the dormitories between us, which gave us about thirty beds apiece. When there had been a pillow-fight or some similar festivity the night before, our jobs were considerably harder. Toothbrushes might be retrieved from inside gym-shoes, face-flannels might be mixed up with socks and bedding might be almost anywhere.

The floors were polished every day, and then we turned our attention to the four landings (until they looked like glass) and after that the four bathrooms in our department, which sometimes resembled a stormy day at Dover.

The morning went all too quickly. Blodwyn was scrubbing the boys' changing room (another very cold job) and Gladys was tidying and cleaning the new wing where the Headmaster and his wife lived with their two small children.

" Oh the work of this place! " Gladys would exclaim sometimes and throw up her hands in mock despair, but she loved her work all the same.

I will not say I actually *loved* mine, but I made a friend of it. This may appear odd, as on the face of things it would seem to have been uncongenial. But I found it fairly varied and interesting, and if I missed my dancing and reading and listening of Whitestaunton, well I was far too occupied to mope over them.

Sufficient unto each day was the work thereof, and it was usually a bit of a race to get through to time.

It was midday and after before I had finished my share of the cleaning and staggered into my room for a hasty wash, a clean dress and a quick hair brush. . . . Then I helped the butler to serve lunch and waited on the masters and Matron on the dais at the end of the dining-hall.

This over, I assisted at the wash-up in the butler's pantry. It was about two p.m. by the time we came down to our own meal. The butler had every afternoon free apart from the one on which I was off duty, so one of the girls helped me to lay up and dispense tea. Cutting the bread and butter for it was my work alone however, and no amount of practice seemed to make perfect, it was slow and laborious. To this day I hate the job and would perform almost any other household duty in preference to it.

From about five-thirty p.m. when I had finished washing-up the tea things, to six-thirty when I began to prepare for dinner, there was a slight respite. It was then I read or wrote my letters. Later I was too tired.

Dinner was at seven-thirty, often there were parents as guests and it was eight-thirty before the coffee could be taken into the drawing-room. By the time the cups had been collected and washed up and preparation's made for the morning's breakfast, it was ten o'clock, sometimes later.

Apart from my half-day (which did not commence until about 3 p.m.) and my visits to the school chapel every other Sunday, I worked almost continuously from 6 a.m. to 10 p.m. seven days a week, for three half-crowns less insurance.

But I was happy. My workmates were cheerful and appeared to like me. The boys were entertainingly natural, some quite lovable, some positive demons. The Headmaster was a good man, pleasant and able, who treated his staff courteously. The masters varied, but all were easy enough to look after and fairly appreciative of services rendered.

The Headmaster's wife, she of the red hair, was tiresome at times, and she was definitely mean, but I daresay she was forced to keep expenses down in those cut-throat times and servants are notoriously careless with other people's property. The Matron was all a matron should be, wholesome, wise, pleasant and kind, the same to the staff as she was to her boys, motherly and reliable.

Looking back, I have come to the conclusion it was a good school, ably run and with a pleasant atmosphere. The boys were well fed and housed, the curriculum seemed wide and varied, fencing and roller-skating were included in the games. Gladys found a pair of skates to fit me and presently I would spend the hour between tea and supper careering round the gym at a great pace. Soon I was doing figures of eight, and waltzing and tangoing. Roller-skating was faster than ballet. Sometimes Blodwyn and Olwen would join me and their antics made me roar with laughter. There was no electric light in the gym which was never used after dark, so we had to perform to the light of flickering candles set in the window-ledges behind the horizontal bars, while Blodwyn pretended to make a great to do about having to clean up the wax in the morning.

I soon found that skating to music was much better than without, and the two Welsh girls being as vocal as most of their race would sing to drown the rumble of the wheels. Their favourites were " The Blue Danube ", " Daisy, Daisy " and " We are the Robbers of the Woods ", from *Chu Chin Chow*. This last was a great favourite and as they sang faster and faster, " Carve him up, carve him down, slice him through from heel to crown ", I circled the gym at a terrific pace and we all finished up breathless, they from singing and I from my exertions.

In what strange ways can one find real pleasure.

H. J. Massingham in *Where Man Belongs* has said:—

" The interest of a man's work makes time irrelevant; lacking it, the brick-layer thinks of getting through the time, rather than the work."

Time meant literally nothing to me at Swanswick, I had not *time* to consider it. I was interested in getting my jobs done, and not for any Union would I have left them undone or even half-done. Everything now seems to be governed by " man-hours " and " minimum wages ", and the law is laid down as to just how much of himself a man shall put into his work. I cannot help feeling that is wrong, and *not* conducive to happiness.

While I was writing this book I suffered a return of my digestive troubles. My doctor said it was over-work, the eternal round of meals for hungry men, of housework and cooking and mending, together with the considerable secretarial work which has resulted from my writing, was putting too severe a strain on my strength. I must get some regular help, he said.

What I really required was a woman or girl who would come in for a few hours each day for perhaps three or four days a week. That would have been sufficient, just so that I might keep abreast of my manifold duties instead of letting them get on top of me. No one in the village was available, most of the women do two or three jobs. Some go out to milk, some help with farm-washing, others work out on the land. At the time, there was no one free to come. But I had read of a National Union of House-Workers, who (according to one of our politicians) had been organised to maintain the solidarity of the home-front.

I made enquiries. In return I was not asked for my requirements, but sent a list of their conditions. First of all, a maximum of 44 hours was to be worked. There was to be a holiday of three weeks' duration *with pay* annually. A girl of eighteen with twelve months' domestic training was to be paid £3-11-6, and if she lived in, a bed-sitting room of her own, or a private room in addition to her sleeping-place must be provided.

Financially I was forced to decline these terms. This was asking almost as much as we pay a head-cowman, with a wife and family to keep; few small, mixed farms could afford to pay out close on £4 a week for domestic help in addition to the other staff. A " help " moreover that would be missing for three weeks in the year and had to be paid extra for overtime—if they could be prevailed upon to work it. Furthermore in these days of house shortage and house-sharing it is almost impossible to be able to conjure up two rooms for the use of " the help ".

A girl of eighteen has to be exceptional before she is worth that kind of money and those sort of conditions. I have not met a girl that age worthy of them yet. I am the last person to condone the the exploitation of labour but no amount of " conditions " can replace the spirit of service.

Gladys of Swanswick, old retainer that she was, had probably never earned more than thirty shillings a week all her life. She had always had a roof over her head and a fortnight's holiday each year on half-pay so that she might go home to see her people in Swansea. But she was happy in her work. Her heart was in it. She knew the school *needed* her. She knew all the masters' tastes and foibles and the habits and characters of the boys. She knew their names and what kind of parents they had. She did not count the hours of work, or watch the clock or the calendar. She was *necessary* to the well-being of Swanswick. The friend of Matron and the trusted confidante of the Headmaster and his wife. They knew they could leave things to Gladys when they went away at holiday time.

Gladys would look after things, Gladys would break-in the new dormitory maid, Gladys would keep on the right side of cook. Gladys never belonged to any Union of Houseworkers. If she had, she might have earned more for less work, but would she have been any happier? Her work was her pride and happiness, humble and insignificant though it might appear to a planning politician. She was happy and she helped to make others happy, she had found her rightful place. Isn't that the test, the one *condition* that should apply to work?

Recently I saw the headline in the London Press:

" Many evils now face youth at work."

It went on to say:—

" Honesty is sneered at. One lad entering a large London engineering firm finds that ' scrounging ' is almost universal. He also discovers that everyone expects him to dodge as much work as possible—if he works steadily he is despised as an oddity or accused of ' sucking up to the bosses '. It is unknown for anyone to work voluntarily for one minute after the hooter has gone."

If this is true, as I fear it is, it makes very sad reading indeed. But fortunately there are still craftsmen, self-employed artisans, men on the land and individual artists, for whom pride of work has not yet been totally destroyed by " conditions ". They are often conditions which result in robbing the worker of any real pride in his work and thereby robbing him of his greatest source of pleasure at the same time.

Yes, I was happy, and the only bad moments I knew were when my sister's infrequent letters upbraided me for lacking in back-bone, taking a dead-end job. Once she came to visit me. As she was living only at Brighton, the thought has since occurred to me that she might have done so more often, but I daresay she had plenty of interests and time went by as quickly for her as it did for me, if in a rather different manner.

In my scanty leisure I read little. They were only the books the boys read such as Kipling's *Stalky & Co.* and Rider Haggard's *She*. When it was fine I wandered down the wooded valley below the school, inhaling the autumn scents and admiring the colours of the fallen beech leaves and the dying bracken. Once I saw a fox, which transported me back to Whitestaunton, and here, in what was known as the Rock Valley, I saw my first badger. I turned a corner and we came face to face for a few seconds. I stared in delight and then he turned and lumbered off among the undergrowth. The Rock Valley was a remarkable walk. It was situated within the school grounds, and was a narrow, tree-lined defile, strewn with rocks and boulders. Many years later, a badger was the means of introducing me to my most valued friend, to whom this book is dedicated.

That autumn evening at Swanswick I thought the stripey-faced Brock a delightful animal and I was happy that he was one of my neighbours.

I soon found a friend to accompany me on these short rambles, for I never had time to go far afield. The English master had a red-setter, Chris, who never seemed to get enough exercise. When confined to the house he would get into all manner of mischief, and I was assured by both Gladys and his master that it would be a kindness to take the dog out whenever I could. I needed no second invitation.

He reminded me of my own dog Mack, from whom I seemed to have been so long parted. He was a fine enthusiastic companion for a country walk who fully understood the joy of living.

Sometimes, when my work was finished for the night I would slip out to the Rock Valley for a final breath of fresh air. Then I became friendly with the moon and talked to it, not perhaps as Endymion talked. But this same moon shone on London and Whitestaunton, impartially. . . . I found it had its moods. Sometimes it was coldly aloof, sometimes low and friendly. When it sailed through the clouds like some silver ship on a dark blue sea, I recaptured the music and enchantment of my days with the *Golden Treasury* at Whitestaunton. There was little room for poetry in my life now, and as for " the

Dago", well he still occupied my heart to a large extent, but I had begun to realise just how far I had to go.

My workmates could not share in my love of poetry or moonlight, even though I got on well enough with them in other respects. Gladys called me a "funny kid" because I loved to go out and see the clouds silver-edged and the greenhouse roof striking back silver-fire from the moon. I loved to see the sky netted with the tracery of twigs and branches and the silver-pennies of the evergreen leaves wink back at the night wind.

The moon behind the chimney-pots transformed my day-time world, giving to the school buildings an almost Moorish appearance. Pools of silver and bars of shadow broke up the gardens and gleams of warm light from the drawing-room windows on the terrace would vie with the unlit ones of the dormitories which now caught the moonbeams and threw them back at me.

I thought of this same moonlight shining unappreciated on London, where few people ever looked at the sky (until the War years) and where indeed it was obscured by a haze of artificial lights. Then I thought of it smiling down on Whitestaunton, touching the Roman villa to silver, reflected in broken fragments on the swan-ruffled lake or sparkling on the waterfalls of the Yarty.

It would be making mysterious and wonderful the woods where only last spring I had paused to inhale the honeysuckle scents, and listen to the cascade of music from the nightingale.

XI

Onwards and Upwards

MY first Christmas away from home was both memorable and happy. Some of the boys had parents abroad, or for some other reason had to spend the holiday at school. All the staff felt rather sorry for these outcasts—after all, Christmas is one time the ties of home pull stronger than at any other —so we vowed we would give them as jolly a Christmas as possible.

Evergreens were brought in and we all worked together; Matron, the resident masters, Gladys and the dormitory maids, to make Swanswick look like an illustration from a Christmas card. The snow that fell a few days before the twenty-fifth completed the picture. A Christmas tree dominated the dining-hall, and the chestnuts of the Rock Valley were denuded of their nuts to make Swanswick's traditional dish of chestnut cream.

Then I tried my hand at making sweets, and finding I had a natural aptitude for this " fiddly " kind of cooking, set to work with a will, and with Gladys, Blodwyn and Olwen playing kitchen-maids to me.

We made peppermint creams, fondants, fudge, toffee, candy and coco-nut ice. The Headmaster appeared when we were making this last, and insisted on sampling it before it was properly cold. It was coloured green and pink, white and chocolate, and made with fresh creamy milk, pure white sugar and freshly dessicated coco-nut, was simply mouth watering and totally unlike the dry candied variety bought in the shops.

I cut out the peppermint creams with the top of a sauce bottle, which was just about the right size. " Necessity," said Gladys portentously, " is the mother of invention."

" What's Mona up to with my best pastry-board? " enquired Cook through her ear-trumpet.

" Look out, you clumsy fat-head," said Blodwyn good-naturedly, " got icing-sugar all over my best-dress you 'ave—There's messy it is." " Poor dab," says Olwen, " You been *sittin'* in it—if ower Mam could see us now she'd die laughin'."

I was too busy to feel homesick. I had saved enough from my

pittance to be able to send small presents to my parents and my sister. I even found a few coppers to spend on Gladys and the others. They were only very tiny gifts, a comb, a powder-puff, a small mirror. To make them seem more I wrote a doggerel rhyme with each one, which was read aloud with delight at the breakfast table on Christmas morning. I was " a one! "

We all received five shillings from our employers (it seemed like a fortune in those days) and the present of a turkey for the servants' hall.

The atmosphere might be new to me, but it was all so acceptedly friendly that I did not have time to ask myself whither I was going. A day seemed a long time at this period in my life and I never stopped to ask myself if I should be cleaning dormitories for ever. Perhaps I instinctively knew that I should not, and therefore did not bother about it further—when the appointed day came I should go " Onwards and Upwards " as the Camden motto decreed. But my sister was stinging in her scorn. I was in a " dead-end job " and why didn't I " look ahead! "

I studied Blodwyn, Olwen and Gladys, knowing I was one of them and yet not of them, and being fascinated by their simplicity and goodness. Certainly they appeared to find life sunnier than my late schoolfellows—was it life's way of making up to them for the things they had lacked at birth—this philosophical disposition?

I loved their delight in simple things (was it not something akin to my own), and, to finish the analogy, their mirth which had no bitter springs.

Their inveterate superstition delighted me, partly because I was detached from it. A dropped knife was indeed a catastrophe, one of us must come running to pick it up—or it would be left there indefinitely—*anything* rather than that the one who dropped it should suffer an alarming disappointment in consequence of having picked it up herself.

One must never spill the salt without taking the precaution to blind the Devil by throwing a pinch at him over the left shoulder. One must never observe the new moon through glass, nor walk under a ladder, or turn the mattresses or cut finger nails on a Friday.

They read a very simple and homely type of woman's literature each week. It was full of tales of servant girls who prospered even to the extent of marrying their bosses. There were erring daughters turned

out in the cold, cold snow—but all turned out well in the end—bound
to! There were mothers who came down in the world when the
daughters went up, so that one of them at least ended up:—
" A Servant in Her Own Daughter's House! "
But THAT all came right in the end too.

" There's lovely it is—I knew she'd 'ave him in the end, see? "
On Sundays the *News of the World* furnished the entertainment in
the servants' hall. These Welsh girls seemed absolutely unperturbed
at being so far from their homes. They carried a little of Wales with
them in their incorruptible speech, their sing-song idiomatic language
and in their love of singing at work.

They began their letters home, " Dear Ower Mam, I hope this finds
you as it leaves me at present ". (All except Gladys whose literary
standard was a trifle higher, and who treated with good-natured amusement the backwardness of her compatriots.)

If I said anything amusing I was " a one ", a " proper caution " or
simply " a card ". Of my home and circumstances they knew little,
except that my mother was kind and friendly, for had she not sent each
one of them a card at Christmas?

" There's nice of 'er, and 'er a stranger too, well I never! "
Shortly after Christmas, our butler decided to leave. He had had
enough of " professional " places, the work was twice as hard in
them, especially when they had a social side as well. No, he was
going to find a small private house, where he would not be run off
his feet.

Mrs. Red-head decided to economise, a parlour-maid was less
expensive than a butler, and even if she did not look quite " the thing "
she could do the work just as well, often better.

Yet another Welsh girl arrived. Her name was Joycie and she was
greeted by, and greeted us, with rapturous affection.

After she had discussed the post with us at some length she exclaimed:
" This place must be the Registry Office's delight, Mun! "
Joycie took pains to train me to the parlour work. She was one of
the kindest girls I have ever known, and her openhandedness was
amazing. Much as she liked us all, she did not think she would stay
very long, she wanted to be nearer her young man for one thing, and
she wanted more money to save for her wedding for another. But
before she went, she determined she would help me to " better myself ".
When she eventually left she thought I could take over the parlour-

maid's job and the higher wages. So she helped me to master the intricacies of "butling". I must take from the left and serve to the right, and learn what wine goes with what.

It was nicer now that we were all girls together in the servants' hall. But all good things come to an end, we are told, and eventually Joycie worked out a month's notice and departed for a better job.

My employers did not take her advice and move me up into her position. They explained that they considered fifteen and a half too young for the responsibilities of a parlour-maid, besides I was not tall enough—certainly I was nowhere near as tall as Joycie. I now used a little make-up, as discreetly as possible, and had cut my hair shorter, but I knew I lacked any kind of "presence", I was much too short and dumpy. Joycie had been tall, slender and smart.

I remember once in Gladys's bed-sitting room we had been discussing the reason why one of the nicest and most eligible of the masters had never married, and Joycie had said:

"No such thing as love there isn't—only passion!" And then seeing the wide-eyed almost unbelieving expression of dismay on my face, laughed, and added:—

"Go on! I'm only pulling your leg—don't be so tup—course there's love, and don't I know it?"

Joycie's successor was a crotchety old Scotsman with a permanent grudge against young maids. First of all he could not tolerate the "high-falutin" name of Monica. He declared that in any properly run household I should be called Mary, and that was an end of it. Mary he called me henceforward. Where the Irishman had been friendly and easy-going, and Joycie kind and co-operative, this old gentleman seemed to take a perverse pleasure in making life as difficult for us all as possible.

He even succeeded in antagonising the cook, defended though she was by an almost impenetrable deafness.

My employers seemed satisfied with me on the whole, though when I look back I think I must have been a very raw recruit, and anything but a model servant. But when at last I told them I could not work with this sour person any longer, they refused to accept my proffered notice.

By the end of February I could stand it no more. One man had entirely altered the happy atmosphere of the staff at Swanswick. Gladys kept more and more to her own room, taking all the meals she could up there. Blodwyn and Olwen sulked and cook withdrew entirely into her shell of deafness.

I was always wondering what wrong I should do next. I began to think more and more of escape and began reading advertisements and writing letters.

One half-day I went into Crowborough and in a fit of depression decided to go to the pictures. I discovered, while still in the vestibule, that I was a halfpenny short of the required ticket-money, so I came away.

I told " Farmer " about this one day and he declared that " they would have trusted you for it—you were silly not to go."

But there was the chance of a humiliating refusal, just because I was poor. Had I arrived in a car, fur-coated, I am sure there is little doubt the manager would have " trusted me " for the amount of a whole seat (and one of the best ones) if I explained that I had left my wallet behind.

I always hated to owe even a half-penny. I remember the day well. The film showing was a Garbo one, and I missed seeing the great star by a half-penny.

The incident stays in my mind, not so much for the principle involved, but because I had for the first time looked on the cinema consciously as a form of " escape ". I wanted to forget my tyrannical overseer, my poverty and lack of prospects—I wanted to live in a brighter world for just an hour or two.

Now I never think of the cinema as a form of escape, but of instruction, enlightenment, and very occasionally, pure entertainment. But I am still conscious of the fact, that for many, especially in the cities, it is the quickest way out of their own drab, unsatisfactory little world. This is wrong, and it should not be so, but the fact remains at the present.

At last I gave in the notice which my employers pretended to ignore, and when my month was up I said good-bye to Gladys and the girls, took a last walk down the Rock Valley, and then walked with my scanty luggage to the nearest station. On my way I passed the playing fields where I could hear the Games-master's whistle, and see the striped jerseys of the boys scattered over the pitch.

It was to London I returned and to the home of a school-friend to whom I had at length turned for advice and help. I had left Swanswick without my last month's wages, as Mrs. Red-head had refused to consider my notice, but now, with Gladys giving her my new address, the pound note and few shillings that were my due, were sent after me.

Before I had been with my friend a few hours, her mother had found me a job with neighbours of theirs. They had a business and needed help in the house, the wages were a step upwards, being ten-shillings a week and I lived as " family ".

I had a good and comfortable home. There were six in family so there was always plenty to do. I felt shy and awkward and a little " out of it " but it was not their fault. The house was a small labour-saving one in a brand new suburb. It was certainly not in the country and yet it seemed a long way from London.

It was now March and the gardens all along the road were bright with almond-blossom, with flowering plum and cherry.

I knew I was at the centre of things, in the home of literature, drama, music and ballet, but I could not penetrate to any of these magic circles. My means were insufficient. My ten shillings a week, less insurance, would barely keep me tidily dressed and supplied in stamps and shoe-leather. It ran to very few bus fares or cinema seats, let alone plays and concerts. At Queensbury I was as far from the centre of culture as I had been at Whitestaunton. I was, in fact, further, for there I had access to the true basic culture of all, the study of nature.

As the spring advanced I felt more and more out of place, and more and more as if the most important things were lacking in my life. Security, freedom from want—a roof over one's head, these were not the be-alls and end-alls of existence. What did London matter, her arts and artifice, her teeming wealth of material and spirit? What was London but collections of the inanimate? What could London offer that could compare with the wind from the sea, the dewy turf underfoot, the cry of the curlew? Here was no sense of freedom, of living, of Man's essential oneness with the rest of nature. Man was a pigmy here—dwarfed by bricks and mortar. If the hills and forests appear to dwarf him also, at least there he was part of a picture—and his size was comparable with that of the daisy, the acorn or the field mouse.

In the city he was dwarfed by everything but the alley cats, and the few sooty birds.

These were bad days for the urban population. Of course there was hardship in the countryside too, but poverty there is never so grim as in the town. Country gardens are productive, the milk is not devoid of almost all its feeding value, rabbits and lesser kinds of poultry and game are more plentiful, there is wood for the picking up and free flowers for the window, there is the harvest of the hedge-rows, downs and meadows to vary the diet. A spare and simple existence may be the lot of the poor countryman, but at least it is not a life shorn of all beauty and dignity.

Of the state of the " man in the street " at this time, Malcolm Elwin has written:—

" Free education had enormously increased the potential reading public, and books were much cheaper—but fewer people read serious books. Newspapers chattered that books had never been in such demand, but with characteristic absence of discrimination they did not specify the sort of books in demand. The phenomenal sales of Edgar Wallace were sufficient indication. Crime and sport were the two main preoccupations encouraged by the cinemas and popular press. In churches, parsons conducted services to empty pews. At elections less than half the population bothered to exercise the right of franchise. With lives divided by superficial pleasures and making the money required to purchase these pleasures, nobody wanted to think. It was an age destitute of integrity and dignity, in which mediocrity and conformity were the essentials of success, while lazily, unintelligently, a nation drifted to disaster."*

This is the description of the between-the-war years when I was growing up and trying to take my place in the world.

One bright April morning, while the rest of the household were all out about their various business, I answered the door on no less than three occasions to door-to-door hawkers or beggars.

The first was a North Countryman, shabby and down at heel, and with black and broken teeth visible when he spoke to me. I gave him a shilling for a packet of sewing-needles.

The second-comer was an elderly man peddling lavender, and to him I gave the last few coppers in my purse.

When I opened the door for the third time I had no money left, and I gazed with dismay at the woman who stood on the threshhold asking me if I would like to buy a polishing pad or a nail-brush. She was very poorly dressed, but quite beautifully spoken. I hated to be unable to buy anything from her and felt totally unable to turn her away without

Life of Llewelyn Powys.

giving her anything. So I asked her inside and offered her the milk and biscuits put for my own " elevenses ".

She told me that she had had a university education (certainly her speech would appear to bear her statement out). When I asked her how she came to be earning a living in this way, she told me a story of an invalid husband and two small children.

She declared that her education meant nothing to the people whom she had asked for work and that an ability to scrub floors would have stood her in better stead, only when she had gone after that kind of job they had said she was unsuitable—there were plenty of " rough " women to be had.

Then she asked me what I was doing at domestic work—even if I did not wear a cap and apron and was working for the friend of a friend, as I told her. I was not married, I had no dependants to consider. Why didn't I cut loose, take a risk?

She left me puzzled and troubled. I began hunting through the columns of the *Church Times*, bent upon getting myself another job, preferably in the country. There seemed nothing. I inserted an advertisement, describing myself as a young lady of secondary school education, fond of the country and animals, who was willing to consider almost anything.

I received two replies, one from a clergyman in Hampshire who wanted a nursemaid for his two children, the other came from a " rabbitry " with a Hertfordshire vicarage as its address.

The latter received my first attention. The " rabbitry " was a collection of cage-like sheds which housed angora rabbits, kept for their wool, which was combed and spun by the daughters of the house.

I lunched with the family off a bare deal table in a stone-floored kitchen. The vicarage was old and rambling and the family seemed as poor as the proverbial church mice. But there were daffodils and wall-flowers in the unkempt gardens, and the rabbits were beautiful with their silky coats and bright eyes.

But alas the job entailed the ability to drive their little car, and I was not yet sixteen, while the age for a female to obtain a driving-licence must be eighteen. It was too long to wait.

The Vicar from Hampshire met me in the buffet of one of the London railway termini, and we discussed terms over a cup of coffee. His manner was pompous and pedantic, but he was offering me work in the country. I was to be paid ten shillings a week still, but was gravely assured that my duties would not consist entirely of housework as hitherto—though I should be expected to assist with—er—er—a certain amount.

Whether or no he was satisfied that I was a suitable applicant for the vacancy, did not appear during the course of the interview, but the very fact that I had advertised through the medium of the *Church Times*, seemed to militate in my favour. Yes, I was engaged. There was no enthusiasm, I was to go on a month's trial.

My name did not appear in the *Church Times* for another sixteen years and then it was in one of the best book reviews I have ever received.

The representative of my publishers who forwarded the column to me said, " The *Church Times* seem to approve of *Hundredfold* and you in a big way."

In between I do not believe I had thought much about the *Church Times*.

The Vicarage was a spacious and delightful country-house, but it required a full staff to run it properly. Instead there was an Indian Missionary girl called Faith and myself to share between us the work and the looking-after of three children.

I was responsible for " upstairs " and she was responsible for " downstairs ". I did all the washing and she did all the cooking. When I had been interviewed in London, no mention had been made of a new baby, but I soon found that washing napkins was an important part of my duties. In addition I did the mending and ironing, most of the shopping, taught the children their first lessons and took the baby out. At garden-parties, meetings and " teas " and the other manifold activities associated with a vicarage, I was waitress, baby-minder and general factotum. In addition to this a kind of kindergarten school was begun in the village hall for the young children of the Vicar's immediate friends and neighbours.

It commenced at ten and finished at twelve, five days a week.

The ages of my charges varied from two to six, children who were better " out of the way " in a morning, but hardly old enough for " prep " school. Some were only at the stage of playing with beads and shells, while others were learning to tell the time or do simple sums.

This part of my new job I found most enjoyable but it was often something of a rush to get the daily washing finished and hung out and my own two charges ready by ten o'clock each morning, and I must not keep my " school " waiting outside.

When I think of that Vicarage I always see a long row of napkins of muslin and turkish towelling strung out in the kitchen-garden with the Vicarage and church tower in the background, and the sunlight peering through the oaks on the Common.

It was a beautiful place and a very beautiful spring, perhaps as fine as those I had known elsewhere. Awakening often with the dawn, I could lie in my narrow little bed in the end room and watch the acrobatics of a red-squirrel who haunted the trellis-work below my window. Roses rioted all over the garden and the cuckoo was my first morning greeting, calling sometimes before the sun was up, lonely and provocative from the meadows beyond the laurel hedge.

How I treasured those moments before the rest of the household were awake, when it seemed the world belonged to me. These moments were stolen out of the day—a day so crowded that I had not time to be myself—just the Vicar's nursemaid-help. Sometimes I would try to read for half an hour before getting up, but more often than not, one of my charges in the next room would awaken and cry out for me, and my day had then well begun.

The eldest, Peter, was intelligent, quick and sometimes quite lovable, but he had been hopelessly spoilt, and indulged in violent tantrums, in order to get his own way indeed almost the first thing he did when he saw me was to hurl an orange at me. I caught it, and whipped it back, exhorting him to be quick! He dropped it and I called him a " butter-fingers " and ordered him to try again, while Faith looked on silently.

He forgot his antagonism at the new face, in the interest of finding out that an orange made a good ball. It had been touch and go for the moment, but the crisis passed, as did many others!

Paul, the younger of the two brothers, on the other hand was sly and backward, and although turned two years old was dirty in his habits. The young baby, Caroline, was alternatively " minded " by Faith and myself. The Indian girl appeared subdued but thought herself extremely fortunate in that she, an orphan, had been elected from the Mission School to live with an English family.

She was quite a good cook and when she found I was fond of curry my popularity with her was sealed. She would often make me strange native dishes out of " left-overs ", and though I doubted their effects on my digestion, they certainly made good eating.

Peter and Paul had all their meals with me in the Nursery. Peter was difficult about his food and I had to use all my strategy to get him to eat anything. The younger Paul, on the other hand, was greedy and gluttonous and threw his food about as Henry the Eighth is reputed to have done.

He was also as mischievous as the red-setter Christopher had been at Swanswick, but one could not tie up a child or banish it to a kennel. He was too big for a play-pen, too small to be left by himself, too backward to amuse himself with picture-books, and too forward to remain in any room if he wished to get out.

He found ways and means whereby he could open every door and penetrate everywhere he should not. Once he poked out and broke every fitting in the Nursery gas-fire, another time he broke into my bedroom and mixed my face-powder with brilliantine.

The only time when I experienced anything like peace was when they were asleep, or I was taking them for their afternoon's walk, with the " little Demon " tucked in at the opposite end of the pram to Caroline.

These walks were undertaken every afternoon, no matter how tired I might feel and in all weathers except the most torrential rains. Peter and I shared a kind of nature-study game, pointing out wild flowers and birds to each other. We invented the " flower fairies ". This method of learning about our natural heritage appealed to the sensitive highly-strung child and when back in the Nursery he would try to draw or paint his conception of the poppy-fairy, the honeysuckle-elf or the traveller's joy gnome.

Peter became so enthusiastic over this new culture that he told his father about it. The Vicar was horrified. He forbade me to fill Master Peter's head with any more such nonsense. I had survived my month's trial and I did as I was bid.

Faith had told me how stubborn and temperamental Peter had always been until I came, yet with his imagination stimulated he could be such a tractable, lovable child.

I asked my mother to send me an old copy of A. A. Milne, and now Peter delighted in, " What shall I call my dear little dormouse? " and " Once upon a time there were three little foxes! "

When the Vicar discovered it, he was enraged over A. A. Milne. I fancied, however, that A. A. Milne knew more about the mind of a child than the Vicar would ever do. My own childhood was not so far away that I could not remember it. I felt there were bonds between his son and myself of which the Vicar knew nothing.

Living in a Vicarage also made me look at religion as I had never done before. I had to face the fact that many practising Christians were not " charitable ", that they spoke without charity of many people, some few of whom I felt convinced were good.

I found that they were very snobbish and that did not seem right for the exponents and upholders of a religion of the weak, the have-nots and the disinherited.

A woman who worked on the land like a man, doing a man's job, once asked the Vicar why she might not go to church without a hat. In discussing the matter with his wife, the Vicar said,

" I referred her to St. Paul."

I referred to St. Paul myself. His rules seemed applicable enough to a civilisation and territory where women did not go with their heads uncovered in any case and where a yashmak was the mark of proper womanly humility and virtue, but I could hardly see that they applied to the here and now, nor that they should be sufficent to make a hard-working, honest kind of woman suffer the wrath and contumely of the Vicar.

I discovered more. I found that the teachings of Jesus, summed up in " the brotherhood of man " ideal, had been largely lost by St. Paul in a welter of dogma and top-heavy ritual. That what had begun as simple teaching and prophesy to bring understanding and hope to men's minds, had, under the tent-maker from Tarsus, developed into an " industry " and a vast and complicated system of ordering the conduct of human lives from cradle to the grave. It was a system which did not allow for changing times and new civilisations, as Christ's original teaching would have done.

The Vicar had not yet seen the bare-headed, short-clad hikers and cyclists being invited to attend Divine Service and stem the retreat that was almost becoming a rout, suffered by organised religion in this country.

As spring advanced into summer, I began to love Hampshire more and more, it was a fine, fair county, containing a brave mixture of old and new. As the summer advanced I found more and more to delight me, harvesting was going on at the very edge of the Vicarage garden. The scent of hay was in the air and I often gave thanks that

I was no longer in London. I had certainly escaped at the best time of the year.

I sent home for my bicycle and on my half-days penetrated into the neighbouring country. Then mother told me that one of my cousins was stationed not very far away. He was in the R.A.M.C. and studying very hard for promotion, but he had asked for my address and expressed a desire to meet me during his free time.

I remembered Vincent well, we had had many a picnic together in my Cardiff days, and once when our mothers had been busy picking blackberries we had gone off in search of Caerphilly Castle and almost lost ourselves.

Already he was a sergeant and working for a commission.

On most of my half-days I met my cousin, going to the cinema if it was wet, holding impromptu picnics on the heath, if the sun shone.

About this time too, I made friends with a woman who lived in a very pretty cottage on the other side of the Common. Her garden adjoined the village green where long games of cricket were played out during the summer evening. She would nod or speak to me if I passed her house on our afternoon walks. It was not long before she asked me to tea.

I had not been at the Vicarage long enough to rate a holiday, but my mother was very desirous of seeing me again, for I had been gone from home more than twelve months, so I invited her to come and see me for a day or two and she could stay with my new found friend across the Common.

When Mother arrived and eventually visited me at my place of work, she was literally horrified at the amount I endeavoured to get through in a day, and it must be remembered that my mother was no mean worker herself.

When she returned to Whitestaunton I realised, not for the first time, that the Vicarage was being run by two pairs of hands, when in reality it needed half a dozen.

XII

The Road West

IT would be idle to say that life at the Vicarage was particularly
satisfactory. Faith scarcely ever spoke to me, visitors treated me
as a servant, and when I took the children out to visit any of their
young friends, the same thing happened. Either I must sit in the
maid's department (more often than not, the kitchen) or be made to
feel awkward by being smothered by the children and ignored by
the adults.

There was one exception to these friends of the Vicar's, however,
and that was a woman who had no children of her own, but was fond
enough of them to invite other people's. She possessed a very intelligent dog, who used to perform all kinds of clever tricks for Peter's
delight.

Our hostess was worldly-wise and kind, and there at least I was
always made welcome and was as much a " visitor " as the children.
One day, she told me bluntly that I was " worth a better job ". Peter
overheard, and with his characteristic lack of tact repeated the remark
to his mother upon our return to the Vicarage.

She pursed up her lips but made no comment. I have an idea, however,
that she was beginning to resent a little her problem child's attachment
to his nursemaid.

I further blotted my copybook at " The Vicar's " by being discovered
reading *Hatter's Castle* in my spare time. This book of Cronin's had
been recommended to me by my sister, and certainly I found it a
wonderful book. It set the scene for a whole series of realistic novels
by the same author, by J. B. Priestley, by Richard Llewellyn and
company. But *Hatter's Castle* when it first appeared must have seemed
rather ahead of its time. I do not know, I only know that the Vicar
considered it eminently unsuitable for anyone who had charge of his
children. I have read it more than once since, and I still cannot see
the reason for his judgment.

Was the Vicar perhaps afraid to face reality—the kind of reality
which this book portrayed?

Despite these drawbacks however, I stayed on for I felt that Peter needed me, and the Hampshire countryside was a solace to me. I loved the heath and the pine, the gorse and the broom, and the fragrant stretches of heather.

One Wednesday I had arranged to meet my cousin Vincent in a nearby town, but something happened at the last moment to prevent me taking the half-day off. The Vicar's wife was going out, and for some reason Faith was confined to her bed. I offered to have another afternoon. Meanwhile I had no way of letting my cousin know. Now by one of those strange coincidences which can have such momentous effect on our lives, Vincent had also been prevented at the last moment from keeping the tryst, but a " mate " of his happened to be cycling in our direction and my cousin gave him a note to deliver to me, explaining his failure to turn up.

It was after tea when the note was delivered. I was sitting on the kitchen window-sill mending one of Paul's garments, and the Vicar's wife who had returned from her outing had just entered the room to give me instructions about getting the supper.

At almost the same moment, a khaki-clad figure drew up at the window and asking if I was " Monica ", presented me with the note.

After supper I was called into the Vicar's study.

The interview opened something like this:

" My wife tells me you have had a visit from a soldier this afternoon."

" Yes, you——"

" One moment, we cannot tolerate your entertaining *soldiers* at the Vicarage."

" It isn't *soldiers*—it's my cousin. . . ."

" One moment," again the hand was raised in remonstrance. " Are you telling me this was your cousin who appeared at the kitchen window this evening—my wife tells me he did not even seem to be sure of your name."

" No, *he* wasn't my cousin. I don't know who *he* was, I've never seen him before. He just came with a message——"

When the interview closed, so was my career as a nursery governess. This was the one and only time I ever received what is so pleasantly known as " the sack ". I often wonder what would have happened if Faith had not been ill and I had been able to have my half-day as usual. Later Vincent has derived some amusement from the situation, and said something to the effect that I was " sacked to success ".

At the time however, I thought it far from funny.

It was a fine morning early in September when I cycled down the Vicarage drive with a suit-case perched precariously on the carrier. Peter ran screaming in one of his tantrums. Monica was going away, he knew it—no one had told him. No one would tell him anything. His mother had forbidden me to warn him of my impending departure, and to me at least, her word was still law.

At the gateway I waved to Peter, told him to be a good boy to Faith and his mother and not forget the Flower Fairies. His screams rang in my ears until the oaks of the Common had been put between myself and the Vicarage.

Well, that was that. Now, at my mother's request I was homeward bound to try to get work nearer Whitestaunton. I did not mind that, the West still held great charm for me, fond though I had become of the Hampshire heaths and commons. I missed the steep hills and their deep, secret valleys, the quiet hamlets so different from these Hampshire towns with their ribbon-development almost joining one to another.

Before Basingstoke I found myself hungry, and the breakfast I had had at seven o'clock seemed to have left little impression on my appetite. Over a field gate I ate the bread and dripping, intended for my lunch, with which Faith had kindly provided me. At Basingstoke I bought some chocolate and biscuits and a pair of dark glasses in Woolworths as the sun was exceedingly fierce and I had a long way to go. Drink I had none, for I failed to see how I could transport a bottle of milk or fruit-squash. I pedalled on happily towards Andover. Map I had none, but the roads were well signposted and I knew where I was making for—it was Salisbury, for Salisbury is on the road to Warminster, and at Warminster I thought I would stay the night. It was about half-way to Whitestaunton, and as I had plenty of time I thought it wiser to tackle the long journey in two parts.

Early in the afternoon I stopped to have a cup of tea at a Roadhouse. The sun beat down fiercely, but downhill at least the speed of my advance was such that I had constantly to brush dead insects from my face and blouse (as I since have from the windscreen of a car). Uphill I lost the breeze of my motion, and over the Downs it began to be a perfect switchback, as much uphill as down. The stretch between Andover and Salisbury seemed endless, for by now I was tiring a little, but cresting the last hill I was suddenly rewarded with the sight of the spire in the Avon Valley. I tumbled off to regard it awhile. Now indeed was I at the gateway to my home country. Warminster was only just over twenty miles away. I knew it to be a hilly road that represented over two hours' hard cycling, but now I was heartened by the knowledge that the worst was behind me. In Salisbury I found the traffic tiring and the busy streets endless, but at last I was pedalling down the Wilton road with my face to the West. The enigma of Stonehenge regarded my passing unmoved. It was early evening, when hot and dishevelled I pushed my bicycle up Bell Hill to Ethel's mother's. I waited long at the door, no one was there. As I waited, wondering what to do and cursing myself for not having warned them I was coming, Ethel's married sister, who lived in a nearby village, approached on her way home from the town. She told me Ethel and her mother had gone away for a week's holiday, but she was sure a Mrs. N. up the road, would put me up for the night. And when I passed her village in the morning, would I call for some apples to take with me, and meanwhile her husband would make out a route for me as she fancied there was a short cut out through Maiden Bradley to Wincanton, and I need not go to Frome and Bruton as I had believed I must.

I thanked her and went on up the hill to Mrs. N.s'. Here I will never forget the welcome I received. Her daughter, who had been a mere tot when I was at school, had now attained schoolgirl status herself and was at the moment very interested in hockey and talked to me enthusiastically of the game all through supper. I remember that supper well. It was the first proper meal I had eaten that day and it was partaken in a room overlooking the Marsh with the fields and brook of my old home. There was plenty of good bread and butter, some of the best ham I had ever tasted (or was it because I was so hungry?) and some fine tomatoes. Afterwards I saw the sun sinking behind the woods from the vantage point of one of the softest of feather beds. Stretching my aching limbs between bleached, darned but spotless sheets, I thought no bed had ever been so welcome or so comfortable.

In the morning my breakfast was brought to me in bed, and it was not *half* a meal either! As I was strapping my case on my bicycle Norman appeared at the door. In the manner in which such matters get about he had heard I was in Warminster and had come round to give me God speed before I was on my way once more.

He was completely unchanged and I felt he must find me very altered with my hair off and my grown-up clothes, but all he said was:

" Still the same old Monica," which somehow cheered me immensely, I did not wish to be found changed by Warminster of all places.

As I left Mrs. N.'s hospitality I turned to ask the reckoning. She hesitated, and I mentally totted it up—a warm welcome, a good supper, a comfortable bed and an excellent breakfast, with willing service throughout and garage for my bicycle.

" Would two shillings be too much? "

Used to kindness though I was, this staggered me completely, but she would not take more. The old saying about it being " the Pore wot 'elps the Pore " zig-zagged through my mind. When I arrived home I sent her daughter my old hockey stick, that being all I could think of to square the real account.

On my way to Maiden Bradley I passed the sacred Field again. I gave it a long searching look, telling it without speech that I had not forgotten my vow to return. It was a golden late-summer morning with very little wind to hinder me, and although all before me was uncertainty I felt life was good, and I was grateful for the mere gift of living.

My road took me by the tall spires of the woods, passed Kit's cottage where I picked up the apples and a route neatly printed for me on a postcard. Then up by Shearwater Lake I pedalled, where lordly pheasants crossed the road in all the glory of their dazzling plumage. Up and away from the sparkle of water, through a dry valley, and then round between an arm of down and an arm of woodland until I came to the delectable Maiden Bradley where I drank of the fountain with the inscription:

" Drink, Travellers, drink of Bradley's purest rill
Which, strange to say, runs quite a mile uphill;
Then to your panting steeds let all attend,
An honest horse is surely man's best friend."

For the word horse I substituted " bike " as scanning with the verse, and then panted on up the high pass which lies between two shoulders of down. How well I was to come to know this stretch of lovely but lonely road, in the years to come.

Presently, away on my left shoulder I saw the chalk-marked ramparts of a great earthwork; its escarpments ran on as an outlier of the Wiltshire downs meeting the Vales of Dorset. On my right was the

Cottages, Dunster

The Cheddar Gorge

graceful colonnaded front of the Hoare mansion at Stourhead, and just beyond I caught a glimpse of the village of Stourton embowered in trees. Then I turned into a road which said:

"London 104.   Exeter 60."

I turned towards Exeter and pedalled on.

An up and down road led me from Wiltshire, through a little piece of Dorset into the County of Somerset, so that in the space of a very few miles I had crossed three counties. This fact impressed me greatly. I was also much taken by the place names on the signposts on either side of the road. They greatly added to my sense of adventure. Names like Pen Selwood, Stoke Trister and Buckhorn Weston, filled me with happiness, as did the glimpses of the blue expanse of the Blackmore Vale, from the hill tops.

I approved of my first sight of Wincanton, its streets were broad, clean and, from my point of view, mainly downhill!

After this first town in Somerset there were more names to delight me, Milborne Port, Compton Pauncefote, Sutton Montis and Weston Bamfylde.

On my left as I approached Sparkford there brooded a tumbled mass of the most inviting hills I had ever seen. They sprawled in all shapes and directions, the one to the fore was wooded and delectable, the village lying beneath it, whose church tower I could espy between the trees was sign-posted as South Cadbury. I did not then know that the great hill was Cadbury Rings (or Camp or Castle as it is alternatively called), the legendary Camelot.

At Sparkford I was grateful for the shade of an avenue of elms culminating at a milk factory. Here I noticed a signpost to North and South Barrow and wondered how they came by their names, were they really north and south of some great barrow. The land was flatter in that direction, stretching towards Castle Cary, and earthworks tended to lie on the Dorset side of the road as I could well see. I pondered the derivation of the name of a village which was to become my loved home one day. But I knew none of these things then, and was aware only that the day was good and the road exceedingly beautiful.

At the other end of Sparkford was a fine gateway with a long avenue of elms to delight the eye. Here the road forked, left to Yeovil, straight on to Ilchester. I went straight on.

I had lunch at a farmhouse that advertised meals, midway between Sparkford and Ilchester. Then I pedalled on across the flat lands of the Yeo, through country that was to see a great Royal Naval Air Station spring from the rich pastures less than a decade later.

I found Ilchester sleeping among its bridges and churches, where the sluggard Yeo wound beneath the willows. Then I was out upon a long road, running straight over hill and dale westwards. I recognised it for a Roman line. It was the Fosse Way.

A long, quiet, but mainly uphill stretch led me towards the tower on the wooded hill of Montacute, but I passed it away on my left, and the long green promontory of Ham Hill followed after it.

Soon I was crossing the river Parret, just before South Petherton. Here it is a pleasing stream, not yet far from its source in the hills beyond Crewkerne. I remember stopping on the bridge to buy an ice-cream from an " Eldorado " man. With my bicycle leaning against the stonework of the bridge I licked my ice-cream appreciatively, while gazing down into the water, here so peaceful and clean, a far cry from the muddy Parret with its turbulent " bore " at Bridgwater. The late summer meadows were serene, the dappled cattle imparted an air of peace and plenty. For the first time since leaving Hampshire the full import of the word " Wessex " took hold of me. Hampshire was lovely, but still too near such great places as Southampton, Bournemouth, Portsmouth and Salisbury and even London itself to have that atmosphere which makes all West of Wincanton seem more than another county, another land! From a hill towards Lopen I could now see the Blackdowns, stretching from Chard to Wellington. Happy hills! with all their secrets, the delectable hamlets, the fortifications of Neroche, the laughing little Yarty, their glades of daffodils and bridal paths of garlic!

Seavington greeted me with the sight of a duck-pond beside the road, and of clean pleasant cottages, stressing once again that a country life is sweet. A mile or two beyond the village I noticed a plantation of trees marching over a well-shaped hillside until they came to a sudden sharp halt midway down an arable field. The sight was so arresting that I stored it in my memory so that ten years later I was to come back and photograph it for one of country books, under the title *Farming Landscape, Summer.*

Soon I was passing the charming thatched forge at Whitelackington, whose Manor House was the scene of a great muster when The Duke of Monmouth held court beneath its fine chestnut tree during his royal tour of the West in 1860.

I pedalled hard up the long, slow, deceptively steep hill which separates Whitelackington from Ilminster. And so down, freewheeling into the Minster on the Ile, whose church is so imposing from without and so disappointing from within, and whose Grammar school is housed in a pleasing medieval building, hung with wistaria blooms in the springtime. Then, plod, plod up the hill out of the town to get me on the Chard road, where I passed " Willy's Rope Walk " which I thought might be a misprint for " Rope Works ", but which I later learned is the correct name for a place where rope and twine is manufactured. At Bridport, long famous for such manufactures, the " walks " used to be the pavements of the town, where the rope was stretched and dried outdoors, even as it is in our own Castle Cary twine factory to this day.

After passing a white farmhouse with a charming garden which stands out even in this district of charming gardens, I found myself approaching the turning to Combe St. Nicholas, where the long uphill lanes present a fairly gentle pass through the Blackdowns, saving the traveller going into Chard and up over Snowdon Hill.

The deep banked lane wound on and up, and I walked and walked, my head now filled with thoughts of home, and my heart with rejoicing to be approaching it.

A friend lived in this village, and as I had to pass her house I stopped for a drink of water. She greeted me with:

" Buzz! what on earth have you been doing—you've got flies all over you! "

Then she took me in and introduced me to her brother and sister and we began talking on photography, a subject in which I was just beginning to be interested, realising that as I had no talent for drawing or painting, I must rely upon a camera to record the natural beauties I so longed to perpetuate.

I could afford to rest now, not to hurry, or look at the clock. There were only two or three more miles to be traversed, I should be home in time for tea anyway.

When I started off again, I hesitated whether to take the lane to the left or right. The left would take me up to the Blackdown crest, and then via " Postman's Lane " into Whitestaunton. " Postman's Lane " led through the woods, round by the Farm and Rectory to emerge in the centre of the village in full sight of church, manor archway, lodge and school. This route obviously for a triumphal return, and mine could hardly be termed that. The right-hand lane, after making a similar steep crossing of the top of the Blackdowns, meandered quietly between high banks through the hamlet of Northay, descending quietly through the woods, with a gleam of the Yarty threading the meadows beyond. Then the road followed the manor wall to the lodge's back door.

That was the route I selected. I saw no one but the ancient Mrs. Potter of Northay, still wearing one black boot and one brown, as I had always remembered her. The lane to Whitestaunton was as empty of any kind of traffic as it usually is (even to this day); from the stone walls supporting the bank which in turn gave on to the woodland, sprouted numerous ferns; the beeches made a colonnade from which to view the stream and the meadows. I put my brake on hard, where the road dipped steeply into my hamlet. Before making the final descent I wanted to make sure it was all there as it had been thirteen months before.

Yes, all was in order, the curving sweep of mellowed wall, the shadow of the Roman steps, the green wildness of the Villa ruins, the copper beeches of the Manor lawn.

The afternoon sunlight came flooding through the beeches as it does nowhere so well as at Whitestaunton. The still lake mirrored the swans, and reflected the old Norman church tower, a gable of the old manor house peeped through the greenery, while beyond, Manor Hill rose as a soft green backcloth to the peaceful sylvan scene.

Whitestaunton! how fortunate was I to possess such a home to which to return. As my bicycle bore me down under the shadow of the manor's lichened wall, I beheld our dog Mack asleep on the little crescent of lawn beneath the wistaria leaves.

Then he heard my approach, gave a grunt, preparatory to " sending off" the intruder, changing it to delighted squealing barks upon recognising me. What a welcome!

As I lifted my bicycle over the step, mother emerged from the kitchen as fresh and dainty as ever. Undemonstrative, as mothers go, but with an appetising meal laid ready and a great deal to say to me as usual.

The new butler had my old bedroom and I must sleep in the little backroom. I did not mind, it overlooked the lane down which I had just ridden, and if I slewed my neck round enough when I had my head out of the window, I could still see the Roman villa and the lake. This time of the year, the lane would be hung with bright gossamer each morning, gossamer hung right across the road from one side to the other, an unforgettable sight in the new-minted sunshine of a September morning.

I helped Mother to change the flowers and polish the brasses and tiles of the little church, and to treat the coffin-stools and bench-ends with linseed oil against dry rot. I never saw a church kept better than Whitestaunton when my mother was in charge of it.

We lived without lack, if without luxury, while I started the old round of answering advertisements. One well-known firm of manufacturing chemists who asked for a young lady of secondary school education as a counter-assistant, turned me down because I was not tall enough. The supply of labour was so plentiful that they could afford to do that! During this last war I saw some peculiar shapes and sizes of womanhood behind their counters and thought with amusement of my own interview, when the specified height had been five feet, five inches.

The supply of " labour " was still far greater than the demand, this was a time when the unemployment figures were at their highest. In the year 1934 about 750,000 ex-servicemen were still out of work. Mr. H. J. Massingham, commenting on this fact, wrote:—

" This is a characteristic extract from the Press of the time—' By the merciless operation of the law of supply and demand, about 750,000 ex-servicemen are out of work.' Obviously this ' law of supply and demand ' is an exorable demon who demands his quota of human misery exactly like the Moloch of the Tyrians and Carthaginians."

This false god to which the happiness of so many families were sacrificed on the altar of economics saw me out of work for almost two months, it seemed such a long time that I almost gave up hope. But although out of work, I was not " unemployed ". I helped to look after the home, cooked, cleaned and shopped in between cycling many miles for endless interviews, or on interminable wild-goose chases after positions that had been already filled.

Mother wished to apprentice me to dressmaking or hair-dressing or something that might be called a career, but there was the question of expense and the uncertainty of my father's employment.

Then one late November day, reading the advertisements in a local paper, I saw the announcement that a new cinema was shortly to be opened at Yeovil. Yeovil was quite a busy town and at the moment there was only one very small picture palace that seated about three hundred people.

The air was damp and misty and the woods hung in tatters as I cycled the twenty-one miles to Yeovil. My mother had not thought much of the job—it seemed " low kind of work "—if I got it—I'd be sure to have to wear some silly kind of " head-dress " and a uniform that would show my legs—the hours would be dreadful, and totally what I was unused to.

A new cinema must need new hands though, and a job was a job in those days, so to Yeovil I went.

XIII

Continuous Performance

FOR the first dozen miles or so, my road to Yeovil was an exact reversal of that taken on my way to Whitestaunton from Oak Common. Once over the Parret bridge at Petherton Cross, however, I found myself on a road entirely new to me. The old Fosse Way, companion of my travels down from Ilchester, threaded the hills to my left and was soon far behind, while the Yeovil road wound beneath the base of Ham Hill. This long green escarpment is the cradle of many fine Dorset houses, churches and farms. The vast acres of mellow stone, hidden from the roadway by a clothing of fine turf, have proved the birth-place of many architectural beauties, which unlike the charity of Portland, begins at home.

Half London was excavated from the clean white stone of Dorset's rugged island of Portland, but when Dorset beautified herself with tower and tithe barn or even humble cottage, it was not to Portland, but to Ham Hill she turned.

The workings have honeycombed the long green promontory above Stoke under Ham, but the marks of Celts and Roman were there even before the quarries. Now it is difficult to know what are barrows and what are turf-grown stone-tips, what are entrenchments of the Roman camp and what are quarry-workings.

After the high green mass of Ham Hill I found myself cycling beneath the conical tree-crowned Mount of St. Michael, above the village of Montacute. East Stoke as well as Stoke Sub Hamdon had proved pleasant enough villages with most of their houses and shops constructed from the local warm-tinted stone, but the biggest joy of all awaited me. Past the powerful looking church of East Stoke which seems to embody most of our ecclesiastical building ages at their best I came to a string of ordinary red-brick council houses.

At the end of them I found myself face to face with a high pair of wrought-iron gates, and there, at the bottom of the long, dwindling-perspective of an avenue of fine yews, I beheld the magnificent frontage of an Elizabethan mansion.

It was a veritable story book house, a place to dream about. I tumbled off my bicycle and peered between the bars of the great entrance gates. The many windows winked at me, the clustering chimneys beckoned and invited. I did not know then that the motto above the door was:—

" And Yours, My Friends."

How often have I since returned to Montacute, how well have I come to know the great house both inside and out, but how long will it be before I have forgotten that initial tantalising glimpse of the West Front on a misty autumn day. The Yeovil road gave me a friend I cherished dearly.

Montacute itself, once free of the council houses, proved to be a charming village and I can well understand it being one of the earliest acquisitions of the National Trust. Montacute owes much to the late Mr. A. R. Powys who for more than a quarter of a century was the secretary of the Society for the Preservation of Ancient Buildings. His father was for long the vicar of Montacute, so the young Powyses had ample opportunity to know and love the beauties of this Somerset village.

Praise of it creeps into Llewelyn Powys's *Somerset Essays*, he cannot even keep mention of it out of the Dorset volume. John Cowper Powys and his brother Theodore whose writings have entertained and enriched so many, knew their first nature rambles about these hills and valleys and played the daring games of Rider Haggard's leap among the stone chasms of Hamdon Hill.

After Montacute, Yeovil was drawing near to me, but I had not yet finished with the countryside. I passed the fertile farms of Lufton, alas, though I did not know it then, so soon to be torn up to make a permanent camp for the Military. I passed Houndstone corner, as yet undefaced by a crimson painted restaurant whose gaudy notices proclaimed:—

" Tourists Come In and Eat! "

I entered the last village on the road to Yeovil, going by the euphonious name of Preston Plucknett. This village, alas, is now almost one with the town, ribbon development having covered the intervening miles between the town centre and the village's ancient Tithe Barn. In the year 1934, the Preston Road houses had not extended nearly so far, and the group of Abbey Farmhouse and Barn were a delight and a challenge.

Then I thought Preston Plucknett a wonderful village to find so close to the outskirts of a town. Now the town has all but swallowed it up. In 1934 the Westfield Estates had not been built, and the Seaton Road houses, which were to accommodate the workers of Westlands Aircraft factories, were only just then in the course of construction. I did not know that where I could see the hordes of workmen raising a new colony to house a new industry, there had been recently discovered the remains of a very thriving Roman settlement. Beautifully tessellated pavements from these accidental excavations can be seen in Yeovil's museum. After the workmen's report, a party of archæologists, under the leadership of Mr. St. George Gray of Taunton, reconstructed the story of Roman life in Yeovil, before the ground was hidden again by the new estates.

Yeovil, while appearing so large and busy after my seclusion at Whitestaunton, in no way awed me, as London had done. There were crowds it was true, and scarcely room to walk on the pavements, or cycle down the narrow main street. But they were friendly, brisk yet hearty crowds. While not appearing so purposeful, they had yet more purpose than London throngs. Their business appeared to be living, and enjoying the process, not tearing along towards a problematical tomorrow.

Here was bustle and activity all right, but none of the soulless rush of the metropolis. Reality was always in sight of *these* people. The green core of Wyndham thrust itself into the town, the cattle-strewn rampart of Summerhouse Hill raised itself behind the Town Station, from every tilted shopping street it was possible to see the real country close at hand.

Although Yeovil has altered and expanded to an amazing degree during these intervening fifteen years, it is still possible to see the green hills ringing it about, and Summerhouse and Wyndham and Babylon Hill still beckon and invite from between the closely packed houses.

Yeovil, having suffered several major fires when our building ages were at their best, had little to offer me architecturally, but I liked its busy, clean atmosphere well enough, and the bustle and smell of the market, almost in the centre of the town.

I found the offices of the cinema company and after a happy and successful interview was told to start work on Monday, the tenth of December. I had been engaged as an usher, with prospects of the

" chocolate job " to follow. The next thing was to find somewhere to live. I had decided that I could easily cycle home at week-ends—but every night, after eleven p.m.? well, no. The cinema manager agreed, forty-two miles each day was too much. If I cared to do it once a week, that was my own affair, meanwhile he gave me a letter of introduction to the vicar of St. Michael's, who would tell me if any of his parishioners had a room for me.

One of them had. She was an elderly lady living in an old house in Market Street, a house whose garden reminded me instantly of that at Walnut Tree Cottage. Indeed, it was just such another house, but larger.

My new landlady was kind and helpful, charging me only six shillings a week for a large bed-sitting room at the front of the house. The use of gas and coal were extra. I did some mental arithmetic (my wages after deductions were sixteen and eightpence a week) and I decided I could afford it.

My working hours were from one-thirty to ten-thirty p.m., this left me my mornings almost entirely free. They were mornings in which I could read, write, or explore. It meant a long day, but I did not dislike the prospect, it would be so good to be independent again.

Cycling once more westwards, I joined the throngs of labourers who had finished their work for the day on the new housing estates. The November dusk had fallen. It was mild and drizzly, and although still the wrong side of Christmas, there was somehow the promise of spring in the air. A workman shouted to me that my bicycle lamp was out. It was indeed, the battery seemed to have given up. I screwed up my eyes and pedalled on through the damp darkness, hoping no policeman would spot me. The rain set in heavily as I bumped at last down Postman's Lane. I had come home with a job, anyway.

On December the tenth I started work at the brand-new, raw-brick edifice in the Triangle, Yeovil; known as the Gaumont Palace. On all the hoardings proclaiming its newly-born existence it was called " The Luxury Cinema of the West ". Word had even got round that there was to be an organ, but it stopped short of that final magnificence.

When I presented myself for work on that memorable Monday I had to step over an earnest young woman who was joining the crimson carpet with an industry and dexterity that held me spell-bound. My! but she was an artist at her work. Then I had to dodge a huge centrepiece of ornamental lighting that was being swung into position, high in the centre of the newly sprayed ceiling.

Men were manœuvring the seats of the " sixpennies " into position, someone was hammering frantically in the direction of the balcony.

On the bare screen, Tom Walls and Alfred Drayton flickered grotesquely, the brilliant " cleaner's light " making them appear faint and hazy, while the film was tested for " sound ".

Engineers and operators shouted to one another from seats in the auditorium to doors marked " Strictly Private ". Cleaners were wielding giant vacuum cleaners, a man with a paint pot was endeavouring to whiten the edges of the steps leading from the foyer to the " shillings ".

" How'll we ever open on Saturday? Search me! You, floor-staff, Miss? Up the top of the balcony—straight ahead—the rest of them are up there. Look out! Mind them nails! Open Saturday! Be a ruddy miracle if we do! "

But we opened on Saturday, December the fifteenth. The sound men had been working all night, the manager had hardly seen his bed for a week. To a constant accompaniment of hammering and shouting and the hum of vacuum cleaners, the floor-staff had been drilled in their behaviour.

For five days we were instructed how to hold a torch, so as not to dazzle patrons, how to proceed with filling up the seating on a busy night, how to conduct ourselves, how to proceed in case of fire.

We were fitted with our uniforms, plain serviceable dresses, of scarlet poplin (so we were easily recognisable in the dark, we were told) and no sign of the " ridiculous headdress " threatened by my mother. I smiled with relief.

The opening ceremony passed without any major catastrophe. I have an idea to this day that I sadly mixed some of the Invitation Cards, and sent the Corporation into the wrong rows. But at least the Mayor was where he should be—right in the centre of the Balcony. Two Gaumont-British " starlets " Glennis Lorrimer and Barry Mackay were there to lend glamour to the proceedings, bouquets were presented and speeches made.

After the guests and dignitaries, came the people of Yeovil to their new cinema. There came the glove-cutters, the engineers from Petters, the factory girls from Aplin and Barretts, the apprentices from Westlands, the housewives and children and a sprinkling of people in from the surrounding countryside to do their week-end shopping.

Our first offering *A Cup of Kindness* gave them a happy enough start. With it was a heavily sentimental " tear-jerker " called *Reunion* which starred Onslow Stevens, Lila Lee and the irascible Claude Dillingwater. It was a perfectly balanced programme for those who came to be " taken out of themselves ", and not to think too much.

That very first opening-day I noticed something about the crowds who came up over the foyer steps to produce their shillings and pence at the chromium plated box-office. They came with the certain expectation of a few hours' happiness. To some it was their one weekly treat and outing, to others it was an escape to a world more wonderful and exciting than their own could ever be, and so therefore, for the time being at least, more *real*. All these people, these not very critical, analytical, or self-searching people were coming for a few hours " break ". They had come to laugh and cry over something other than themselves. Here was release and refuge, both.

Much can be said against the influence of the cinema, against the false standards of conduct and thought it may be partly responsible for setting, against its preoccupation with sex and crime, and the fact that it has been used by the masses as a substitute for thinking. But to its credit can be laid the hours of comparatively harmless happiness it has given so many people, the certain relaxation, the glimpses of art (even when of an inferior kind) that many lives would lack entirely.

And to its credit must be laid the interest in great music, literature and art at which cinema-patrons have ultimately arrived, by no matter how devious a route. Is it not better that they hear *Madam Butterfly* through Grace Moore on a sound track than that they should not hear it at all? How many towns of the size of Yeovil would patronise Grand Opera in any case? Is it not better that the villagers from Merriot and Stoke under Ham should know Tschaikowsky as the man who wrote a concerto for Mary Astor to play in a Bette Davis film, than they should not know his music at all? They might never have seen the works of Gauguin apart from *The Moon and Sixpence*, but a garbled version of a painter's life is better than no interest in him at all, in my opinion. If we wait for the best, for perfection, the man in the street may never come to within reach of it, but if we meet him half-way, sometimes more than half-way—he may be led to it—in the end.

The fact that people came to what I had already begun to look upon as " my cinema " to enjoy themselves and be happy, made the work, as far as I was concerned a great pleasure. How could it be otherwise? A happy atmosphere begets happiness, once set, it is not hard to maintain. In those early days, the newly-trained staff worked well together. We were not a team of " glamour-girls ", with platinum bobs, false-eyelashes and scarlet finger-nails. We were girls who might have been in service, in shops or in factories, but for the slump. Our work was just a job, that was all. Our cashier was a hard-working mother, not Hollywood's idea of a box-office girl at all. She was a woman who needed the part-time work because gloving was so bad at the moment. Many of our patrons were known to her by name.

By and by, however, this staff left for one reason or another. Some wanted more money (after all the wages were very slight for even the least ambitious), some wanted more reasonable hours, some found the work too tiring. From one cause and another however, the original staff left one at a time, and presently I was the only member of the original " floor-staff " to remain. The new girls did not receive the instruction and drilling that we had done, and in my opinion the standard of service commenced to deteriorate, as to this present day it has in so many concerns connected with a large public.

After my first Saturday night's work I went out into the Triangle and saw the buses lined up to take some of our patrons to their outlying homes. There were destination boards to Odcombe and East Coker, to Sherborne and Milborne Port, to Mudford and Marston and South Barrow.

It was strange to see the name again—South of the Barrow. How many of the places for which these buses were destined, had I cycled through? How many of them should I get to know before I had done? They rolled away from the lighted cinema frontage into the darkness of country roads and lanes, while their occupants compared shopping notes or discussed the merits of the programmes they had just seen.

After the cinema had closed for the night, it was too late to think of cycling to Whitestaunton. Besides, after walking for hours on carpets as yielding as sand, my feet ached intolerably.

But by ten a.m. the next day I was passing Montacute House once more.

And now my weeks fell into a pattern, altered only by the change of programme at my place of work, or the changing seasons at Whitestaunton.

Mondays found me sailing down the long steep lanes from Combe

St. Nicholas, trudging up the hill out of Ilminster, flying over the Parret bridge, pedalling beneath St. Michael's hill at Montacute, and finally bumping to rest at the bicycle shed under the Gaumont stairs.

On Tuesdays I got into the rhythm of my simple housekeeping at Market Street. On Wednesday mornings, more often than not, I did my essential shopping which often included errands for my mother. Thursday, except in the case of unparalleled attractions, offered a change of programme (super films were kept for six days), it was also the town's early closing day, and the shop-keeping population often attended the cinema in the afternoon. Friday was market-day, and there was the usual influx of country people. Friday brought in the farmers, it eventually brought in my own farmer. I loved the breath of real countryside the market gave to the streets. I liked to hear the voices of pigs and sheep, and it was even exciting when a bull broke loose and the streets cleared magically!

Above all I liked catching the snatches of speech exchanged in the thoroughfares or shops. It seemed that the countryman who lived only a mile or two from a thriving town like Yeovil spoke just as rich a kind of dialect as the farmer in the heart of Whitestaunton, or the man ploughing under the shadow of the Downs.

Saturday was a long strenuous day. If the film showing was anything of a " draw " at all, we were usually filled up early in the afternoon. There were always stray children to be attended to, and harassed, basket-laden mothers, who dropped things down behind the seats, or shed a scarf or glove in the gangway. More sweets were always bought at the week-ends. Money changed hands more readily with the pay-packets almost untouched. Saturdays came and went and we hardly saw " the going of them ".

Sundays, come hail rain or snow, May or December, saw me out on the road to Whitestaunton again. When the cinema closed on the Christmas Day which happened to fall on a Friday that year, I went home on the 25th, came back for the Boxing Day (when we did brisk business) and then cycled home again for the usual Sunday, the day following. That week I had pedalled more than eighty miles over the roads of South-west Somerset.

I came to know my road so well that now, when motoring along it I find myself memorising every bend, every change in camber, and every shape of field and copse. I know at once if a tree has been felled, or a house built, but I am happy to say it has not changed a great deal and it is still possible to see a water-vole dive off a lily-leaf and swim like a silver streak towards the buttercupped bank of the Parret.

I was soon given the work of chocolate-girl which made my employment so much more interesting. This, however, kept me outside in the foyer most of the time, and I found it difficult to see very much of the films. By moving my tea-hour slightly however, I managed to see a good deal, and it was very rarely that I missed a newsreel or a "documentary" short. The non-fiction in films as in books has always appealed to me.

As much as the films, the people who paid to see them, excited my interest. There were so many types and characters. Some of the greatest entertainment could be had from the periodic visits of "county" families, often come to finish a day out after a Point to Point meeting, a Show, or some thing of the kind.

There would be a great deal of argument as to what was showing, at what time, and who was in it. They rarely thought of consulting someone who might have enlightened them. Then there would follow a mass movement toward the balcony steps, where they would be asked to produce their tickets. A wild hunt would follow. Mummy had them, no she gave them to Jim, no Hester had them——

"Oh Mummy, you simply MUST find them." "Where *can* they be?" "Oh Darling, you *are* too tiresome!"

Then would come the loud-voiced flash of inspiration, "Darlings, I didn't *buy* them! I've just remembered—we were talking, and I went right past the box!" (a fact I had noticed long ago). Then followed the younger daughter's comment, clinching the whole matter, I thought, amazingly well.

"Oh Mummy, you *EGG!*"

What a lovely word, how very apt! The cashier exchanged glances with the girl on the door—"Eggs" described them so well, eggs coddled, addled or scrambled—their exaggerated accents and peculiar behaviour. Henceforward the staff knew them as "eggs". In our family at least, the term has persisted, and I find it very apt.

The "Eggs" came to see George Arliss in films like *The House of Rothschild*, or Ronald Colman as a very gentlemanly *Clive of India*. They had a natural penchant for British films or at least British stars. Hollywood was largely unexplored territory to them.

Not so to the masses of our public however. They were as much at home in the America of the Hardy family, or of Shirley Temple, as they were in the streets of their own town.

Shirley Temple's *Baby Take a Bow* was the forerunner of amazing " house-fillers " for us. They were largely pictures in which I could see less than nothing, but the Yeovil public lapped them up. Clark Gable after *It Happened One Night* was a close runner-up.

These were some of the last years of regular appearances of great stars like Ann Harding and Norma Shearer, or the incomparable Garbo. Some great names then, are great names still—they are the " stayers " like Irene Dunne and Spencer Tracy, Myrna Loy and Frederick March.

Leslie Howard was making his reputation and holding it quietly in the face of all comers. He delighted us in *It's Love I'm After* and awed us in *Outward Bound*, he overshadowed the dynamic Bogart in *The Petrified Forest*, swaggered through *The Scarlet Pimpernel*, and gave us a fine romantic Romeo to Norma Shearer's Juliet.

Bette Davis made a timid entrance in George Arliss's *The Man who Played God*, stayed for the success of *Of Human Bondage* with Leslie Howard and embarked on a career of unparalleled successes.

Costume romance was supplied largely by Conrad Veidt, by the new young Robert Donat and Douglas Fairbanks, junior. An up-and-coming young man called Errol Flynn was given the lead in Sabatini's *Captain Blood*, Matheson Lang forgot there was such a word as retirement.

Sir Aubrey Smith continued to portray everyone's idea of a typical elderly Englishman, while players like John Wayne, Jean Arthur and Alice Faye were just emerging from the ranks of " second-feature " players, Jack Holt and Richard Dix continued to be seen with some frequency, while John Gilbert was still one of the screen's leading " great lovers ". English screen actresses were very ladylike and English screen actors smacked rather too much of the theatre. Madeleine Carroll was making the best of two worlds, being decidedly well bred and English, and decidedly cinematic at the one and the same time.

Ginger Rogers had broken into musicals on the arm of the fleet-footed Fred Astaire, and was busy spreading the magic cult of " glamour " which was later to drop on Betty Grable and company.

Ann Sheridan was about to personify " Oomph ", and Vivien Leigh reveal that English actresses could act after all. But in the main

Wistaria on the Lodge, Whitestaunton

Gold Hill, Shaftesbury

filmgoers turned from the well-bred artificiality of English stars, and the " phoney " glamour of Hollywood " cuties ", to the warmth and passion of the ladies from the Continent.

Anna Sten came up in a blaze of publicity to decorate Tolstoy's *Resurrection*. To have a lazy eyelid and a broken accent was a passport to stardom. Sari Maritza, Militza Khorjus, Dolly Haas and Tamara Desni were " imports " on both sides of the Atlantic. Ingrid Bergman had not yet been discovered and Leni Reifenstahl turned from her dreaming legend of *The Blue Light* to directing a film of the 1936 Olympic Games.

Elizabeth Bergner came simpering into the British filmgoer's heart, while London born Lilian Harvey made one success after another in the German studios.

These were the days of Edna Best and Herbert Marshall, when Nova Pilbeam was the child in *Little Friend* and Jimmy Hanley had the small part of an errand boy in the same film. Only a few weeks ago I saw him in a personal appearance at our cinema, having come the whole way to the " top of the tree ", since then.

I watched a fashion in musicals set by Jeanette Macdonald and Nelson Eddy, taken up by Marta Eggerth, Grace Moore, Nino Martini, Jan Kiepura, Gigli and Tauber.

Evelyn Laye came to the screen with *Evensong* and Jessie Mathews with *Evergreen*. The inimitable George Robey and the late and much lamented Mr. " Jetsam " enlivened a film version of *Chu Chin Chow*, with lovely Pearl Argyle leading the ballet.

Gaumont British brought us *Jew Süss*, *The Passing of the Third Floor Back* and *The Wandering Jew*, all with Conrad Veidt in the lead.

Many well read books were " translated " to the screen, from James Hilton's *Lost Horizon* to Dickens's *David Copperfield*, from Victor Hugo's *Les Misérables* to Hervey Allen's *Anthony Adverse*.

In the two last named Frederick March pulled off a hat-trick of stardom that began with *Dr. Jekyll and Mr. Hyde*, and was capped by last year's Academy Award for *The Best Years of Our Lives*. March is by no means my favourite actor, but I think he must have had successes in more meaty parts over a longer period than almost any other screen actor of comparable age.

Charles Laughton roared at us from *Mutiny on the Bounty*, Bing Crosby crooned at us from a host of trivial " opuses " whose names I cannot recall, Peter Lorre sent shivers down our back in *The Man Who*

Knew Too Much, and Boris Karloff made our hair stand on end as the monster in *Frankenstein*.

Hollywood was "magnificent and stupendous" with its De Milles, its Dietrichs, its Von Stroheims, its *Lives of a Bengal Lancer*. Britain was unpretentious but entertaining with the Aldwych farces, with Jack Hulbert and Vera Pearce, Marcel Varnell and Will Hay ; we roared at *Oh Mr. Porter* and *The Camels are Coming*.

Out of the welter of memories of those days there stands out Robert Donat, a new and compelling personality in Dumas's *Monte Cristo*, the natural appeal of Jean Muir in a magazine story called *Desirable* and the superb photography of *The Blue Light* and *Man of Aran*.

I remember too, Maxwell Anderson's *Winterset*, a film with a difference—and a film which did not pay; and Norma Shearer and Veree Teasdale with the pop-eyed Joan Crawford in *The Women*, another film that was an artistic success and a financial failure as far as our public was concerned. But above all, I remember an unpretentious second feature, almost entirely acted by children, called *No Greater Glory*.

A foreword to this film stated that every ruling power in Europe should be compelled to see it and draw a moral from it.

Here was the tale of a horde of poor children who took sides to stage a mock war over the possession of a vacant lot on which to play. They took their rivalry seriously, and warfare of the contending gangs becomes more open and more dangerous. One of them, the boy called Nemachek, a weak young lad of European extraction, is sent on a secret mission while suffering from a severe cold. He is ordered by his parents to stay in bed, but at the appointed time he staggers forth to fulfil his duty.

He dies of pneumonia. Even while his friends mourn at his funeral, a company of building contractors moved in to take over the lot for which he fought and died.

I have never met anyone who has heard of *No Greater Glory* nor who remembers George Breakstone as the slum child, and I thought the film must have passed unnoticed, until, shortly before he died, James Agate mentioned it, urging it should be shown again. He had not even remembered the title correctly, but his description of the film was unmistakable. I was glad that someone had appreciated its significance.

Here I must apologise to those concerned if I have misspelt any names or misplaced any dates, both errors are possible, as I write from memory only and have no text books from which to check my facts. Before I resume personal aspects of my life at the cinema—a life which was to last half a dozen years I would make the following observations:

The English countryside has never received anything like justice on the screen. René Clair in *The Ghost Goes West*, made use of English sky and clouds in a way that might be copied to advantage by native directors. We have more recently been given glimpses of the Cotswolds in *Tawny Pipit*, Kent in *A Canterbury Tale* and Sussex in *The Loves of Joanna Godden*, but always apologetically and half-heartedly.

What a wealth of English scenery stretches from Land's End to Hadrian's Wall, from Blakeney Point to " The Lakes ". Why are they not drawn upon? Why are we so ashamed of our countryside? It is not all built upon and marred, after all. It is true the sun does not shine for us as it does for the Hollywood Western, but I wish our producers knew what cloud-shadows over the downs can look like, or that a set cannot build anything to equal the play of light and shade in a West Country copse.

We have a land like no other and the surest, easiest way to educate people to the value of their heritage is by the medium of the cinema. I would ask for natural colour, and no " background music " other than that of the waterfall, the click of the binder, or the wind in the corn. And if our film of the countryside is to be a non-fictional piece of entertainment, please let it be free from the eternal facetious running commentary, and let the pictures speak for themselves.

Much has been said about the cinema being an " art ", and it has been suggested that " art " is the enemy of box-office. We hear the continual glib phrase, " What the public wants ". The sponsors of this phrase too often mean " What we give the public ", for the public can only judge by what it gets. Given the *opportunity* of seeing good, the public will ultimately want it, but it seems to me that *opportunity* is everything. How can they judge if they are never allowed to try?

As a matter of fact the success of films like *The Blue Light*, *The White Hell of Pitz Palu* and more recent offerings like *Monsieur Vincent* and *Paisa*, show that the public do not waste such opportunities as they are offered. It is unfortunate perhaps, that the films listed above are continental, wholly or in part, but the Continent it seems, pays more attention to art and less to box office, and nothing appears to suffer, least of all entertainment value.

If one " leg-show " pays, then leg-show follows leg-show, ad infinitum, a similar " cycle " of crime and brutality follows. One " Western " has a host of imitators, one successful " horror " film starts a fashion. " We will now sit ourselves down " say the Producers (or words to that effect) and find the ingredients that make a ' best seller ' for the box-office."

When Shakespeare began to write *Hamlet*, or Tschaikowsky his Fifth Symphony, I do not imagine either of these gentlemen decided they would write or compose a best-seller. What they created were works of art—the best in their creators at the time. Because of their sheer merit in sincerity, in craftsmanship, in human appeal, they became " best-sellers ".

However much tastes may vary, the public on the whole will always respond to that which is *good*, even when they do not pause to analyse what makes it good. It is the bounden duty of those concerned in any art to give of their best always. Public taste is in their hands—the public can only be as good as what it is offered.

In this respect, the cinema has a long way to go. In the past it was thought that money had a great deal to do with the matter, if enough was spent, the results were bound to be good. Now we are coming to realise that the less money film companies have to splash on " epics " the better chance we stand of seeing good work on our screens, for where there is insufficient means for distracting " padding ", more " heart " will have to be put in the work to make up for it—real characters, real situations and real backgrounds will need to be used, and real merit will have to appear when wealth, once the cloak of mediocrity, is no longer to be relied upon.

When Italian directors, artists and technicians found themselves in such reduced circumstances after this last war, that they had to go out into the streets and countryside of Italy to make their films without adequate studios and equipment, the results were minor masterpieces like *Open City*, *Shoe Shine*, *To Live in Peace* and *Four Steps in the Clouds*.

I do not imagine that the little French film *Le Diable Au Corps* cost a fortune to make, but how rich it was in acting, in charm and in human appeal. Such films and their entertainment value in the truest sense of the phrase can never be measured by the amount of money they cost to make.

XIV

The New Country

COMING to see *The Gay Divorcée* or *The Firefly* were people
who came at the same time week after week and sat as nearly as
possible in the same seats. From these habitual filmgoers of
Yeovil and district it was possible to pick out characters, one might
even trace the history of a courting couple.

First they would meet in the foyer, almost as if by accident, and end
by going inside together. A few visits later and it might be arm in
arm together. Then they would come in having met on the way,
diffidently at first, and then more openly, hand in hand. He would
buy her chocolates and the best seats he could afford. The love-affair
would run its course. Sometimes they would quarrel and come to the
pictures separately or with other partners. If the romance ended in
marriage (as it frequently seemed to), there was less spent on chocolates
and even on seating. Sometimes this economy was effected before
the ceremony to save money for it; sometimes it was enforced afterwards by the proximity of a "happy event". When the family
arrived, they might take it in turns to visit the cinema, while the other
stayed home and minded the baby. In many cases we missed their
patronage almost altogether, although from rare appearances it was
plain they had not left the town. I do not think abstinence was all a
matter of economy, their lives had now become so full of other matters
that the "escape" offered by the cinema was not necessary.

There were amusing incidents in plenty, there were jealous girl
friends and fiancées who watched their man closely in case the usherette
on the door should make eyes at him. If he thanked her too graciously
for tearing their tickets, the girl in possession would jerk him away
sharply. Many is the glance I have exchanged with the ticket-girl
over such an incident! Because we worked in a cinema, we must all
be sirens!

Matinée patrons were often almost blinded by the sudden transition
from bright sunlight to the darkness of the cinema. They would
grope and stumble in spite of the usher's torch-light. Often they
would attempt to settle themselves in another patron's lap, or on a seat

that did not exist. Toes would be stepped on, hats knocked awry, and muttering and grumbling ensue. Sometimes a woman with a well-laden basket, half-blinded into the mistaken belief that the row in front of her was unoccupied, would knock off the hats of all the people in that row, her bumping basket doing fearful execution, while the victims wondered what manner of fate had befallen them, until eventually the culprit lowered herself into her appointed place.

On my own part, and before I ceased to be an usher, many a half-blind patron has been led by the arm, had her seat lowered into position and been firmly placed in it, to save undue interruption of the programme, and possible bad language on the part of other patrons.

The film titles were often a cause of merriment. Pity the poor commissionaire who when asked over the 'phone " What is on? " had to reply: " You Can't have Everything ", " Tell Me tonight " or " It's All Yours."

I heard *Les Misérables* called a few things which the author would never have recognised, while Marlene Dietrich suffered at the hands of the local dialect. The staff were often the worst offenders in the matter, and the manager himself was not always exempt. One time-sheet which I typed out had the item " Friml Favourites " altered to " Film Favourites " by a conscientious commissionaire who had never heard of the composer of *The Vagabond King*.

By this time I was helping generally. I had bought myself a second-hand typewriter, had taught myself to use it (after a fashion, as I still do) and was able to help with secretarial work when the occasion demanded.

I was kept far busier with " chocolates " than I had been when on the floor staff. True there was not quite so much running up and down, but I rarely knew a really slack period. When I appeared inside the auditorium, during " Sales Intervals ", i.e. during the news, the trailers, advertisements, etc., I had to carry a very heavily laden tray. A page-boy was supposed to assist me, but at the crucial moment he was usually required elsewhere and I found I must carry out my sales unaided. I had made it a rule never to sell during a big picture, unless it was some raucous " musical ". If people could not settle themselves with chocolate before the main feature came on I decided it only fair to those who wanted to listen and look uninterrupted, that they be made to wait until afterwards. Apart from this one little foible, my only concession to art if you like, I endeavoured to be as obliging as possible.

When " Inside ", I simply hated being asked for something I had not got, so I tried to bring half my counter in with me. If a " line " was asked for more than once, I added it to my next order to the manufacturers. In this way both my stock and my custom increased. As the years passed, I developed quite a steady little business and some of my regular customers would come in to buy their confectionery at my counter even when they were going to the opposition's picture, or not going to the cinema at all. I used to find this very gratifying, and it encouraged me to further efforts.

I dressed my counter with care every afternoon before the cinema opened, pestering my commercial travellers for attractive " dummies ". At first my chief suppliers were Cadburys, Rowntrees, Nestlés, Lyons and Frys, to which I later added Barker & Dobson, Cliftons, Kunzle and Caleys.

Eventually of course, the business I had built up was killed by the war and chocolate rationing, but that is to anticipate.

I was not only interested in my own side of the business, but I began to consider the ordering and publicity departments of the cinema and to take a keen interest in the projection room. I did not find my all-embracing interest shared by the majority of the staff. After the first few months of our existence they came and went with a monotonous regularity. I think Welsh Joycie from Swanswick would have said our Gaumont Palace was the employment bureau's delight.

We had started out with a drilled floor-staff, an ex-sergeant-major as chief commissionaire, an excellent second in command (who incidentally was one of the best-read men I have ever met), and an able third commissionaire and a bright little page-boy. At the end of the first year, only the men and myself remained of the original staff. In the operating box, only the Chief was the same. The morning staff of cleaners remained largely the same year after year, barring illness and occasional sudden death. Theirs was a job for life, a few extra shillings each week to buy the fish-and-chips, or pay for a charabanc outing to Weymouth.

Although I hardly regarded my share of the Gaumont Palace work as " a job for life " I was prepared to take every interest in it. I was prepared to learn about every aspect of it, and that no doubt was the secret of my contentment.

I had little patience with the girls about me whose theme song was " Roll on tea-time ", or " Roll on supper-time " or " Roll on the week end! " They wished it were a new picture, or they wished it was

Saturday night, or next week. It seemed to me that they were " roll-ing-on " and " wishing " their whole lives away. I could not under-stand it myself. The whole business of film-making, showing and distribution was so absorbingly interesting, and if the films palled there was always the study of the patrons!

Now all our staff were not like the above, as I shall show presently, but it was a very common fault and one which is responsible for many of the labour ills of today. I have always believed that if one takes an interest in one's work, the *time* takes care of itself.

No wonder six years passed at the Gaumont, almost before I had known it. But they were not an entirely unbroken or uneventful six years.

When I had been at the cinema about a year, the young butler at Whitestaunton took himself a wife, and as they wanted the Lodge in which to live, my mother had to find elsewhere for herself.

After some searching we came across a very nice farmhouse at West Coker, half of which was being let to a suitable tenant. . . . We obtained this half-house for a very reasonable rental. It was a beautiful place with a large garden, complete with greenhouse, tennis-court and ornamental pond. Our side of the house consisted of three large down-stairs rooms, three bedrooms, a bathroom and two large attics.

It was these attics which gave me the idea. I turned the more suit-able into a " dancing-room ", had a few shillingsworth of leaflets printed and began to teach the village children dancing at sixpence a lesson. My " class " averaged about twenty every Saturday morning, so I was earning ten shillings a week on top of my wages. Here was wealth indeed!

My pupils were very keen, and I devoted some of the proceeds to buying new records. We did simple jigs, reels, hornpipes and minuets and then with the aid of a book or two, turned our attention to ballet.

In response to the demand I later began a series of ballroom dancing classes on my " early night ", when I was home from the cinema about nine o'clock. These I held in a room over the New Inn, hired for the moderate fee of one and sixpence an hour.

My pupils were very keen. There had been nothing like that in the village before. One mother came to see me to ask me if the exercise would help a backward child. I took the girl and gave her ten minutes to herself after the others had gone, until she grew more confident and less clumsy in her movements. Long after I was forced to give up the classes, through my mother moving once more, the child's mother used to come into the cinema and ask me if there was no way I could continue to teach her daughter dancing, as she missed it so.

Just when things were going so well with my dancing class my father appeared upon the scene to ask Mother if she would join him at Bournemouth. He had a very good position (the best he had ever had), the matter of finances would be so much easier if we no longer tried to keep two homes going. The upshot of all this was, that Mother gave up the house at West Coker, and I returned to Yeovil.

My time in this new village had not been wasted however, for it proved the gateway to hitherto unknown Dorset. I would walk with the old dog Mack in the direction of Crewkerne, or over the wooded hills that lay between Coker and the sea at West Bay. I remember the poppied peace of Sunday afternoons in the summer on these Dorset hills, I remember the sweetness of the syringa by the lake in our farmhouse garden and I remember seeing a badger for the second time in daylight, in a field near East Chinnock. My mother joined me in the discovery of East Coker, which we promptly designated as one of the prettiest villages we had ever seen. I later discovered that J. B. Priestley in a list of English villages, shared our view. In daffodil time especially, the group of church, manor and alms-houses beneath the budding boughs, is hard to equal for a picture of unspoilt England. But almost all the village was equally beautiful, the farms and cottages were built of the warm Ham stone, and in settings of tree and garden, worthy of their architecture.

We were long enough at West Coker to spend one unforgettable Christmas there. It was everything a country Christmas could be. I decorated the panelled walls of the dining-room with ivy-trails, hung mistletoe, picked freshly from the nearby orchards, over the generous doorways, and heaped vividly berried holly about every picture and ornament. A large Christmas tree stood in the alcove with the stained-glass in the window and there were real yule-logs for the ample fireplace. We had not then had the electricity installed and the soft light of the oil-lamps completed the warm atmosphere of our festive room.

My sister and her husband arrived from Brighton on Christmas Eve. In addition to our presents, hung about the tree, mother had packed and neatly numbered lots of intriguing little parels. We were to find out the joke later.

She had sent away for every free sample she could find advertised in the current press. We drew lots for these " surprise parcels ", and I remember receiving a sample of roofing-felt, asthma cure, and someone's adhesive that was guaranteed not to come unstuck. My sister received a sample of liqueur wine in the tiniest of bottles, and a harmless hair-dye; my brother-in-law drew a booklet on how to improve the mind, together with a sample of baby-powder; Mother had some corn cure and a trial package of cosmetics. Even the dog Mack had a sample of charcoal biscuits for dogs with indigestion and by the time we had done some " swapping " we all had something more or less acceptable.

There was a turkey for us at the bakehouse in the village, and some of my dancing class were about to wassail us. It was everything a Christmas should be, except that it did not snow.

When Mother went to Bournemouth I had to give up my dancing-class in spite of many protests. I went back to my one room in Market Street, and practised my *fouettés* in the Gaumont staffroom before the other girls arrived.

Most of all now, I missed my Sundays at home, and soon my thoughts turned to cycling to Bournemouth just as I had been used to cycling to Whitestaunton. It was just over twice as far away, that was all.

For some time I pondered. It was a good four hours' journey. To leave Yeovil, as had been my wont on a Sunday morning would give me very little time at home. No, the best plan seemed to leave on my journey after the show had finished on Saturday night. For one thing, once I had " cashed-up " after the last sales-interval, I could leave the cinema instead of waiting until the very end of the programme as I had had to do when I was an usher. With average luck this meant I could get away about ten o'clock, and be in Bournemouth about 2 a.m. I did not mind the journey if Mother did not mind waiting up for me, or waking up for me at that hour.

So it was established, and Saturday nights saw me pushing up Babylon Hill just ahead of the end-of-show buses, taking the patrons home for the night. I pedalled in moonlight and darkness, on nights of frost and rain. I was rarely later arriving in Bournemouth than 2 a.m. and often as early as one-thirty! My legs often ached, as Saturday was our busiest day of the week at the cinema, but after what was left of the night's rest I was always ready to go with my mother on some expedition to shore or heath on the Sunday.

One Saturday night, pushing my bicycle up West Hill, Sherborne, I saw headlights approaching me at a great rate. The car swooped down the hill on the wrong side of the road, and almost certainly out of control, forcing me to leap for my life, while I dragged my precious bicycle with me.

The car grinded against the high curb, rocked, righted itself and plunged on, leaving me holding the handlebars of my bicycle firmly enough, but with the back of my machine, something of a wreck. My case was ripped clean off and its contents scattered about the hedgebank, the bicycle's back wheel was bent, some of the spokes broken, and the tyre in ribbons, it was not going to carry me another mile that night.

I was dumb with vexation, and even while I disengaged my lamp to collect my possessions and ascertain the full extent of the damage, a nightingale in the trees above me burst into a torrent of song. The irony of its serenade did something to restore my equilibrium. Why if the curb had not been so high thereabouts I might have been killed! I was incensed that the driver had made no attempt to stop and that I had been unable to take his number. What an unsporting thing to do. Of course he knew he had hit me, his lights would have shown me up for one thing, and he would have heard and felt the impact for another.

I leaned my damaged bicycle against the hedge and walked into the middle of West Hill to stop the first car going into the town.

It was a leisurely Austin Seven manned by a horn-rimmed, earnest young woman. I told her my tale and she drove me to the Police Station.

Here endless minutes were wasted while I explained the situation, but it seemed little could be done as I had not taken the car's number and by now it must have passed through the town. It was now just eleven o'clock, but I was fortunate in finding a cycle-shop open, because the owner acted as a garage for the clientele of the local cinema.

He found a bicycle I might hire, there was not much choice, and after I had explained the whereabouts of my own, promised to collect it and have it ready for me about midday on Monday when I should pass through again on my way back to Yeovil. The accident cost me a pound, which I could very ill afford, it also gave me a very late and uncomfortable ride to Bournemouth.

The hired bicycle fitted in all the wrong places, my knees appeared to be under my chin, and the distribution of weight was all wrong. In addition there was no carrier and I had to tie my case with my mackintosh belt to the handlebars. As I resumed my broken journey the nightingales were still very vocal in the Dorset woods. I was home even then before 3 a.m. but it was the longest forty miles I ever rode.

I came to know the road to Bournemouth as well as I previously knew the road to Whitestaunton. The nights were empty and frequently misty, and I knew when I was coming to an inhabited place chiefly by the glimmer of lights ahead. Cattle browsed quietly on Lydlynch Common, a clock would chime at Sturminster Marshall, and the Stour would flow quietly beneath its old bridges and over its level, misty meadows.

On a Monday morning I would vary my return route, according to the time of my start and the state of the weather. If I was feeling really adventurous I would come the slightly longer way home by Wimborne Minster and Cadbury Rings. Here the mile-long avenue of matchless beeches was a never ending source of delight to me. Sometimes I came through Poole, sometimes up through Wallisdown and round by Corfe Mullen with its ancient church. Each Monday I would leave the sea, the piney cliffs of Canford and the creeks and inlets of Poole for the inland hills of heather and gorse and the fragrant plantations of birch and conifer.

I came to love " Dorset Dear ", and yet I never could abide Bournemouth, and only went to it because my parents and my dog and my home were there.

I came to love the meadows by the Stour and the hanging woods of Bryanston. The great humped back of Bulbarrow awed me (I never had time to stop and climb it) and I gazed with wonder at the great chalk-scarred fortifications of Hod and Hambledon Hills which guarded the gateway to the Blackmore Vale and the rich interior of Dorset's dairy-land. I began to realise that these downs of Dorset were almost at one with the chalk hills of Wiltshire, and that they stretched in an almost unbroken chain towards Shaftesbury which in its turn commanded Mere, which was the gateway to the Wiltshire Downs about Warminster; and so on to Salisbury's great plain. So was some sense of geography born in me, and I realised a oneness of the territory which those builders of the *valla* on Hambledon had sought to guard.

Marauders had come sailing up the Stour from the direction of Christchurch ; had not the Saxon Hengist lent his name to Hengistbury Head? I became excited by my discovery and would like to have known more, but I must forever pedal on to the work that waited for me and not turn aside after vain things.

I came to know every thatched cottage and each avenue of trees along the roads between Yeovil and Bournemouth. Blandford was my " half-way " mark, the signposts were my friends, when I met the street lights, I knew I was drawing near Bournemouth, when I met the hedgerow elms I knew I was drawing near to Sherborne. It was a good ride.

As time went by I varied these week-end rides home with visits to Warminster. In the aggregate this was some twenty miles nearer, and by the same procedure of leaving after the show I could arrive at Ethel's house shortly after midnight.

Apart from the hilly little town of Wincanton, there were no built-up areas on this ride, and the last dozen miles, going towards Warminster were among the loveliest I had then ever encountered.

During midsummer nights I could often get as far as the great hill of Camelot before complete darkness fell, and it became a race to see how far along the road I could be when the first stars came out. After the plain village of Mudford with its well-proportioned church beside the river Yeo, I passed the manor and farms of Marston Magna and the rose-gardens of the fine village of Queen Camel. At Sparkford I would join the road I had once used on my return from Hampshire. When I had contemplated the fork to Yeovil on that September day, how little I had dreamed then that I would make the town my home for so many years.

In the glimmering " dimmit-light " I would pass by the great gate-way and avenue of Hazelgrove, and once again come to the turning to South Barrow, while the legendary Camelot slept on my other side. The hills of the Dorset border, so beautifully moulded in their infinite variety of curves, loomed dark against the summer sky.

The road to Wincanton led beneath one of the loveliest hedgebanks I have ever known. It stretches up the long, gradual hill approaching the turning at Yarlington. Here it seems, grow most things in due season. Here was a profusion of gorse and bracken beneath the lordly beeches. Here were primroses in the spring, and bluebells and even an odd laburnum. In the autumn, maple and the " bloody twig " of dog-wood vied with the fire of the beeches. In the summer, the length of the bank was pricked out with glow-worm lights in a profusion I have not met with elsewhere. On a midsummer eve this bank is beautiful with the beeches etched like a rich design in lace against the luminous sky, the tiny balls of glowworm fire peeping beneath the tangled undergrowth.   In autumn the bank is a riot of colour, from deepest crimson to the gold of the gorse, in spring it is a poem in pastel shades.   In winter only, is it a bank like any other bank, betraying nothing of that happy harmony and contrast in the growth that makes up its composition and results in a picture hard to equal.

Between Wincanton and the top of the Pen Selwood ridge I used to pass a house which was always unlighted.   Week after week it remained silent and empty, though of a fair size and in good repair.   Repassed the following Monday in daylight, it presented blind windows plentifully festooned with cobwebs, the garden full of weeds, rank and overgrown, the barn doors swinging open, like some relic from Imber. This good house gone to waste always puzzled me.

Now, twelve years later, I still pass it, looking the same as ever and it still puzzled me, until, conscious of the acuteness of the housing shortage I asked a nearby farmer the meaning of its emptiness.   He replied that it was not empty, but had always been inhabited by a hermit, a man who is not fond of light, for the blinds are always up to the window, and no light is ever seen from them after dark.   Occasionally, very occasionally, I have seen a thin wisp of smoke issuing from one of the chimneys.

I had to wait a dozen years for the riddle of the neglected house to be explained to me!

After the woods and lakes of the Stourton corner I was out on the open road to Maiden Bradley, where the distance between the farms seems colossal to one on a bicycle and in the dark alone.   That time of night, approaching early morning, all traffic had died on this road, and it was usual for me to turn out my light, I could usually see better without it, and proceed as one with the countryside, inhabited it seemed only by owls, bats, moths and foxes, and the small nocturnal creatures of field and hedgerow.

The two points in my journey I loved best of all, was the high pass between two shoulders of down, just before Maiden Bradley; and the dark mysterious stretch of road between the woods and Shearwater.

In the first instance, the steepness of the road compelled me to dismount, and standing there beside my old Hercules, recovering my breath and listening to the night sounds from the beech copse above me, I could look across a stretch of valley and down to the long crouching mass of Whitesheet Hill. Easy to imagine it manned by some of the last of the Celts, those dwellers of the highland, watching, eternally watching for the encroaching Saxon tribes from the fastnesses of Cranborne Chase, where they had turned the flank of the great Bokerly Dyke and were advancing to their great victory at Pen Selwood. Were there eyes behind the mighty ramparts? Did they know the days of their countrymen were numbered, could they see the top of Alfred's Tower above the trees on Pen Selwood, proclaiming that a great Saxon king was to take the place of Ambrosius, Uther Pendragon and Arthur? Did they know that even the Saxons were not the last, that they in turn had to fight the Danes over this very same terrain. Oh wide, empty land under the starry dome of the midsummer sky, what have you seen, what have you known? I gazed down upon it while I fancied I could hear the world turning. For a moment I was part of the scheme of it, an unremarkable female person, leaning on a rusty bicycle.

Then a deep breath, into the saddle again and heigho! down the hill under the low branching beeches, beside the garlic bed, along by the church wall with its crucified limes, and so into Maiden Bradley.

After the sleeping might of those great hills, the woods were close and friendly. I did not mind their whisperings and rustlings, the road made a chain of moonlight patterns between the lakeside trees. In times of full or near full moon, Shearwater was a sheet of silver, beautiful to behold, with two boathouses on the far shore, one on the bank and one reflected in the water.

In the dark I would pedal through Crockerton, with its lovely mill, set in the shadow of Southey Woods, where the clear trout streams slide over waterfalls, and dream beneath willows and alders. On I would go past the mushroom fields, up by THE FIELD with its many happy memories of childhood games and picnics. And there from the top, if the moon were high I might see Warminster Down sleeping on its side, with the white chalk scars showing plainly, and on one side the land of the White Horse, and on the other the great might of the Plain with all its secrets.

To come down into Warminster, to cocoa and a feather-bed shared with Ethel, was like coming into the broad light of day after a night in the woods. The mystery and sleep were banished in the ever sure warmth of my welcome. My friends in Warminster have always been friends indeed, the same now, the same forever.

The return journey on Monday was always a hectic affair, as I was intent only on being in time for work, and the last few miles from Mudford into the town were mostly uphill. On these journeys I would often meet the National bus plying between South Barrow, Sparkford and the town. Always the same driver and conductor greeted me, and when they came to pass an hour or so between buses in the shelter of the cinema they always greeted me with a—

"Hi ya, Warminster."

They are still on the same route today, not noticeably changed, and still as cheerful as ever. Now I pass them in a car, no longer displaying my knees for the passengers' approval or otherwise, but still on the same road, doing the same journey. They seem changeless as the road itself, which winds beneath the hills of Corton and Camelot, taking the town to the country and the country to the town. The terminus of this bus with its two faithful retainers who still salute me as "Warminster" is the lane at the bottom of my farmhouse garden. Even at the tender age of thirty I am constantly amazed at the threads of continuity which contrive to run through the apparently haphazard pattern of life.

XV

The New Enchantment

WHILE I had been patiently growing up in order to be old enough to marry Mr. Samaniegos of Durango I had not noticed that I was growing out of him. Oh, make no mistake, he was still my ideal, but an ideal is too apt to be like a portrait, lovely to contemplate but lacking in life.

Not that I thought much about the matter, I was in fact still so bound up with the idea of my " ideal " that the thought of a real live flirtation neither occurred nor appealed to me.

I did not go to dances, had I been inclined to, the hours I worked would have made it rather difficult and in any case I could hardly afford a dance dress. There was no question of a boy taking me to " the pictures ", I was there already! True I corresponded in a desultory fashion with Norman and even encountered him occasionally at Warminster. He had invited me more than once to dance in some of his amateur productions and I had obliged whenever I could. But Norman had given no indication that I was more than a friend and I had never thought of him in any other light myself. He was as rude, uncomplimentary and impersonal as a slightly elder brother. I very much admired his work and sometimes even longed to be in a better position to take a share in it. If only I had not had to leave Warminster just when I was " growing up " I might have danced to my heart's content, I might have helped Norman to produce plays and pantomimes. It did seem bad luck really, but still I wouldn't have missed knowing London and the Camden for anything. It seemed one could not have it all ways.

So far, I had given no thought to " romance " as it was called on the screen. True most of my fellow employees seemed to have " boy-friends " or " steadies ". None of these specimens appealed to me very much however. They were mostly pimply and uncouth. I naturally wanted someone older and more mature, someone who knew more than myself—someone more like my " ideal ".

Among my dancing pupils for the ballroom session at West Coker had been a sprinkling of boys. I thought at first they were all from the village, but soon found that one or two of them came out from Yeovil in a battered Singer car. It was driven by a young boy of my own age who was an apprentice at the aircraft and engineering factory at Westlands.

He was interested in music and would even bring new records with him. One of his friends could play the piano after a fashion. I took no more notice of him than I did the rest of my pupils, there was never any time. But after my classes had to cease, I found he had not forgotten me.

Each year, our cinema was closed to film-offerings, and presented instead the efforts of the local Operatic Society. I was nineteen when they presented Yeovil with their version of *The Mikado*.

It was fine to open in the evenings only and to be able to sell real " opera " boxes of chocolates instead of the usual blocks and bars. The atmosphere of " theatre " was a change from cinema. Everyone was very jolly, almost all the audience it seemed had someone in the cast. By now most of the patrons knew me. The Mikado himself was a friend of my manager's and had always been most affable to me. It was quite like a personal affair and I loved every moment of it.

The dark-eyed boy with *The Mikado* score was presenting himself at my counter. Did I remember him? Did I? Well, vaguely. How nice it was to find someone interested in music—Yeovil wasn't very artistically inclined now was it? Well, not exactly, now in Manchester which was his home—Manchester? That was just a name on the map to me. I only knew it seemed a long way away.

When Bill arrived on my scene I was neither forewarned nor forearmed. I was not lonely, I had all the friends I wanted. I knew nothing of love, I do not see how one can, until it has been experienced.

My new friend had no money, he was only an apprentice, but his people sent him a small allowance and had bought him the old car. On his birthday they had promised him a new Morris Eight, and the date was only a few weeks away, what about me coming with him to pick the colour and model. A fellow-apprentice had a father in the trade.

I found Bill a change from most of the people I met at the cinema, with the exception of Mr. Mikado with whom I held occasional conversations, this young man was the only person I knew with tastes and opinions near my own.

Soon I had ceased to cycle home at week-ends, Bill drove me instead.

We went skating at the Bournemouth Ice Rink, Bill was almost a champion and I had my roller-skating days to help me on. We drove deep into the New Forest and then came home to take Mother to the Pavilion.

The next step was teaching me to drive the new car. I was not mechanically minded, but picked it up at last, with strict instructions to double declutch always, and so change gear noiselessly—an attribute alas of few women-drivers.

For the first time in my life I was able to share most of the things I loved with a companion of a like mind. I did not notice it at the time, I slipped into it easily enough, taking the new-found companionship entirely for granted. There is an old saying about not knowing heaven until we lose it.

Both Bill and I were young for our age, in some ways, it was as if we had both just left school; of experience in love, neither of us had had any. There was no thought for the future, and sex entered into our companionship no more than that it was pleasant for a girl to be out with a boy and vice versa. It added just that much extra interest to the friendship.

At Christmas, Bill went home by train, leaving me the car in which to visit my mother. I did very well considering it was my first time out alone and I got mixed up with a Point to Point Race meeting crowd on my way back on Boxing Day.

Bill returned from his holiday at home with some disquieting news. He had told his mother all about me and she had been most chilling. When he had tried to find out why she disapproved of the whole idea of his new friend, she had said it was because I worked in a cinema. Checking the impulse to cry " Whatever for? " I tried to reason it out from *her* point of view.

Of course it was not a very elevated job like a school-teacher or a scientist, or even a hairdresser or a mannequin, but I could see nothing of which to be ashamed. True a city cinema might employ " butter-flies " for want of a better name, but the girls at the Gaumont were just ordinary unsophisticated country girls with precious little " glamour " about them. True some of the younger members used nail-varnish, but many of them were married women doing part-time jobs to help along the finances at home. I told Bill what I thought.

" Of course, it's utterly mad," he said, " I tried to explain, but Mother doesn't understand, my sister has told her that only loose girls work in cinemas." (Here I stared at him horrified). " And Dad is pretty wild and says he will stop my allowance."

I was overcome at the unfairness of this attack by unseen, unknown assailants.

" If Father stops my allowance, the next thing is I shan't be able to run the car," continued Bill.

" Well, that is that," I said with more lightness than I felt, " I shall just have to get out my old bike again."

" If you do, I shall get one too," Bill assured me. " I didn't realise until I was on the train coming home, what life in Yeovil used to be like before I knew you—why there was nothing—absolutely nothing— what the devil did I used to do with myself? I can't think!"

Come to that, what did I use to do with myself before I had met Bill? I couldn't think either!

Soon after Christmas, Bill, while eating chocolate which I had provided, suddenly said:

" You know—I've been thinking, there's nobody like you— you've got a funny face that looks nothing from across the street, but when you're close to—as close as you are now, you are quite beautiful."

" What? " I exclaimed, scandalised at something that seemed little short of heresy. " Not only that," went on Bill calmly, " You are such a good pal—you're a girl in a million."

I stared at him openly. This was praise indeed. No one had ever said anything like this to me before—Norman had always treated me with a kind of good-natured offhandness—" Still the same old Monica". Bill was intelligent and wholesome, well-educated and brought up, if he meant what he said, then there was some hope for me—all my dis-approving school companions, and even my sister, must have been wrong about me!

We went in ice and snow to Exmoor—my first visit to that wonder-land of natural scenery and wild life. We went in the wind and rain to Milton Abbas and the green heart of Dorset, we crawled in the mist and fog across the beetling brow of Mendip. It was a long, hard winter, but it did not keep us in, together we adventured and explored. We drove in turns, sharing the expense of petrol, bringing our own contributions of food. One memorable Saturday, he turned up with a present for me, a present on which he had lavished his entire month's allowance. It was a beautiful Spanish shawl.

"To go with your gypsy hair," he explained, thereby coming as close to poetry as I had ever known.

We knew each other for five months, from the late autumn round to the dawn of a bleak spring, and did not know we were in love until it was almost time to part.

For my own part I had no experience of such pain before and did not know what to expect. I thought such a parting could be bridged with letters and a promise to wait, I did not know what wounding lay in store for me.

At first Bill appeared to be the more strongly affected. He said he would refuse to return home and would get work in Yeovil to remain near me. I pointed out that that would be throwing all his years of apprenticeship away. His people were adamant about his return, he had a few more months to do in a works nearer home. His friendship with me doubtless had something to do with that decision.

One of my most vivid memories of that parting was that *My Man Godfrey* with the late Carole Lombard was playing at the time. I had long looked forward to seeing it, but now I found all my joy in it shattered. I had the strangest possible feeling as I watched it over my tea in the back of the balcony. It was as if something of me was missing.

As the days passed, the feeling grew and became worse instead of better. Time was no cure, and whoever said, "Out of sight, out of mind," had never been in love.

I found myself thinking of Bill far more now than I had when I knew he would be popping in any moment, with some new piece of music, or a fresh record in his hand, or a place marked on his road map that we were to seek out and visit next.

My mornings awoke me to a sense of loss, my last thoughts before going to sleep were, "I wonder where he is and what he is doing?"

He was *not* a good letter-writer. Neither, in point of fact was I. There were a certain number of trivial items I could tell him most days, but as he had finished with Yeovil there seemed little point in doing so. I could not put any deeper feelings down on paper (indeed I had not analysed them myself), I could tell him I missed him and that was true and easy enough, beyond that, it was not easy to go.

Did I indeed love this boy of my own age, when my "ideal" had always been someone so much older and more "cultivated"? I did not know. The sun was still shining and the moon at night; Yeovil's streets appeared the same, but something had happened to me, for nothing was as it had been before. There was no one to turn to and exclaim, " Look at that—look at this ! " It was now March, but for the first time since I had come to notice such things, I could take no interest in the approach of spring.

Bill complained of my lack of letters and yet I wrote almost every day. He still complained, and I could not help wondering if they were being intercepted. He began to suspect as much himself.

The weeks dragged on. For the first time in my life I knew real loneliness. I was no worse off than I had been before, but it was in direct contrast to the recent happy companionship.

In April I received a letter suggesting I take a week's holiday and visit Bill's home. He knew I had a week due, for during the winter we had often discussed what we would do with a whole week in the country in the summertime together.

To visit an unknown house with hostile inhabitants in a distant country seemed a pretty tall undertaking for me, but anything was better than this inactivity, when it seemed the mainspring of my life had run down.

If this was love (and I was forced to admit that it must be), then I did not like it. Love was meant to be romantic, poetic and joyful, and now here was I with an empty, lost feeling inside me, which I did not care for, at all.

And this was the price I paid for a few months of happy companionship, a few chilly picnics, and some hours skating and driving. It hardly seemed a fair exchange. Far better never to have met him, to have remained as I was before and never to have known the shared tastes and discussions, the explorations and the laughter.

I had heard all about the " Better to have loved and lost " adage, but here I was tempted to disagree. After all I had never *asked* to meet Bill and have him fall in love with me. He had not been in my scheme of things at all!

We had not even talked of marriage, he was as yet only on the threshold of his career, it would be years before he could think of marriage. I had not thought of it myself, only to shy from it in dismay. What run a house? have children? cater for a man and all his needs, wash and cook and order and entertain—how COULD I—how could *I*? True Bill found little wrong with me, but then he was an exception. My past experiences had planted a fine growth of inferiority complex in me, and the thought of Bill's parents, and Bill's other friends and relations caused it to thrive exceedingly.

I would see Bill however, just once again, I would try to read the truth in his eyes, to find out where I really belonged. He had told me he loved me, not once but many times, and when he had kissed me it seemed real enough that he loved me. No other man had kissed me, not even the usual good night kisses which I am told do not mean anything. Long ago, when planning out my lines of conduct in life, I had decided that kisses should mean something.

I packed for Manchester with a quiet determination. Bill wanted to see me, he had asked me to go, and I would not be afraid.

The four friends of whom I shall write later now rallied round, with advice, assistance, and loans of various articles and garments. I withdrew all my dancing-class savings from the bank, they amounted to some six pounds and represented a good deal of effort, and at last I caught the night train for the North.

The carriage was full, and sleep was impossible, and early the next morning I arrived at my destination, sleepy, hot-eyed, crumpled and dishevelled to find no one to meet me as had been promised. I found a taxi and made my way to Bill's address. A neat maid answered the door. Bill was out, gone to meet me, it transpired, at the wrong station, and his mother was not yet downstairs.

I stood up to his mother as well as might be expected under the circumstances. She said first of all that I looked older than her son—perhaps I did, I do not know, the journey had made me feel considerably older—that I was unsuitable, that Bill was too young to marry, he must concentrate on his career, and I had distracted him.

"Not intentionally," I replied. "I know just how important a career is, never having had one myself! And marriage has never been mentioned."

This appeared even worse, and apparently she thought Bill must have seduced me and I had come here to blackmail him. I was protesting my innocence of any such charge or intention, when Bill appeared, and very ill-at-ease he looked. But at length even his mother relented saying:

"Well, as you've come, you might as well have a good holiday while you are here. I've told Bill to take you to N—— to stay, there are plenty of boarding houses there."

As soon as we could escape we did. I could understand his mother's feelings so well. I suppose I didn't look suitable, with my cheap borrowed clothes and my lack of style, though when she spoke to me she could tell I was a sensible girl and not what she had at first imagined (why will mothers of sons always expect the very worst?) but that did not alter the fact that she wanted someone very much better for her only son. The house was imposing, beautifully furnished and well run. I learned that his father was a magistrate, and many other facts about the family which increased my apprehension. Bill assured me that his feelings had not changed in the matter.

" Now Mother's idea is to separate us. I know her well enough when her mind is made up, and it's made up over this, but there is one way we could defeat her—by you getting a job up here yourself. Then we should be able to see each other while we are waiting."

Leave the West Country, Yeovil where I was so happy, go so far from my mother, my home and my dog, go to a place where the people spoke a different kind of English, where even the wild flowers were not the same? It was a tall order.

Bill could see my hesitation.

" All right! no need for you to do that if you feel it is TOO drastic, just threaten Mother with it. Tell her that if she doesn't promise to give me the wherewithal to come down to Yeovil every holiday, and let me read your letters unopened, etc., you will diddle her by staying up here. Go on, that's the thing to do."

I dutifully did it. This time his father was present also. He was a heavy, quiet man who said little, but regarded me balefully out of close-set eyes.

" You are *most* unlikely to obtain work here, many of our own people are out of work," said Bill's mother coldly.

The next day I sallied forth from my boarding-house retreat, armed with every newspaper I could buy, and returned at the end of the day with two jobs.

The first was as chocolate girl in a new theatre, subject to the recommendation which I knew would be forthcoming from my Yeovil manager. The second, much more to my liking, was as an apprentice in a book-shop. The money was very slight, but I believed I could exist upon it while I learned, a love of books was my only recommendation.

The man who offered me this work was a small, pleasant man with twinkling eyes. Instead of asking me about experience and qualifi-

cations, or discussing premiums and wages, he asked me one or two
searching questions about my home life, my taste in literature and my
views on life. He also asked me to quote from one of my favourite
poets and I gave him a Shakespearian sonnet:

" Shall I compare thee to a Summer's day."

I never saw John Gort again, no never in my life, and when we met
and spoke with each other it was not for more than thirty minutes.
But he wrote me almost every day of his life for three years after that
one meeting. He was attacked by a severe illness, during which his
letters fell off and ceased sometime before he died when the war was
at its height.

He never knew that I " made good ", that his letters helped me. He
died before the publication of my first book, but the book he always
wanted to see written, *Romany Cottage, Silverlake*, was dedicated to
him posthumously with the permission of his wife and sons. He also
told me to write a book of *Rural Reflections* but not to attempt to get it
published before I was thirty, or I should want to re-write it when I was
older and wiser. *Rural Reflections* was actually published four months
before my thirtieth birthday, and how I wished I might believe that he
could know of it.

When I returned to Bill's home with the story of these two offers of
work, there was a speedy capitulation. Bill's mother said, if I would
go home like a nice quiet girl at the end of my week's holiday she
would agree to anything. Bill should meet me at my Mother's in
Bournemouth at Whitsun, and August, and of course she would not
interfere with my letters.

I agreed to all this, but Bill was uneasy. " Oh, God," he said, " if I
were only finished messing about training, and was earning a living
wage."

" Don't be such an unnatural son," I commented. " Your parents
are both thinking of you—you can't expect them to think of me, I'm
nothing to them and you are everything. If anything goes wrong let
me know, we will find your fare—Mother and I, and we'll consider
matters again."

It was left at that. My week soon passed. In the old familiar
Morris Eight, and taking turns to drive as usual, we went here, there
and to most places of interest in Bill's vicinity. I did not like his
countryside as much as my own, it was too urbanised and one was

never out of sight of the factory chimneys and slag heaps for very long, but I enjoyed being with him again.

Here I would stress that there was no physical passion between us, in spite of the "inloveness" of our situation we were both apparently almost unawakened. When I see "children" of sixteen or so, all over each other and "courting strong" I wonder, did Bill and I come of another species, why were we as we were, are they more normal, or were we? Some of the answer lies in the fact that Bill and I had so many interests in common that we were always *doing* something together. There were none of those long, romantic pauses which have to be filled in with kissing, or more. When we were not skating or rowing, swimming or climbing mountains, we were jabbering away nineteen to the dozen about some nice point in the *Golden Treasury* or some play or film we had just seen.

In many ways it was a wonderfully happy partnership, how it would have fared had it progressed I find it impossible to prophesy.

At the close of my week I went home. After this, I thought the loneliness will not come again in the same fashion, our association has stood the test of time and separation, we are still the same to each other. We could wait.

The pain and loneliness did come again of course. When I saw spring change into summer and realised that Bill and I had never seen Somerset together in the warm sunshine with the woods in leaf, I could have wept. My faith in some distant future began to be shaken. My letters were soon returned unopened. I sent a telegram but there was no reply and then after several weeks my *Golden Treasury* was returned addressed by handwriting other than Bill's. With it was a note from his father to say that further communication from me would be destroyed unopened, and that his son had gone away.

To hold my *Golden Treasury* in my hands had the most defeating effect of all, while Bill had it, he had some of me, even as I had his wonderful Spanish shawl. It had been a pact, something like that contained in Sir Philip Sidney's ditty in the *Treasury's* well-thumbed pages:

> "My true love hath my heart and I have his,
> By just exchange for one another given."

Our absolute separation was brought home by this return of my *Golden Treasury* more than by any other single thing that had happened.

It was more of a blow than the curt note that accompanied it. My last shred of faith had gone.

I wondered over and over again what had really happened. Had Bill simply weakened, coming to the conclusion that the whole thing was not worth the trouble? Had his parents succeeded in making him change his mind about me? Had someone else perhaps come upon the scene to capture his interest and take my place?

Whatever it was, I felt I was completely beaten. There was no hope left, I had felt and hoped all I could, I was emotionally exhausted, almost numbed. When the girls suggested he would come back, when Mr. Gort wrote that he might claim me when he came of age, I could only reply, "Never". I knew it was all over, that I had lost him, that it was finished.

For many years I did not open my *Golden Treasury* again. My sense of loyalty and constancy were bruised, my ideals in the dust and my faith bitterly shattered.

Whatever happened, it must have been easier for Bill than it was for me. I was left "at the scene of the crime", every road and lane about Yeovil held associations for him, for me. He had even had his special seat in the balcony—I was not sorry when my mother suggested I went to Bournemouth for a time. "You could get a job near home, you would not feel it so much, the rhododendrons are lovely," she wrote. So I gave in my notice, packed up and cycled to Bournemouth once more. I was none the happier for knowing I was running away.

XVI

The Five Friends

IT was at the week-ends I had most missed Bill. Once how eagerly had I looked forward to Saturday night. If we were going home to Bournemouth we would leave immediately after the show, in order to have a clear Sunday ahead of us, even as I had endeavoured to do when I cycled. If we were going on one of our exploratory trips, I would be up until late on Saturday night, cutting sandwiches for the morrow, putting thermos flasks ready, priming my little camera with film, setting out warm clothing and seeing that all was in readiness for the early start in the morning when the Morris Eight horn would be heard soon after breakfast.

Now Sunday was a desert stretching between Saturday's blissful fatigue, and Monday's new round of work. During the week my four co-worker friends might rally round and help me to forget that I was forgotten; but on Sundays they had a life of their own.

There were ten usherettes, their personnel continually changing, but from the current ten I had made four very good friends. We were all much of an age, all doing the same sort of work, and yet we all wanted something different from life.

First there was Muriel. She lived with her widowed mother and a young brother and sister only a few doors away from me in Market Street. Later she helped me to settle into " Romany Cottage ". She had the real " green fingers " and both her mother's garden, and later mine, responded to her care. What she wanted most in life I think, was to be loved. It is not a bad " want ", and many would do well to pay more attention to it. To want love and be prepared to give it is a fair foundation for human happiness and surer than ambition or greed or even the desire to remake and reform. Muriel was the kind that marry fairly early in life, to have children and make a loving mother. She was also very attached to her own mother and could not bear to be far away from her for long. I spent more time with Muriel than with any of the others, partly because she lived so close to me, and partly because she was of such a happy disposition. On the early summer mornings after Bill left me, we often went out walking or cycling together. We would walk out through Newton Copse, looking down on the fine old house of Newton Surmaville, and make our way lazily to the banks of the Yeo, and there lie and talk and plan.

One morning we cycled to Glastonbury and back, before work started. To behold the Tor in the sunshine for the first time, as we crossed the level moors from Butleigh, was an unforgettable experience. One felt the joyful sacredness of the place of which another writer has said:—

"Only in Jerusalem was a wider influence born."

Together we crossed the sunny vale of Avalon, cradle of the Anglo-Saxon race, pausing to gaze deep into the still waterways that threaded the buttercup fields and gave the roadways innumerable bridges.

After this little Holland, we climbed the steep sides of the Tor and surveyed the sad road back to Wells, along which the last of the Abbots had been dragged on a hurdle to his execution on Tor Hill. This was the same road along which Monmouth's ragged army had marched and counter-marched. A sad road, with sad associations? Perhaps. But it was hard to be sad on such a morning, with the green leaves dancing like flags on the breeze, and the water in the rhines winking up at us from the cattle-studded meadows, while the Butleigh Monument bearing Hood's triumphant vessel, stood up against the dark woodland and the bright clouds.

The second friend, Betty, had come, strangely enough, from my own birthplace of Cardiff. She was staying with an aunt in Yeovil, trying to make a new start and forget a searing unhappiness left behind her. For almost on the eve of her wedding, her fiancé had died of pneumonia. For some time she had kept her secret well from us, but when at length she told us why she had left her lively city for what she often contemptuously referred to as our "Somerset backwater", we felt we understood her better.

Although I had lost my love to some unknown cause and not a fatal illness, I felt there was some point of sympathy established between us. We were both "in the same boat". She was a most likeable girl, smart, vivacious and warm-hearted. She reminded me a little of Joycie from Swanswick. The same bright eyes and milk and roses complexion was there; the same wholesome, milk-maidish kind of beauty.

She had the habit of talking with her hands in an almost continental manner, and once at the tea-table sent our communal tea-pot flying.

She was a gallant girl who richly deserved happiness, her spirit was so fine.

After Muriel and Betty, came " Collie ", the youngest. Her real name was Evelyn, but no one ever called her that as we already had a girl of that name—the last of the five. Collie was a corruption of Collins her surname, and as I was always called " Scottie ", we made a canine pair, which Betty took advantage of by giving us dog-brooches at Christmas. If we argued with our elders (for Collie and I were the youngest of the bunch) we were told to go to our kennels.

Collie was the life of our party. She was incorrigible, no snubbing ever damped or daunted her. She carried the schoolroom with her. Though her exterior might be as sophisticated as you please with the assistance of various aids to beauty, her interior was that of a schoolgirl.

She had us fairly hooting with delight at the howling errors she would make in the simplest matters of general knowledge. She would confuse " magician " with " musician " and declare that one boiled an egg until it was soft. She was good-natured and impossible to offend. We were all very fond of her. I once walked with her as far as Montacute House. After staring at the magnificent terrace, the oriel-windows, the gables, statues, pillars and gazebos, she suddenly opened her handbag and after a certain amount of rummaging drew forth a phial of lavender-water.

" Just right for this place," she commented, sprinkling us both lavishly with the perfume. " Now I *feel* right." She looked at the house and then sniffed the lavender-water deeply. " Fits somehow, doesn't it? "

Now I never go to Montacute but I think of lavender water. Yes, it did " fit " somehow.

One Christmas the staff had " clubbed together " to give our manager an ornamental blotter for his desk, and we decided that Collie as the youngest should present it to him. But the very afternoon we had chosen on which to make the presentation, he had us all paraded on the carpet to give us a lengthy lecture on our behaviour. Nothing was right that afternoon. The day before someone had got in without having their tickets torn. Did we realise the seriousness of this? The Revenue and Excise men would be on to us. Why were we so lax? And another thing, there was far too much laughing and talking and not enough attention paid to our work, girls were missing off their posts, fire-drill was not smart enough, we were always late back from tea—

and so forth and so forth. The harangue continued almost interminably. We shifted from one foot to another while anxious patrons peered in through the still padlocked doors to see if the cinema intended opening that afternoon.

Collie dropped the blotter which she had held so long behind her back. " Not now, not *now*," I hissed.

We were admonished to stop fidgeting and attend to the lecture. We sighed. When at length it was over. Collie thrust the parcel under our lecturer's aggrieved face.

" Please sir, a Happy Christmas from the staff."

I could not bear it, I broke and fled. We dared not look at each other, but dispersed to our posts, leaving our astonished employer holding the parcel, while the commissionaire, clearing his throat, hastened to admit the first customers.

" There is a time and a place for everything," said Betty to Collie at tea-time.

" What Collie did this afternoon was strategy," I replied. " It may not be according to the book of rules, but it was certainly turning the other cheek."

It was a sheepish manager who thanked us later in the day. He was not without seeing the funny side of it himself. He has often reminded me of it since. No one but Collie could have done it.

Last of my fortunate friendships, there was Evelyn. She was the eldest of the five by a couple of years. In colouring and size she resembled myself, and before now we have been mistaken for each other. She had just married. We watched her unspectacular courtship with approval, we " passed " her husband—he was " one of us ". Evelyn had a dry sense of humour and a surprising interest in current affairs. She would write letters to the newspapers about conditions of employment in cinemas, and show us the result. She was all for us joining a " union " and we did attend one meeting, but were not very impressed. The idea of fighting the Gaumont British syndicate for better working conditions and higher wages was one thing; bringing criticism and contumely on the head of our manager from the powers that be, was another. We liked him too well for that. He was a bit of a fuss-pot at times, but he was always ready to discuss things with us, he was fatherly and decent. No, he somehow did not represent the spectre of " Capitalism " as opposed to the working masses, he worked longer hours than any of us.

Sometimes Evelyn would steal a morning off from her little house to take a cycle ride with me. She had a sister who was married to a farm-worker and knew quite a deal about country matters. She was a perfect mine of information when it came to where to find the best apple-orchards or the biggest blackberries.

Sometimes I would go back to an impromptu lunch with her and admire her wedding-presents and her brand-new furnishings. Her hospitality was both boundless and genuine. It amused us to be taken for sisters at work, her own sister was as much unlike Evelyn as mine was unlike me.

When the idea of " Romany Cottage " first took hold of me, it was Evelyn who cycled with me to Sherborne to interview the land-agents, and it was Evelyn who advised in the matters of household equipment.

Such were the friendships I left when I went to Bournemouth. Within a month of my arrival, my father had been suddenly taken ill with cancer, operated upon and was dead. It was all over so quickly (he had never had an illness before) that Mother and I hardly had time to examine our feelings on the matter. My sister who arrived too late to see him before he died, gave his epitaph in:

" What a wasted life."

I withheld judgment, then as now. He was happy in his wife and daughters, he loved his home. He had his moments out with dog and gun, or in the earlier days playing cricket and riding, when he must have felt that life was good. He could lose himself over a good tale by A. E. W. Mason or John Buchan, as much as he could over a bottle of whisky. The complete lack of ambition which often so estranged himself from my mother and sister, was no barrier to an understanding between us. He knew himself, we did not.

Mother stayed where she was. We were in a pleasant house in Branksome Park, a house set among shrubs and rhododendrons and with a garden overlooking a real orchard. It might almost be in the country.

" Might " was of course the operative word. I discovered I had sold my birthright for a mess of pottage. In exchange for company and a home of my own I had cut myself off from my true roots. Mother could delight in the crowds by the seashore, in the fine shops, the flower-beds of the square, the band playing in the gardens. Alas, I could not.

The only way I could tell how the agricultural season was progressing that summer was to take a boat out into Bournemouth Bay, or stand on the top of Canford Cliffs on a clear day, and view the harvest fields across at Studland and Ballard Down.

At County Gates the boundary came down and set us in Hampshire, but just down the road we were back in Dorset, and it was towards Dorset I always set my heart. The Old Harry rocks were the portals to the dream country of Purbeck. There was a land of heaths and wild inlets, of dreaming stone-slatted cottages, of the brooding Corfe and the ancient Kimmeridge, and of a matchless, lofty coastline. I stood on Canford Cliffs or Branksome promenade of this upstart town by the sea and remembered that once it had been known as " Bournemouth—near Poole ".

Poole had been an important place in the affairs of England when Bournemouth did not exist.

I got work immediately in this seaside town, where the great god to be worshipped is the " holiday-maker ", as often as not from London and the Midlands, and knowing nothing of local culture. They bring their own with them, as the Maids of Swanswick took Wales with them wherever they went. But this culture had no roots, nor traditions.

Their culture consisted of selling a few miles of sand and sea and of covering the cliffs and sandhills, the heaths and meadows beyond with the temples of this culture.

Hotel life taught me a great deal, I watched and I learned from my father. Money could buy anything—service, civility, affability. Real kindness, real charity, was there any? The sea and the sand, the air and the pines were there to be sold to the highest bidders. They were welcomed and made to feel at home, as long as they parted with their money.

Give me the honest vulgarity of Blackpool in preference to this pretentious elegance, this disguising of plain commerce under the name of " spa " and " resort ".

I longed for the ripening fields of wheat, the changing shades of Babylon Hill and the fat cattle beside the winding Yeo. I was given instead the alien pine and the exotic rhododendron until it became difficult not to feel smothered alive by both of them.

Mother had let several rooms in her house to typical Bournemouth old ladies, and as I acquired a job immediately, our finances were stable enough.

My first work was at a local cinema. Thinking to find it the counterpart of the one I had left, I was staggered to find how it differed in atmosphere.

I soon learned that in a city like Bournemouth the workers have separate and almost inviolate " grades ". First, after the skilled careers like window-dressing, secretarial work, hairdressing, assisting a doctor or dentist as receptionist, there comes hotel work. Some of this is rated very highly, especially if you are the seen and not unseen (i.e. kitchen staff). Then comes serving in an ordinary high-class shop, or being in their cash-desk. Then come the more menial occupations ; the serving in little shops, or in the " chain-stores ". This was only a little above laundry-work or running a lift, or working in a factory. Cinema work came somewhere between being behind the counter at Woolworths and working in a laundry.

Who says class distinction is restricted to " society "? I had considered the matter of fresh employment carefully, deciding to attempt to " better myself " from cinema work if at all possible, and now seemed just the opportunity. I had more than two years' excellent reference from my manager for selling chocolates and helping generally. Surely with experience behind me I might go onwards and upwards?

There was no hope of being accepted in one of the big stores. Mother insisted upon me trying, but I was not sorry when I was turned down. The work possessed no appeal for me whatsoever. It seemed to me utterly unreal and altogether absurd that any girl should want to spend years of her life among clothes and fashions, flattering silly women with more money and time than they had sense, and addressing them as " Modom ".

Was that how we were meant to live?

Some of these establishments needed a premium from me to help them to teach me how to sell things. In some cases I should not be earning for two years, and I was nearly twenty.

My father warned me against hotel-work with the words, "It's a dog's life ". So I did not try that, and rather than be out of work for more than a day or two, I slipped into a vacancy at one of Bournemouth's largest cinemas.

I searched the faces of my fellow-workers for one of a like mind to myself, and found not one congenial spirit, no, not half a one. When I thought of the girls I had left behind at Yeovil I was amazed that the mere matter of fifty miles could have wrought such a change in the type of girl employed by the cinema.

Here were no ex-nursemaids, no home girls, no married women. These Bournemouth Belles were glamour personified. They regarded my unbleached hair, my natural nails and my unplucked eyebrows for an infinitesimal space of time, and then dismissed me as a curiosity.

It seemed I was once more out of step. At boarding-school I had been too forward, here I was too backward. Few of them believed I was almost twenty, their average age was between fourteen (part-timer) and seventeen. I had never heard of a " blind date ", and if I thought it was a kind of fruit I learned by careful attention that it is what happens when your girl-friend tells her boy-friend to bring along *his* boy-friend—for you.

These girls on their way up from laundry and multiple store to the promotion of lift-work or kiosk-management had no interest in their work unless it be as a possible medium for meeting new boy-friends.

On the outside they were groomed to the last eyelash, within, they were completely raw and uncultured. They were the product of a new civilisation. Arriving at work on foot and by 'bus, in high heels, eye-veils and elaborate make-up, they were amazed to see me wind-blown and panting, wheeling my old bicycle round to the car-park. Afterwards I had to wrestle with a very ridiculous pill-box head-dress which looked mighty peculiar atop my mop of hair and homely features. Although ruled by the same corporation, the plain-silk-poplin dresses of Yeovil did not seem to be the thing for Bournemouth.

From the staff-room, high in the roof of the cinema building, I was able to catch a glimpse of the dancing sea, a vast unspoiled plain of silver stretching Channelwards. At those moments I loved the sea, but I hated the town that had sprung up to cater for people who mistook rhododendrons for real country, and who turned their backs on the sea to watch the crowds on the Promenade.

As soon as I was able, I obtained a post nearer home. It was " just down the road and round the corner ", at a small but select grocers.

During my lunch hour I could accompany the cashier, a timid little girl who had only just left school, to a picnic meal on the beach. These hours were happy and almost paid for the drudgery of the shop. For drudgery it was. We stayed open until seven-thirty every night, and eight o'clock on Saturdays. We started at 8-30 a.m. and the time allowed for meals was niggardly. There was no official tea-time, and we must wait until we arrived home.

I found so much to learn, however, that I was not unhappy and the three other members of the staff were kind enough to me, but unfortunately the Manager was not quite so kindly disposed.

After work I sometimes went swimming with other members of the staff, delighting in the warm surf, the tang of seaweed and the distant glimpse of Swanage's cliffs. On such occasions I thought deeply of Bill, wishing with all my heart that he might be with me to share these joys of summer; a season we had never known together.

Half unconsciously I sought his face in the crowds. Would he ever come back for me? No, never. Give up hope, give up hope, hope is such a painful thing, resignation is so much easier.

But every time the postman came I unconsciously looked for the well-remembered handwriting on an envelope.

Always I was disappointed. But there were letters bearing a Northern postmark, letters written in a fine, clear hand, whose importance (because they were not Bill's) I at first underrated. They were letters which in all their beauty and wisdom I would have gladly exchanged for one scribbled, loving line from Bill.

But even then, though I did not fully appreciate their worth, these letters from John Gort whom I had met in a book-shop for less than half an hour, seemed too fine to destroy.

I have never made it a habit to keep letters, I always try to reply by return and then to destroy them. The exceptions have been a few written to me during the course of the last war which I have retained for historical reasons—these and John Gort's.

One such letter begins:

" DEAR FRIEND MONICA,
" I observe with much satisfaction that you are becoming much more *positive* in your attitudes to and expectations of life. It is a line of thought I wish you to continue in and cultivate to its fullest extent. Later, when your confidence in the infinitude of Goodness has really established itself to stay, you will find you have ' arrived '.

" But you must be constantly on your guard against the nature of your reactions to disappointment which may sometimes arise. They come to all of us. See to it then that they do not in any way shake you in your confidence in GOOD or in your ideals, as they did formerly.

" See to it that they leave you immovable. Disappointments do not really matter much in themselves, but our reactions to them matter a great deal. It is always the reaction which makes, mars or breaks——"

Now why did he bother with me? Why did a busy, cultured man, with a full and happy home life, bother to spend hours (as he must have done ultimately) to encourage, help and advise a raw, uneducated young girl whom he had seen for but a very short time?

Perhaps an explanation can be partly gleaned from his own letters.

" I, as a person, or instrument, as a ' means ' need not concern you. In due course you will forget—as long as you ' arrive ' at happiness, contentment, fulfilment, that is all that matters."

He must have known I was much in need of help, and he knew I believe, as no one else has ever done, how difficult it was to help anyone with a hard exterior and a painfully vulnerable interior.

But he did not give up trying. Two or three times each week his letters arrived.

Once I sent him a snapshot of myself and my fellow-workers sitting on the beach. It was taken with my own camera, by the lad who served on the bacon counter.

Mr. Gort wrote:

" It was good to meet with you again, you are as I had remembered you, except that like the little boy in A. A. Milne you have sand between the toes. You have good feet, happy feet, and I should say they may one day convey the burden of someone with a message for humanity, and there comes into my mind the verse:—

" How beautiful upon the mountains are the feet of
him that bringeth good tidings."

A message for humanity forsooth! I, who had never known where I was going, who had simply pedalled on, in hopeful expectancy of a destination. I, who had no translatable message for *myself*, I, who was like a straw in the wind—a message for humanity, it was laughable— but well, it was nice too, to be thought so well of, even if one had done nothing to deserve it.

XVII

The Sixth Friend

IT was high summer and my sister was staying with us when the worst calamity of all befell me, one which I could not have foreseen and which even now remains with me in something of its original shock and horror. To be wrongfully accused of theft. The injustice of it!

My Mother had asked me to bring her some custard-powder back. When one member of the staff purchased something, another usually wrote out the ticket, and discount was allowed. When I remembered my Mother's request, the lad on the provision counter was busy serving, I took the two packets of custard-powder out to my basket so I should not go without them, and returned to my work.

Before either Jimmy-on-provisions, or myself on dry-goods was free to enter up the transaction, the manager beckoned me into the store-room and proceeded to accuse me of theft. He had seen me put the custard-powder in my basket.

Of course he had, there had been no attempt at concealment.

" But don't be silly "—— I began.

How well can I still hear the man and recall his unjust accusation.

" Be silly? Who are YOU to tell me not to be silly—Who do you think you are? Who are you calling silly? I'll learn you to call ME silly! "

Apart from my natural indignation at the injustice, how funny the situation can appear now, and how tragic it was then. The last straw, in fact. Bill, Daddy, and now this!

I had learned to fold-in sugar bags and tie parcels neatly, to weigh currants and sort out greengrocery, and here was I with it all wasted.

In vain did Jimmy-on-provisions come out and do battle with " the old man ", on my behalf. In vain did he point out that we often did it, that there was no attempt at concealment or fraud.

The little cashier was so taken aback that she could only whisper: " If you go, I'll go, he doesn't like me either, and I know you and Jimmy have paid for everything you've ever had."

It was almost lunch-time.

" The old man never liked you," said Jimmy. " You telling him he was silly has riled him proper, he doesn't intend to keep you."

" I wouldn't stay," I said quickly.

" He told Bertie only the other day that you were cheeky. Bertie said you lent a bit of class to the place—I had to laugh."

I could not laugh myself, I remembered I was going home to Mother with her custard-powder all right, but without a job. Oh, dear, how could I face it—and the explanations—and my *sister* there. Oh it was too much, too much! Then I realised that the tears were streaming down my face and I was shaking from head to foot. A wealthy woman customer from one of the fine houses overlooking Poole Harbour had just come into the shop.

" What's the matter, child—whatever is the matter? "

Jimmy-on-provisions explained to her. " The kid's had a raw deal, Mrs. S——, we are really sick about it, and her dad died only a few weeks ago."

" You come home with me," said Mrs. S——. " Mr. Provision Counter says you have shortly lost your father, now you cannot go home and add to your dear Mother's worries by presenting her with a face like that. You are coming to my house and we will freshen you up a bit."

I had previously thought this lady rather tiresome, and our manager did " kow-tow " to her so, as if she were royalty, but I allowed her to lead me and my bicycle round the corner to her resplendent house, while Jimmy locked up the shop for the lunch-hour.

She led me into a cool spacious room, with the harbour visible from its windows. A schoolgirl daughter was lounging on the lawn in a hammock. I was shown into a well-appointed bathroom. Afterwards a trim maid brought me a cool drink, laced with something more potent than lemonade.

I was beginning to feel worried, for I had promised Mother the custard-powder in time to make a pudding, and in addition I was taking the meat home from a local butcher, who fortunately did not close during the lunch-hour. I excused myself as early as I could, and began to pedal home frantically.

Now I had to explain my reasons for being a little late, but first I delivered the meat and custard-powder. Then I realised that I still had not paid for the latter, this apparently being the last thing anyone was worrying about at the moment!

I told my story while the chops were sizzling in the pan. When I had finished, my sister walked out of the little kitchen without a word.

Between the strain of the morning, and the unaccustomed lacing of brandy (which is what I have since taken it to be) all my self-control broke.

" What's the matter? " I demanded of my sister. " Why don't you say something? You don't believe in me, do you? You never have done? I know what you said about Bill—I'd no sex appeal—and you ran Mr. Gort down, because you said he was a ' pick-up ', we'd never been properly introduced. I never do anything right, do I? Why don't you say so? You think I'm like Daddy, don't you—that I'll always be like Daddy? You hinted at it often enough——"

She suggested I was being hysterical and said that we had enough to worry about, without me coming home with this kind of news.

I wondered vaguely what she could have to worry about. She had a nice home, a kind husband, a car, money for holidays, all the dresses she could wear. She was nice-looking and always well. She had nothing to worry about compared with me—who was plain to the point of being peculiar, who was not smart and could not keep the love of a boy like Bill.

Mother told me to sit down and eat my dinner and stop making a fuss. I did not feel like any dinner. I was admonished to get on with it or I should be late for work.

Late for work! I could not go back there again—not even to finish the week out. True the staff were sympathetic enough, but I could never work for that manager again—never!

When, after a pretence at eating my lunch I cycled out of our drive again, it was not to go back to work, but to go back to Yeovil. I had known happiness there, I would again. Memories of Bill should not be allowed to matter, should not be permitted to keep me away from a countryside which I knew, and to which I felt I belonged. It was foolish to have to run away, but now I was going back. I had no money worth mentioning in my purse, no luggage on my carrier other than my handbag, but I was on my way back.

It was a very hot day and I had had no lunch, I was twenty and had not tasted " strong drink " before, I had never been inside a public-house, Mrs. S——'s lemonade had given me a queer, off-the-ground feeling.

Out on the Dorchester road the feeling increased, when I looked along the road, the traffic ran together out of focus. Somewhere beyond the fork to Wimborne, where runs a dual carriageway now, I remember wobbling and falling, and the next thing I was sitting on the grass verge beside the road while a lorry driver was lifting my bicycle into the back of his vehicle.

He said I had fainted and he was going to take me home. I said I was cycling to Yeovil (true my legs appeared to have turned to jelly or something equally as unsubstantial). He would have none of it and presently I was deposited at my Mother's house.

This was the final straw as far as my sister was concerned. It was some time before she spoke to me again. A doctor arrived and prescribed bed for a week—nervous exhaustion, dyspepsia and all sorts of minor ailments. He had a " How long has this been going on? " attitude. After a glass of physic I went to sleep.

Early the following morning, I arose, packed and then said good-bye to Mother. Before I resumed my interrupted journey to Yeovil I made a telephone call.

" Could I come back? "

" When? "

" Today? "

The answer came back. " Right away if you like."

As I cycled back across Dorset, along a road so often traversed by Bill and myself during the past winter, I thought of all Mr. Gort had said. I remembered the kindness of Mrs. S—— in her big house, of the lorry-driver, of Jimmy, the provision hand, and the little cashier. What was there for me to complain about? Why, very little.

My sister's openly expressed contempt, my Mother's hurt bewilderment? They would pass and I could not help them.

I was going back where I had been content, I could be content there again. In some small way I even knew I was wanted—wasn't my job still waiting for me? Collie would be there to make me laugh again, and Betty to chat about Cardiff, I could discuss books with Evelyn and go cycle rides with Muriel.

My spirits rose as I pedalled westwards, even without Bill, it was still quite a lovely world.

My welcome back to Yeovil left nothing to be desired, and in a day or two the old threads had been picked up as if I had never gone away. My four friends were as staunch as ever. But at least one of them astounded me by the announcement that she'd had a hard time combating a rumour that I had gone away for a confinement.

" My dear," said Betty, " some people will think of *anything*. ' Don't judge others by yourself,' I said to her—and added—Scottie's only been away a couple of months and she looked no more like a confinement than I did, when she went."

I screwed up my face at Betty. " But that's hardly the point, " I argued. " You didn't need to defend me from such a filthy charge. You could have just said I wasn't that kind of person."

Betty looked out of the staff-room window, at the summery crowds in the Triangle. "There's no such thing as *that* kind of person, Scottie."

I was not sufficiently mature to understand her then, but I recount the incident as proof of the utterly baseless scandals which can arise so easily in small communities from ignorance of the true facts.

If my friends had said, " She ran away to have a baby," Yeovil could have understood them better, than if they had explained, " She ran away to avoid meeting Bill's ghost in Middle Street or on Summerhouse Hill."

I found the old staff-room more pleasant and friendly than ever, after my experience of its counterpart in Bournemouth. The five friends settled down to their old routine again but with this difference, Mr. Gort now dropped in to make a sixth. For soon it began to be impossible to keep his letters to myself, and I began to share them with the other four.

In one of my letters to him I had described a picnic with Muriel, and he replied:—

" I find the description of your outing is vivid and intensely interesting. For two young girls to have remained by themselves in such a secluded spot for as long as what I take to be ten hours, is really wonderful. Most young women appear to bore each other stiff when left alone together for half that time. What pleased me most of all was that you found your happiness from just ' being '. What is the trend of to-day? It is hurry, bustle, scurry. Few people leave themselves time to think. You and your friend Muriel are fortunate to have each other, such friendships are both rare and valuable."

Later when I had thanked him for some of his letters, he wrote:—

"You could not have interpreted the qualities you mention, were it not for your responsiveness in recognising them as sincere. We can understand and appreciate only that which we possess ourselves (even if in a different degree). The clearer the crystal, the more brilliant are its reflections."

One day Collie in an unexpected flash of wisdom asked, "Can't you get Mr. Gort to help Betty? It must be so awful to lose your fiancé like that, just when you're going to be married."

He subsequently wrote:—

"Tell your friend Betty, that the jurisdiction of the Universe is upon God's shoulders, governing, controlling and correcting, every cause and effect *harmoniously*. Tell her Divine Love has met and always will meet every human need. Tell her to be still and *know*."

Betty, reading through this letter, and blinking back her tears, declared, "Scottie, this friend of yours is a *good* man." Yes, he was a good man indeed.

Lightheartedly the five of us accepted him as a sixth friend, at Christmas we sent him greetings signed by all five of us, and in return he demanded a place at Muriel's wedding celebrations.

For after Evelyn, Muriel was the next to get married. The rest of us decided to stage a party in the staff-room unknown to her, on what was to be her last night at work.

Muriel was safely down the "sixpennies" and so well out of sight of the preparations. I had devised a "mixed-grill" as presenting the fewest difficulties regards cooking and serving. The page-boy was left in charge of my counter, while I set the long refectory table.

On my way down to see my counter was all right, I encountered Collie in the balcony, she was sniffing audibly.

"What's the matter?" I hissed. "Got a cold or something?"

"I'm *sure* I can smell sausages frying," she said.

"That's not at all surprising, considering I just put them on the gas-ring," I countered.

"Supposing the Manager smells them?"

"That'll be too bad, particularly as I've borrowed his saucepan to fry 'em in."

"Oooh——"

What's the matter?   Faint heart never won fair supper!"

When the last patrons were in, and I knew Muriel was about to be relieved on her post to come to supper, I went round the foyer collecting the ornamental vases of flowers, which I now placed lovingly all down the centre of our long table.

A place was laid for the Absent Sixth, as requested.

I cashed up hurriedly and called the others.   Muriel was the last into the staff-room.   When she saw the preparations she began to cry.
" What's the matter? " asked Collie.   " Don't you want to get married? "

" Perhaps," suggested Betty slyly, " she doesn't care for sausages."

" It's that I don't want to leave you all," said Muriel between sniffs.
" We've had such happy times."

We sighed and beamed at each other.   She didn't want to leave us not even for a husband, and such a nice lad too.

" Ain't Nature wonderful? " commented Collie.

Muriel's marriage began the break-up of what Mr. Gort called our " Happy Gang ".   Evelyn retired from work to start a family, and presently Betty returned to her native Cardiff.   We kept in touch with each other, but after some years of a very happy marriage she died from cancer following childbirth.

There was now only Collie and myself left—and Mr. Gort's letters. My return to the West Country seemed to strengthen in many ways my bond with John Gort and I soon found myself confiding in him to the extent of sending him some of my old poems and stories.   Some of these had been written at Whitestaunton, a few at school when I should have been doing my " prep.", and some had been written during my months in Hampshire, while cockchafers blundered against my lamp and I listened anxiously for noises from my charges in the next room.
Of my poems Mr. Gort said:—

" If the temporary necessary world does not side-track you, I feel there is that in you which one day may burst forth into splendid flame.   The world in general *and its opinions* makes you cold and cautious, afraid to express what is in you, or when expressed is but half-expressed.   To some, especially untutored urban minds, your West Country poems would make heavy going.   Yet some of the most magnificent poetry ever written in this country—Milton—is heavy going.

"To-day all is hurry, scurry, race, race, and for such a state of mind your poems could not be properly read, understood or enjoyed. One has to be calm, relaxed and above all bring *love* of the subject to the reading of it, in order to sense the feeling and spirit of the author. I might add here, that it is essential to bring love to the reading of your Bible if it is not to remain a closed book to you.

"When one's heart is really in one's work, poetry, music or anything else, one is subject to a kind of divine compulsion—one feels ' under orders '. It is this in no small degree which makes rhyme come from you so easily.

"I would like to keep a copy of your long poem with me always. Will you write me out one? You have put your heart into this—and do not reply as you once did, that ' that is easy '. It is anything *but* easy, and I am surprised at you saying that. To put one's heart into anything, above all to *keep it there*, is one of the most difficult of all achievements. And let me plainly tell you this. *It often gets broken in the process.* Not necessarily broken beyond repair—but broken nevertheless badly. You may have already learned that, but I very much hope not.

"I arrived at my favourable opinion of your long poem, feeling my way there.

"You may not, at your age, and with your short *actual* experience have come to a point when you can easily understand what I try to explain. But sooner or later you WILL come to it, though it be given to the comparative few to be controlled by the heart in the divine way. The vast majority are controlled by their desires only, not really by the heart at all, as they would wish to believe."

This " long poem " of which Mr. Gort makes mention in the above letter, was a fairly recent piece of work, written during intervals of serving at the chocolate counter. I was still nineteen when I put it together, writing a few lines at a time, bobbing up and down from behind my array of chocolates. When I came to transpose it on to my typewriter in a decent manner, some of the writing was so scribbled it defied even the author's translation. I was reminded of Browning.

"When I wrote that, only God and Robert Browning knew what it meant—now God alone knows! "

A word which I finally deciphered as " glow-worm " for long had me completely beaten, it looked like one long series of squiggles.

This was one of the few things I ever wrote which brought me anything like satisfaction. It was a complete labour of love and had no "market" in view. In it, I wrote of things I had seen in the countryside, and I wrote from memory, while working in the midst of a busy cinema, with love for the subject deep in my heart.

Later Mr. Gort commented on the poem in detail and then suggested I sent it to an absent West Countryman if I knew one, not necessarily a person who was interested in poetry.

Consequently I posted it off to a friend from Chard, then exiled in a poor east-end quarter of London. He wrote in reply:—

" I have just spent a half-hour round Somerset thanks to your poem, it was like being home again. I particularly liked the beginning, ' I have seen a May sun rise——' ".

This poem always seemed too long and unwieldly to do anything with, but recently I split it up into short stanzas and prefaced two of my country books with them. My Danish friend was loud in his praises of those verses commencing *Hundredfold*, but as his " bible " was Ella Wheeler Wilcox, I am not entirely certain how to take his continental praise!

Mr. Gort was plainly of the opinion that I could write, but I did not give the matter any serious consideration then—the world was " side-tracking " me too much, as it always has done, and I am afraid always will do.

I was too busy looking after my little business, trying to make a home out of my bed-sitting room and trying to " get-over " Bill. I was hardly equal to taking up writing seriously.

Occasionally I cycled home to Bournemouth, but after the dog Mack died, my visits became less frequent. My Mother was very happy and settled there. She vowed she had made her last move. Everything about Bournemouth suited her and she seemed to grow younger every time we saw her. My sister and I were well satisfied.

A new girl came to the Gaumont, a country girl whose home was in a remote village near Maiden Newton. She invited me to accompany her home one week-end and by so doing I discovered a whole new country opening out before me.

Soon I had fallen completely under the spell of Thomas Hardy's country from High Stoy of *Tess of the D'Urbervilles* to Glanvilles Wootton of *The Woodlanders*. I learned to know " Toller Down so Bleak and Bare " of the poem called *The Homecoming*, and remembered how I had crossed the great ridge for the first time when I cycled from Whitestaunton to Brighton.

In my mind I began to carry a map of Wessex, and almost each week filled in some detail on the territory from Bridport to Warminster, from Priddy to Shaftesbury.

Recently I have been asked how I came to know Wessex so well, considering that travel has been difficult, petrol rationed, and I have always been so occupied with other matters. My reply is that I first drew my map of Wessex from the saddle of my bicycle, motor journeys made since have only filled in a few details or joined up one district with another.

It was on a bicycle I learned the haunted beauty of the hills about Cerne Abbas, or the unspoilt loneliness of the Chesil Beach. To my long cycle rides with my new friend Dorothy, or alone, I owe the discovery of magic little places like Rampisham, Wynford Eagle and Bradford Peverill, Clifton Maybank and Sutton Poyntz.

From a bicycle I received a truer impression of the " lie of the land " than one can do in a car. The imprints of different cultures and geological stratas are more clearly and truly visible at eight miles an hour than at even twenty-eight.

Cycling was often hard work, pushing up Benville Knapp, walking the long hill out of Beaminster, struggling up Rampisham Down, I was yet rewarded with the scent of clover almost beneath my feet, with the cry of the gulls after the plough, and with the feel of the tall wheat beside the pathway, wheat which from a car I could not put out my hand and touch.

XVIII

The Cabin in the Clearing

SINCE writing my West Country poem, above all since discovering Hardy's Dorset, the "lack" in my life had been given a name, and I was all for putting an end to it.

For I knew now what I wanted. Certainly I might fall in love again, even ultimately marry, but it must be to a man of the countryside, he would be my roots and my background. Bill had belonged more than half to the city. What would have happened had we married? Now I could even bear to wonder. He was fond of theatres and skating rinks and rather sophisticated entertainment, he would not like to be long away from the "centre of things". But our idea of the "centre" was different. To me, it was where things were growing and living—I was beginning to find myself.

London and Bournemouth had taught me my lesson, the country was my rightful place, and in future I would stay where I belonged. Of how I came across a gamekeeper's cottage hidden deep in the Yeo valley, I have written in another book, whose kind readers have prompted this one.

My letters from Mr. Gort that had once commenced with "Dear Friend", had now altered to "My Dear Romany". He recalled my past camp-fire outings with Muriel, my lonely night journeys, and concluded:

"I believe you really have some Romany blood in you——"

When I moved out of my room in Market Street for the last time, he wrote:—

"I am delighted that you are taking over your new home on September the nineteenth. I am holding no doubt but that you will be very happy. It is a unique position for a girl to be in, and one which should enrich you greatly in many ways if you will develop your glorious opportunities for being alone. At your age I also longed to be quite alone—you have all my sympathy and encouragement."

The generosity of my friends and my own planning and saving had provided me with a very fair home which I christened "Romany Cottage", much to Mr. Gort's delight.

As a child, sitting high and dry above the Folly Brook in Warminster I had dreamed of a home of my own. Not for me was the cottage of knick-knacks and shining delft or the cradles and chintzes of other little girls. I had been reading G. A. Henty's *The Cabin in the Clearing*, and that was the kind of home *I* wanted.

Mine was to be the log-cabin in the backwoods, with the fox by the woodpile and the shy deer peeping in at the door. I had visualised meals cooked in the open and eaten beneath the sun or the stars.

To a very great extent "Romany Cottage" was this childhood vision come true. It proved however to be more than my ideal home in ideal surroundings, it was the gateway to an entirely new world for me, a world I had known existed, if only from glimpses by the wayside, or the pages of Thomas Hardy and Mary Webb, but a world I had never really explored until now.

For now began my real education in what Goethe has called—

"The things that are abiding."

Of this new world being daily opened to me, Richard Jefferies has written:—

"There is a life in the hamlets and villages around, in the little places that are not even hamlets, which to the folk who dwell in them is fully as important as that of the greatest city. Farmhouses are not like the villas of cities and city suburbs. The villa has hardly any individuality, it is but one of many, each resembling the other, and scarcely separated. To-day, one family occupies it, tomorrow, another, next year perhaps, a third, and none of these have any real connection with the place. They are sojourners, not inhabitants, they are drawn thither by business or pleasure; they come and go, and leave no mark behind. But the farmhouse has a history. The same family have lived in it for perhaps a hundred years. They have married and intermarried and become identified with the locality."*

When, walking in my garden at "Romany Cottage", I looked across to the moated farmhouse at Wyke I learned the true significance of those words, which never could have been brought home to me by the mere printed page.

* *Hodge and his Masters.*

I roamed the Yeo valley from Sherborne to Clifton Maybank and it seemed the countryside more than met me half-way; it was only a matter of time before it claimed me entirely. There was still, however, the matter of my living to be earned and as I knew nothing of cheese-making or tractor-driving and was still a little inclined to be afraid of cows, I had to remain with one foot in the country and one in the town.

It was by no means an easy life, the sheer physical endurance it required and the economic self-sacrifice alone ensured that. I had so few shillings to spend on food, after my rent and rates were paid, and my dogs fed, that I had to study nutrition the hard way. Meat came my way but seldom, and then largely in the form of a rabbit snared by the neighbouring Shepherd who was my very good friend. I lived almost entirely on whole-meal bread and butter, eggs, and fruit and vegetables, with cheese taking the place of meat. My only treat was an occasional banana and cream for my tea. There was no room for fancy goods and tinned products in my economy. Yet I always had enough to eat and my health was never better.

" Romany Cottage " taught me a whole new set of values. I found some of them expressed for me, in the words of the dialect poet William Barnes, himself a Dorset man, in the poem better known now as the song " Linden Lea ":

> " Let other vók meäke money vaster
>   In the air o' dark room'd towns,
> I don't dread a peevish master
>   Though noo man do heed my frowns ;
> I be vree to goo abrode,
>   Or teäke age än my whomeward road
> To where, vor me, the apple tree
>   Do leän down low in Linden Lea."

My apple tree leaned down low with fruit for me and I wished I might stay with it all the time, but for the time being sheer economic necessity forced me to continue as I was, seeing as much as might be of the countryside in my free time.

The daily ride from " Romany Cottage " and back, in all weathers and through all seasons, ensured that I adopted a rural attitude to living, even while continuing to work in the town. When I went to the cottage I had no thought of writing about it, and it was not until almost a decade afterwards that I put my impressions of those Dorset years into a book.

I am told, both at home and abroad, it is the book by which I am likely to be remembered. And if I ask myself why, I think the answer is not far to seek. Love was in my heart as I wrote, the love of which Mr. Gort waxed so eloquent, if eloquent is not too easy a word for some of his expressions of help and wisdom. The writing in that book was bound to be raw, I had only one published volume before it. Experience of my craft was almost nil, and I wrote entirely from memory with the aid of some rather faded snapshots taken during my actual sojourn at the cottage. Yet now, if someone says,

" So and so has read your books and knows of you—has the greatest admiration for your way of life," and I ask which of my books it was made such an impression, the answer is always the same—

" *Romany Cottage, Silverlake.*"

In the most casual conversation, in gatherings in distant parts of the country where I believe I am not known, there is always someone who says,

" ——we knew of you through *Romany Cottage*, so and so read it and liked it, oh so much."

Perhaps many people, men especially (in this case men predominate in writing to me about the book), have fancied such a simple country existence of their own, few have the opportunity (or the courage to *make* the opportunity) to try it. But they read into my book an experience they themselves might have had, have indeed secretly wished to have. They are not reading about *me*, but about themselves, hence their enjoyment. To some extent this is true of all books. The reader must read himself into it, and it is especially true of autobiographies and biographies. " How does his life compare with mine? " is the question in the reader's mind.

In her *Wheels on Gravel*, Alyse Gregory, widow of Llewelyn Powys, has stated:—

" There are three processes necessary to the best writing. They are to feel profoundly, think independently, and express yourself in words that convey to others with eloquence and lucidity the full quality and import of your emotion—it matters only that it should have grown up out of the depth of your own being, should have been reflected upon with intellectual veracity, and should remain loyal to what your apprehended life-experience has taught you to be true."

If *Romany Cottage* deserves its laurels it is because most of those above conditions have been observed, through no art or artifice, but through pure love of the subject.

It was nineteen-thirty-eight when I first went to the cottage, the last year of a very shaky peace. To me war was quite unthinkable apart from my Mother having assured me that another war was entirely impracticable. It was not so much with war as with the question of Faith that I was now concerned.

My visits to local churches gave me no help or spiritual nourishment. The sermons were pointless and ill-delivered (from my own knowledge of the Bible I felt I could better appeal to the cowmen and their wives seated in the little carven pews).

Mr. Gort plainly believed in a God, only he mostly called it by the name of Good. " God IS Good," he had said. Myself I was inclined to believe in something, even after reading about Spain and Czechoslovakia, and realising in the light of history that man has always been the most cruel, pitiless, ruthless creation of nature.

Never before, with my friends and harmless pursuits had I had time to ponder on these weighty matters. Here was I, approaching the age of twenty-two and I did not know whether I believed in God or not. Many people will say that the wonderful manifestations of nature, with which I was now in daily contact should have clinched the matter for me once and for all. They did nothing of the sort.

My exiled friend from Chard to whom I had submitted my West Country poem had written:—

" Your expositions are somewhat vague, reminding me of those written by leading churchmen! Even an atheist knows the difference between right and wrong, it is not altogether necessary to have a god to know that. It appears the whole keystone of the business is Faith. How many people can say they really believe? Can you say it? *Honestly now?* After all, there is no such thing as a passive, mediocre kind of faith. It is either whole-hearted or non-existent. To be in the former category one must necessarily observe the teachings of Christ and the rules of Christianity to the letter. Look among your leading churchgoers and Christians and see how many do this. Our supreme example is perhaps the Pope, living in what amounts to positive luxury in his private city of the Vatican, equipped with his own railways, marble-palaces, radio stations, etc. But then this man is the Pope, he is infallible.

" I once heard an atheist orating in Hyde Park, a couple of Irish women tried to argue with him, they were voluble to the point of being hysterical, but it was honestly about the most one-sided argument I have ever heard.

" No doubt you are prejudiced by the old story of the atheist who when in a particularly tight corner, goes down on his knees and starts praying like mad. Obviously, the logical explanations are two—(a) either habit—he had it drummed into him when young, or (b) he's going to try everything, just in case! You must agree, Monica, that atheism is the only religion of common-sense, but when we meet again we will drink a toast, you to your possible Something I to my possible Nothing."

This friend had corresponded with me in a desultory fashion ever since my school-days as indeed had Norman, the musician from Warminster. We met but seldom and about the copy of my West Country poem, despatched just before I settled in at the cottage, he wrote:—

" Whereas country life leaves the imagination free, the town to my mind, tends to make it run in one channel—the grimness of life and the struggle for existence."

Be that as it may, it had certainly set my mind free to think, as it had never been before. Strangely enough the peace and quiet of the countryside did not lure me into an unquestioning acceptance of old faiths and creeds and precepts, I found myself beginning to question every established law and code.

Writing of the Burmese, H. J. Massingham has said:—

" Naturally we expect a whole nation to have gone to the dogs. We find instead the most enlightened land laws in the world, marriage customs which put our property laws to shame, a justice that does not degrade the evildoer, nor exile him from nature and his kindly fellow-men, nor revenge itself on him in the name of society, nor brand him for the rest of his life as a deterrent, nor advertise him as an excitement to the mob. (Are not our murder trials a modern variant of the Roman bread and circuses?) "

Without becoming in any way politically minded I became more aware of the rightness of the " brotherhood of Man ", and not merely of Man, but of all the creatures upon the earth. Hunting them, with anything more lethal than a camera, seemed unthinkable.

I marvelled too, the day I realised that the same set of chemicals in the same soil nurtures oaks and buttercups alike and feeds all the wonderful varieties of natural growth. It seemed such a simple, and at the same time momentous discovery.

I learned too that to try to grasp happiness too sharply, was to lose it entirely. To search and search for the miracle of perfection was a waste of time, but in the course of one's daily life, often when least expected, a glimpse of the " inaccessible " would sometimes be vouchsafed.

Sometimes I found it in strange, unexpected ways, not in the gorgeous sunsets or the drifts of cowslips before my door, but sometimes in a shaft of moted sunlight streaming in through the open door of a cinema exit, before the artificial lighting was on, and while the building still remained to be called into life.

But to consciously try to recapture the same thing again was a foolish waste of time, once it was passed.

I remember one hungry Sunday afternoon, very much enjoying a poached egg and toast for my tea. It was simply delicious, everything about it was just right. Now though it was an unheard of thing to take two eggs at the same meal, I was tempted to repeat the pleasure at once. The second time was not a bit the same. The egg was not done so perfectly, neither had it the flavour of the first one, while the toast was overdone.

The lesson may seem an absurd one but I took it to heart!

So many people write to me now who would like to find a " Romany Cottage " for themselves. Some of them bewail the fact that they will never have the courage, or that times have changed so much that such a venture would today be impossible. Yet all these people to a greater or lesser degree believe that such was a life worth living, and the ideal is an existence simple, healthy, honest, free from hypocrisy or greed, but how many people, as Fielding Hall writes:—

" —think differently—are content with cheerless days with an absence of love, of beauty, of all that is valuable to the heart, if we can but put away a little money, if we can enlarge our business, if we can make a bigger figure in the world."

My life at " Romany Cottage " was not to be measured in terms of money or even of security. My life there was perhaps no more secure than that of the rabbit in his burrow waiting for stoat and trapper and greyhound to threaten him.

The " law of supply and demand " threatened me always. When there was a war in Spain, the imports of nuts was decreased and the price of nut-milk chocolate went up and people bought less of it. So even such distant events affected me, if but distantly. The close proximity of war haunted and hunted me, and poverty threatened me often from very close quarters.

I took nothing for granted, I was thankful for every day I was left in peace and for every month I was able to meet my rent. I was thankful for the apple trees that bloomed for me, and the brook that yielded me free watercress. Life may not have been easy, I have never pretended that such a life was, though at twenty-two it is fairly easy to laugh away one's difficulties, but I was happy, happy in my environment, in my daily work and my daily journeys. Recently I took the Danish-born guide from Wookey Hole to see my old cottage in the valley. He had long expressed the request that he might visit the scene of the book, for, although loyal enough to his native Denmark, and having travelled most of the countries of the world, he prefers the West Country of England to anywhere else on earth. Nothing, he says, from New Zealand to Norway can equal its changing, yet change-less charm.

After viewing the cottage, walking round the garden, separated from the meadow only by a low railing, he looked in the direction of Silverlake Farm, just visible through the thick foliage of bush and tree.

" And you don't mean to tell me," he began, " that that young girl from the farm, walked all that way each day to bring you a pint of milk."

I nodded. " Certainly she did, Emil, in fact, the whole time I was at Silverlake I met with nothing but kindness from everyone. From the woman who returned my dog Spry after he had strayed as far away as Thornford, to the Shepherd who cut me a clothes-line prop, the first washing-day I had at the cottage."

It was true, I met with kindness from these country people, whenever I was in need.   Farmer Legg, afterwards killed by a German plane while ploughing near Silverlake, would carry down my five gallon drum of paraffin oil, which was my sole means of lighting and cooking at the cottage.   A roadman stopped and mended a puncture for me, when I unhappily picked up a sharp object in one of my very worn bicycle tyres.   Molly from the farm brought me a rice pudding the only time I was ever ill at the cottage.

My Mother visited me at the cottage several times, her verdict was favourable, and she even said it was a life she could have been happy living when she was younger.   My sister and her husband came twice, once bringing Mother with them.   It was the first time I had had a home of my own to which to ask them.   We got along very well on the more nearly equal terms of the new association, the past was never mentioned, perhaps because the future loomed now a little larger than life.   It was the time of the Munich Agreement, they were days of testing and crisis for the nation.

My sister and her husband were anxious for their business, they saw their established way of life in danger.   My Mother said little; like myself I think she considered the possibility of war in the light of a bad dream—too fantastically dreadful to contemplate seriously.

Sitting under my great apple tree, reading A. G. Street; watching the rain against my window panes while I composed an answer to Mr. Gort's latest epistle; walking with my two young dogs beside the newly born river Yeo, the affairs of the rest of the world seemed remote and unreal.

Only when I crossed Babylon Hill and descended into Yeovil was their reality borne in upon me.   There I saw the Nazis goose-stepping through countless newsreels until they seemed to shake the world with their marching.   There I saw men whitening the curb-stones, women fixing black-outs to their windows, and little children, herded and ticketed like cattle, awaiting homes in a " safe area ".

But once I had crossed the shoulder of hill again I was in a world of sheep and shepherds, the smell of farms and all the sounds and sights of nature.   I was with the things that are " abiding ".

XIX

"Into the Jaws"

WHEN a schoolgirl I had gone, about 1932, to a lecture on Disarmament given by a very able speaker, and I was much impressed by his arguments which I might say fell on prepared ground, as previously, while at the Camden School for Girls, I had joined the League of Nations Union's junior branch.

A young woman of obvious education had made me angry and bitterly ashamed by standing up and heckling the speaker to the effect that—

"Without war, where would honour and glory, etc., be?" I can remember now the burning shame with which I regarded this heckler. That a member of my sex should make such a cruel, stupid ignorant remark, that she should be so short-sighted, nay, worse than short-sighted, absolutely *blind* as to think that any good came out of the murder of our fellow-men, or that honour and glory could not be found without the foul means of war!

I longed to get up and reply to her, to tell her and all like her that honour and glory exist in serving one's fellow-men, not in killing them, and that adventure still awaits those who would have it—adventures of the body; climbing mountains, plumbing the depths of the sea, challenging the air—and adventures of the mind ; delving into the secrets of nature and of the universe, translating the old poets, philosophers and sages, and bringing their thoughts and reasoning into line with our own.

I burned to reply, but dare not, for I realised that with such an attitude of mind, nothing would *make* her understand. It would be like talking to someone who did not speak the same language. The speaker answered her for me.

"Madam, had you ever been in the firing line you would know that pain and mutilation are the only honour and glory accorded the average fighting man today."

But from that day onwards, the fear that there might he another war, in spite of the unthinkableness of such a contingency, grew like a cloud on my horizon. If people were so blind and misguided in their attitudes to this greatest of all worldly evils, then might not we fall again into the old errors, simply because people did not, or would not think sufficiently sanely and honestly on the matter?

Always I fought against it, when the " war-mongers " declared that what was wanted was:—

" A good old war to clear things up," I refused to subscribe to their theories. Yes, it was a shame about the way the Nazis and Fascists were running loose, but war never *did* and never *could* solve anything; and it left nothing but the seeds of the next conflict, sown in soil made fruitful with human blood, and ready to blossom forth again betimes.

Through the days of scares and crises, I resolutely said to myself, " It will not happen, mankind must have learned by now. They will talk it over, the lust for power will shake down; the inverted inferiority complexes of those who were defeated in the last war will wear off. Give them time, when the threat of war looms high and near above all of us, they will see as we do that arbitration must be used instead, that man must talk it over with man, and come to an amicable plan where all men can live in the world as brothers. After all, if the Bible is to be believed we are all of a common descent, each race of us, and therefore *are* brothers. Can brother kill brother without the charge of murder being levelled against him? Is it any less a sin to kill in the name of war than in the name of peace? ' Thou shalt not kill ' is absolute and equivocal, if the Christian faith means anything, if Christians from the Pope down to the humblest worshipper in the hamlet church really believe their faith, no *Christian* at least, will fight ever again."

I held to this through the years from my school-days until the moment in September 1939 that war was actually declared. Even then I found it hard to believe, when Shepherd leaned over my garden fence and said quietly:—

" Well, it's bad news, Miss."

Mr. Gort had mentioned " war " but once in all his many letters, and then only for a few words. He had expressed satisfaction that I was living in a " safe " place. After my reply to that letter, came this from him:—

" You were surprised that I should mention ' war '. That shows me, perhaps more than anything that you are ' growing ', I should *not* have mentioned it under any ordinary circumstances, it is wrong to do so; it was just, viewing your picture of the cottage, I felt a momentary gladness sweep over me, that you lived in such a place."

As we were to learn " such a place " was no more likely to be immune from the death from the air than the centre of a crowded city, but we were as then unversed in the full extent of the " new warfare ".

Remembering that old silent picture *The Four Horsemen of the Apocalypse*, with its arresting caption : " Into the jaws of hell on earth— WAR," I marvelled yet again, as I have done many times since, that mankind, while being fully conscious of the enormity of its mistakes, should continue to practise them, full knowing the awful cost. Could it be, I asked myself, that the present generation—my generation— had forgotten the spate of war books, poems, plays and films after the last holocaust, proclaiming unanimously the folly of this particular type of human madness? Had they forgotten *Journey's End* and *All Quiet* or the other side of the sad tale in Erich Maria Remarque's *The Road Back*?

They had forgotten, or they had never known, or if they had both remembered and known, then they had failed altogether to take in the import of the burden of such writings, so that they too were wasted and their message lost, just as the lives of those given from 1914-1918 were wasted and lost.

Because I tried, even through the haze of personal fear, grief, indignation, patriotism and all those other emotions which beset us at such times, not to lose sight of fairmindedness and reason, I broke my habitual rule to keep no letters other than those of Mr. Gort, and for the sake of a clearer picture in years to come, I kept letters and notes representative of the times from a number of people.

I have since thought that war would not be so bad, so utterly inde-fensible if some of the laws of human conduct and behaviour learned beneath its stress could be retained in the days of peace that follow. But how soon is the unselfishness, the camaraderie, the willingness to share, totally forgotten? How soon does the old mad scramble of each man for himself and the Devil take the hindermost replace the spirit of helpfulness, charity and service that were the only entries on the credit side of war?

During the war we felt a deep kinship with the Russians, we were ready to share our meagre lot with those refugees and outcasts worse off than ourselves, we were ready to open our homes and hearts, the world-wide calamity knit us all together, as a family will leave off quarrelling to find their house is afire. But once the danger is past, we forget the bonds of brotherhood which momentarily knit us in common hopes and fears, and the one good that might have come from the war, recedes further and further as the time passes.

Here is a cross-section of letters from my friends and relatives received while at " Romany Cottage."

First from the orphan, who for the purposes of this book shall be called " George ", he was a friend of my Mother and later myself, to most he would be thought " queer ": we thought him entirely sensible. He was killed by an accident owing to the blackout. This letter almost forecasts his own death:—

" What a mistake this war is, I felt all along that we should not come to it, and now we have. Everything is spoiled, business lost, plans for the future ruined, and aims in life wasted. For myself, I have worked hard as you know, most of my time for next to nothing, I have denied myself many things and for what? I might as well have laid abed. Look at your son-in-law's case. He has just taken over a fine business, got well started, and now this. What a waste! It seems the only gains go to the ' animal ' minds who cannot think and do not care.

" I dare not cycle in this blackness, it is no help to my eyesight and I am afraid I dread the winter for what it will bring, people do not realise we shall be feeling the effects of the war then. They think only in terms of excitement and uniforms. In a proper world there would be no such things as soldiers.

" Really, this is no letter for you, because you are such an ' up and upper ', but if I cannot write my feelings to you, who is there?

" Yours sorrowfully,
" GEORGE."

To a person with an average sense of humour, the " sorrowfully " may have a faintly facetious ring. I can assure them it should not be taken so. George was genuinely " sorrowful " for the follies of mankind. He died in the winter of which he was so afraid.

Next comes a note from Norman, the musician friend of Warminster days. It is dated a few days before Dunkirk.

" Things are happening so fast I feel I must write to know if everything is alright with you. I hope all is well, it is years since I saw you and it may be years before I see you again.

" I have been in the army four months, such busy months that I have had time to think of nothing but settling down, which is perhaps just as well. I can tell you nothing concerning my unit except that I am in the Pay Office, have passed my Trade Test and am now earning the magnificent sum of 2/9 per day, one shilling of which is sent home.

" We are in the excitement zone here, and can see the coasts of France very clearly. It is almost impossible to realise in this sunshine that over there men are killing and being killed.

" We live from day to day and tomorrow who knows? Last night I was playing for Jeanne de Casalis, next week we are supposed to be holding our big cabaret with Ats. talent.

" I have just heard, we are now on the move, if you answer this letter as I hope you will, please address as overleaf.

" Yours as ever,

" NORMAN."

From a friend of my schooldays who subsequently became a Flying Officer, and to whom I dedicated my first book as, in the capacity of Secretary for the British Amateur Press Association, he had always encouraged me to write such a book:—

" It was good to hear from you and I am grateful to you for adding another correspondent to your regular list. I'm glad you appreciate that the principal joy (and practically the only one) of life in the Services is the receipt of letters. Believe you me, that pleasure is very real, and on mail-less days a blanket of depression settles down.

" After a month in the R.A.F. I see no reason to amend my initial impression—it is a disgrace to democracy. I would prefer to be a dustman than in my present position. As yet I know no more of the job of flight mechanic than I did on the day I joined. I have not yet seen an aeroplane lower than 500 ft. My whole time is occupied in learning to drill, march, march and drill. Thousands of pounds are being spent here each week simply to teach us to ' present arms ', while the hard-pressed Russians are fighting for their homes and lives. What a farce! One would think the exigencies of war would be sufficient to cut red-tape. I fume to think that I missed a fulltime job in the A.F.S. by only a few days. I could have been doing *essential* constructive work——"

The above is the portrait of a man approaching forty, a man who had always lived by his brain, being forced into scrubbing billets, saluting officers—doing anything in fact but what he is fitted for. He climbed out of it however, but not without the consciousness of many wasted years.

Something of the same sentiments can be found in Llewelyn Powys's diary when he says:

" The anomaly of war in this stage of our civilisation is clearly seen by the importance attached to such work as constructing a tank and carrying a bayonet effectively."

To which H. J. Massingham adds:

" War was never the agent of civilisation but of barbarism; it was civilisation which became the agent of war. War has never served either the needs or the progress of mankind, but it has poisoned its well-being, brutalised its soul, impoverished its culture and debased its understanding."

I have heard it said that wars speed up invention, and further scientific progress, and have had such things as " Radar " held up for my inspection as proof of the credit side of war.

What such reasoning omits is that human beings would rather have homes than radar, proper sanitation than wonderful aircraft hangars, food than new-speed records on the air and security rather than atomic power.

While such strides are being made in mass destruction, while all means are being found to put out fires and then create bigger fires to put out, ordinary decent human progress is at a standstill.

Every night in the trapping season, the countryside around is made hideous (even to those accustomed to it) by the screams of trapped animals which may vary from the rabbit for which the gin was originally intended, to the domestic cat or the shy partridge, the straying dog or the frantic stoat. Through the long hours of agony, sometimes in the sunshine of the brightest of spring days, when the cowslips dance in the meadows and it would appear all things are in harmony, the trapped creature, cowering, scraping and screaming, caught sometimes by a limb, sometimes by its snout, sometimes by the fur and skin of its belly, waits for the release of a blow to end its agony.   Time has been when I have killed a dozen rabbits, freed a frenzied cat, and ended the swearing of a blood-soaked weasel within the confines of one meadow. Yet the Sawyer trap was invented, patented, and demonstrated by the R.S.P.C.A. as a means for effectively and humanely killing pests like the engaging rabbit.   Its adoption generally depends upon the passing of a law in Parliament.   So little time has war left for such humane matters, that the old rusty, torturing gins continue, while men wait for time to attend to such matters.

I wish I could explain this to the fox who dragged a gin after him for many years, dying of a slow starvation the while.   I wish I could tell our cat who had her kittens born cold and dead while in the toils of these hideous contraptions.   I wish I could make our excuses to the maimed birds, or the rabbits dying in agony from a gangrenous limb which in his extremity he finally gnawed through.

These are all God's creatures as much as ourselves and if we awaken late to the need to deal with them humanely, if in the interests of our food production they must be dealt with, at least we have awakened, thereby showing some human progress in the right direction—should little matters like time and convenience prevent a step in the right direction being taken?

But for the war we should have the Sawyer trap in place of the barbaric gin, we should have houses, food, clothing, a better standard of education, better opportunities to live fully.   Who can say that war is the " Agent of Civilisation ?"

And who can doubt that it is the opposite, when they read the enclosed which I received from my sister during November 1940:

"——he had spent the night at Covent Garden where there were severe fires and dreadful damage.   He was on one ' case ' from 11 p.m. until 6-30 a.m.   A baker had been starting his evening ' bake ' when his place received a direct hit, and he with his oven went down into a deep crater with the demolished building on top.   When Montie got there, the warden and he could just faintly hear the man calling ' Get me out—I'm burning '.   They worked with the rescue squad until 6-30.   A woman doctor from Charing Cross Hospital stood by and when they had made a narrow channel she was lowered down and injected morphia to ease his pain.   The building was burning fiercely but the firemen dare not play their hoses on it because of bringing the masonry down on the rescue work. It was like working in Hell. Naturally the blaze made a target and bombs fell like hail. The man when eventually they got him out was terribly burned as he had been jammed up against his oven, he also had a broken pelvis and smashed ankle—it is unlikely he will recover, the last we heard from the hospital was that he was very low. All these rescue men deserve the V.C. In the last war a man who risked his life for his fellow-men was a hero and was decorated——"

The men up in the clouds who dropped the bombs, it will be argued, were just doing a job of work, and now sane people blame them no more than they blame our own " gallant airmen " for dropping bombs on civilians in other countries.

I left my work at the cinema in 1940, after six years, broken only by a couple of months at Bournemouth. During my absence they showed a film whose title I cannot remember but it may have been *The Battle of Britain* or something similar, it dealt entirely with " How we drop those beautiful bombs". I surprised my late colleagues and manager by refusing to come and see such a picture on the grounds that it was morally wrong, even if it was " our side " who were doing the bombing. None of those " gallant airmen " knew who or what was down there at their so-called " target ". Even after the raid on Sherborne, when I was nearly killed, I could take no pleasure, no honour or glory from seeing the same done to our enemies. The only real enemies of mankind are the forces of nature—flood, fire, famine, pestilence and death. It is against them we should unite and fight and against them only. Man should have no quarrel with man. Life is more or less hard for all of us, we have the same puniness in the face of the elements and elemental disasters. But how soon we could minimise their effects, perhaps even master them if we would realise we were on earth to help each other.

To some extent the war brought forth this feeling, but as I said before it did not last long—between nations or individuals.

I have a cutting before me, headed : " Sympathy from Sherborne, U.S.A." which goes on to say that the Massachusetts town, in a letter to the Vicar of Sherborne, Dorset, " desired to express their sympathy and to make offers of help to the ' mother ' town. They express hope that the Abbey was not damaged and ask what are our most pressing needs of the moment now that they may send help accordingly."

Of course this spirit is not entirely dead, in spite of growing mistrust and hard words in Press and Politics, people of one country and nation are still ready to extend a helping hand to those of another.   There are those in the U.S.A. who cannot bear to think of us being in want and who deny themselves to send us food-parcels, and even then feel they have no right to be living " comfortably " while we still suffer austerity conditions.   Similarly there are people here in Britain ready to open their homes and share what they have with those unfortunate peoples who lack home or country because of the cruelty and stupidity of man.

A few warm hearts, a few clear minds, and few helping hands, when will they join and band themselves together in an " humanitarian front," an army to fight war and all it stands for, an army to promote peace and goodwill?

XX

A Strange Harvest Home

I ENDEAVOURED to keep the balance between the country and the town, the abiding things and the transient things, between war and peace. For as long as I could I carried on at the Cottage. The chocolate sales fell off as the supplies dwindled, and as I worked on a commission basis, it became increasingly hard for me to live. But before I say good-bye to "Romany Cottage" I would lay before you a picture of my life there in wartime that has come back to me through a devious channel.

Among other people's letters I now come upon one penned by myself, it was returned by the post office, the whereabouts of the addressees unknown. They had last been heard of at Dunkirk and had posted me a brief note from a transit camp to tell me they had reached England safely.

My letter reads:

"DEAR ALL THREE OF YOU,

"Thank you for your pencilled scrawl, I suppose the typewriter has been left for the Germans. You called yourselves peacetime soldiers and now I suppose you think you are heroes. Personally I do not think anything could have been so trying to your valour as walking out to 'Romany Cottage' in the dark, those country noises must have been terrifying to your town-bred senses.

"You ask me how the Cottage is looking. Well, I am writing this in the garden, and the heavenly peace of Silverlake only serves to emphasise the hideousness of what is going on elsewhere in so much of the world just now.

"My garden is a city of birds. The cuckoo does not realise it is June, for he has not changed his tune yet, I must hang a calendar out for him. Molly and her brothers have cut my garden with a scythe and made a kind of rick by the back-gate, it looks like a bad-fire-risk to me! The back-gate is the one used for visitors, remember? The front-gate is the one opening into the field, used only by the dogs when they want to chase the cows.

" There are plenty of flowers out and I can see them now the grass has been cut. The old-fashioned white roses are in bloom, they have a heavenly perfume but are very thorny (there should be a moral there somewhere). The hedges are covered with dog-roses and honeysuckle, and the plum trees back and front are heavily laden with green fruit. It looks like being a good crop. There are a few strawberries beginning to ripen, but I hate to deprive the ants and slugs. The gooseberries have been eaten as far as I know—I sold the crop and it paid my rent for a week. You didn't think I was so businesslike did you?

" The gnats are biting, the sky is a very deep blue and I am covered with freckles. I suppose you remember the place with snow on the ground and Coltman thawing the water to make some tea. You did not mention him by the way, and I'm wondering if he got back safely and if he will really take up farming when it's all over—if it's ever all over. I hope that doesn't sound too pessimistic. It will be one day of course. But I have an aunt at Waterloo, I don't suppose I ever told you. Her husband was a grain merchant. No one knows what has become of them. She was one of mother's favourite sisters and very pretty. They had an only son about my age, no one knows what has happened to him either. Uncle Marcel's people were refugees in the last war and lost all they possessed.

" Here we have the same thing happening twice in twenty-five years. It seems incredible to me, how can mankind be so mad? All those little people in Belgium, how will it ever be made up to them—and there was Poland before. Doesn't human happiness matter? I think it does very much. I once saw Albert the Good as he was called. Auntie Vera and Uncle Marcel told me he was much loved and I find it hard to believe evil of his son. Don't you honestly think Leopold was driven to it—what choice had he?

" Yes, thanks for enquiring I have done a little writing—but only a very little. Please don't tell James Agate, I want to be the first to let him know. And yes, Farmer L. still comes over occasionally. His father died just before you all went overseas which has made things hard on the farm for him and given him a great deal of extra responsibility——"

As I have said, this letter was returned by the post office and I gave up hope of ever knowing what had happened to Lewis and Joe and

Lofty, the three friends in khaki who had walked out to Silverlake in the very early days of the war. Farmer L. often expressed a desire to know how they were getting on. It was a long war. But on the publication of *Romany Cottage* the spokesman for these three was told he was " in a book ". A friend had been reading it and as no names were disguised had passed on the news straight away.

The ex-territorial, ex-hero of Dunkirk wrote to my publishers as the only way of getting in touch with me and the letter was forwarded. I think the author of it was surprised upon receiving my reply to learn that I had moved less than a dozen miles from Silverlake and was not writing from a flat in Bloomsbury or a castle in Spain.

At the commencement of the war all three of these young men, one of them married and one of them engaged, had vowed that a home like " Romany Cottage " was just their " cup of tea ", and after it was all over they would look out for such a place for themselves—each one of them.

As far as I know, their plan never materialised. The leader of the three allowed London to claim him again. The pay packet is usually the deciding factor, and most women seem to be afraid of the country-side—most women who are used to the towns, that is.

And yet there are compensations in a country life that can more than outweigh any so called " sacrifices " people are called upon to make when they give up life in a town.

According to my mail-bag however, more and more young, and not so young people are choosing the country life, years in the services having taught them to appreciate the freedom and wholesomeness of an out of door life.

So many of them have told me they cannot stand another day at an office desk, or a factory bench making goods to export to countries who weren't over anxious to have them, in order that we may exercise a purchasing power for inferior food.

Many of these people have decided they would prefer to come into the country and grow some of that food themselves. In their own way they are doing their best to right a cock-eyed urban economy which for all its efforts is only leaving our larders increasingly empty.

Early during the course of the war I received the following in a letter from Mr. Gort:

" In short, as the star of your next best friend rises, mine *must* in exact ratio decline and pale, and you must *let it*."

My new friend was a problem, he was totally unlike any other friend I had had. He did not meet me half way, nor on common ground, spiritually he was a " taker " not a " giver ". Norman, the schoolfriend in Chard, Bill, and Mr. Gort had all possessed some streak of Bohemianism in them somewhere. They were rational and conventional only up to a point, somewhere there was always a chink in their armour. Mr. Gort at more than sixty years of age could bubble up with boyish enthusiasm in some of his letters. Bill had done mad and beautiful things like opening the " sunshine roof " of our car, " to let the moon in."

The " next best friend " was like none of these. I hardly realised it, I was so used to people being natural and spontaneous that I conducted myself as before, often to the complete puzzlement of " Farmer L."

The cinema was the means of introducing us, for he came in regularly each week on the same evening, at the same time, and sitting whenever possible in the same seat. Sometimes he was accompanied by a young lady, more often than not he came in alone.

He was noticeable because he was different. His appearance was striking and he seemed to bring a breath of the outdoors with him. Sometimes he wore breeches and a hacking-jacket, and yet he did not look quite a farmer.

The face was a little too pale, a little too studious, and not sufficiently weather-beaten. I judged him to be about thirty. What really troubled me when I first began to notice him, was that he came in with clockwork regularity *whatever the film*. Now, lots of other patrons did this, but they were townspeople who " dropped in ", as one does into a public-house for a drink. They did not much mind what they saw, it was the weekly, or bi-weekly outing that mattered. It was part of their routine of living—accepted, unquestioned. It was, in a way, something like their weekly visits to church, part of their pattern of living. They worked hard all the week and their evening at " the pictures " was one of their rewards. What they saw did not matter it was sure to be something to " take them out of themselves ".

It was that last part of the matter that troubled me. Why did a young man of athletic bearing and an intelligent countenance, want such " taking out of himself "? He was of the brand and breed who usually chose their entertainment more carefully, He was not quite an " egg ", oh no! he was not nearly voluble enough for that—on the contrary he was quiet and well-mannered and never used two words where one would do, but neither did he appear to be of the species who did not care what they saw, as long as they could "escape".

The year was 1938, we were still twelve months off the ultimate catastrophe of war, and I had just settled into "Romany Cottage". Shepherds and farm-workers were my friends and farmers my only neighbours.

My problem patron often stretched his longish legs into the gangway, he always chose an end seat for that reason—he was a man who hated to be cramped. I was careful to step over the offending feet and avoid bringing myself and my chocolates to grief, the length of the balcony stairs! I even went so far as to warn the others.

Although I had never spoken to him, the cashier referred to the problem patron as "your man", occasionally varying it to "Your man with the eye-brows".

"I see your man is in again tonight—watch out for his feet, Collie," and then turning back to me—"he asked me if I would get him a box of matches."

"There's some in the machine," I said.

"He didn't have any change, he gave me sixpence."

I took the coin. "I'll take some in on my way up to supper." And then I thought—he smokes a pipe, he may be waiting for them, he is a very regular patron, I had better go now.

"Good evening," I said. He merely nodded, and then added:

"You had better bring me some chocolate with the change." I had come up without my tray, had made the journey purposely in fact.

"Yes—milk or plain?"

"Yes, please," he said.

I went back to my counter.

"Some people," I remarked to Collie who was on the door, "cannot make up their minds—'Milk or plain?—yes, please.' Now what do you make of that?"

"Take him one of each," suggested Collie brightly, "if he's left you enough money."

I took him one of each.

Hereafter he always bought some chocolate, but never knew what he wanted, so I began making up his mind for him—"Have you tried this? do you like that? these are very nice——"

As time passed he returned my "Good evening", when he came in, instead of merely nodding.

" I'd like to shake your man," said the cashier bitterly one evening.

" Whatever for? " I demanded in some alarm.

" I just wrong-changed him, and he never said a word, just stood there, looking at the money and waiting for me to put it right—he's so darned sure of himself—I'd like to *shake* him."

" You'll never shake *him*," said Collie. " He's like the Rock of Ages."

" Yes, I should say he was pretty unshakeable," I agreed.

One very wet autumn night I was late leaving, and the problem patron and I arrived at the back-exit together. The rain was streaming down, and I was covered almost from head to toe in waterproofs, from an outsize pair of Wellington-boots to a real oilskin sou'wester. There was no glamour about my weather attire for cycling to Silverlake. Collie came to work in a transparent plastic mackintosh and a flowered umbrella garnishing her best costume. I possessed no illusions as to the kind of figure I cut, standing in the streaming doorway.

My problem patron had recognised me, however. We exchanged the usual, typically obvious, typically English, remarks on the weather. Then, " Have you far to go? " he asked, taking in my apparel which must have looked like a month's deep-sea fishing off the coasts of Labrador.

" Three or four miles," I told him—" Near Sherborne—Silverlake—I don't suppose you've heard of it, no one ever has."

" I know it," he said gravely. " I've hunted over that country."

" Hunting," I said flatly, " is cruel and I do not approve of it."

He shrugged. " A cat with a mouse is cruel—I never think of the kill, people who haven't hunted, don't understand of course."

" I have hunted." He looked at me unbelievingly. " With a camera," I added.

He plainly did not understand. I also wanted to say that I put his mentality above that of a cat, but I thought it better to change the subject.

" Have *you* far to go? "

He plainly considered this a slight impertinence on my part, and at first I did not think he was going to reply. He was lighting his pipe, and stuffing the pouch and matches back in his pocket. I was reminded of the " What does your father do? " question on my first day at boarding school. Had I committed a social howler?

I tested my bicycle light. " Where *do* you live? " I persisted openly now, riled by his manner.

" You would not know it," he said curtly.

"You'd be surprised at the places I know—at the places I've been——"
I coloured I believe.

He pointed to the bicycle with his pipe. " On that? "

" Yes. I once cycled to Brighton on it."

He smiled. " Oh, I don't live as far away as that." He paused.
" But I don't suppose you have ever heard of South Barrow, or have
any idea in which direction it lies."

I positively snorted.

" It is ten miles from here, in a roughly north-easterly direction.
There is a milk factory on the corner leading down to it from Sparkford
and it's a mile off the main Wincanton road—under the Cadbury Hills."

" Yes, that's right," he said with some surprise. I sensed that he
half wanted to ask me how I knew the place, and if I had been to the
village, or if I knew anyone there. But nothing more was said.

The following week I was struggling with my accounts in the
chocolate-room behind the cash-desk, when the cashier called out.

" Scottie, your man has just gone in."

I looked at my watch. " Really? he's early," I said.

" He's got a girl with him—a smart one, in a fur coat."

" Oh," I thought heavily for a moment, then brightened, perhaps it
meant a double quantity of chocolate. I took my tray upstairs. It was
no good, she only smoked cigarettes it seemed, and I received no
commission on the sale of them.

He did not come in at all the following week; having once spoken
with him at some length I now looked upon him as an old friend and I
began to conjecture on the reasons for him breaking his long established
habit.

The week after that, on Armistice Day, he was in again, and I was so
overcome with relief that the old order was once more in force, that I
inadvertently said:

" Good evening, we missed you last week."

The royal " we " did not deceive him. If anyone had missed him it
was the chocolate girl, not the Gaumont British Picture Corporation.
It was another wet night, the mud was deep and sticky on the roads.
He offered to give me a lift home.

The question of my bicycle was never mentioned; leaving it meant
that I should have to walk into town the following morning. I did
not mind. The first time I had seen the cottage I had walked out and
back, it really did not matter, even if it was November.

We drove in silence, apart from a few directions timidly offered by myself. When we came to the beginning of my track to the cottage I instructed him to draw up. He asked where my home was, and I pointed across the fields. He got out of the car and looked. A passing train throwing flame and smoke into the damp night sky, threw my chimneys into relief for an instant.

" Good gracious! " he exclaimed, " You live down there? I thought *we* were a little off the track at Barrow—but at least we've a decent road! "

" It's all right," I said. " I like it down there."

" It looks lonely," he said doubtfully, " for you to be going to at night. I should think your Mother is relieved when you are in."

" She doesn't know," I said, delightedly. " You see she lives in Bournemouth."

The darkness was pregnant with silence for a moment. He was plainly groping for words. I came to his assistance.

" I live down there all alone—no wireless or anything."

There was a long pause.

" Alone? Good Heavens, girl! Not even a dog? "

" Not yet—the farm bitch is having pups shortly and I hope to have one of them, but it'll be a long time before that'll be any kind of a bodyguard."

" What ever possessed you to live down there all by yourself? "

" I like the country," I explained stoutly. " It was the only way I could get to live in it."

He did not say a word, and I could but dimly see his face. I turned my face up to the drizzle.

" It's getting late and I must go—have to be up early in the morning—thank you *very* much for the lift—it's saved me getting wet quite a lot."

" I don't think it's right for you to live down there alone."

He was now quite decided.

" You mean not proper? " I suggested.

He fenced a little. " Well, shall we say indiscreet? "

I laughed. He was nettled. " That's all very well—but as it happens I am a trustworthy sort of person to bring you home—— "

It was my turn to be nettled.

" If I hadn't thought you were I should hardly have let you."

We exchanged very chilly " Good nights ".

It was weeks before he suggested taking me home again. It was a year before he actually entered my house. By that time the war had begun, and old Nell's litter of puppies had grown to be sizeable dogs, with healthy appetites. I knew only too well as I possessed two of them.

The war had stopped hunting, but it had " started " farming.

My problem patron came in a little less regularly than of yore.

Ramon Novarro while still drawing a tender smile at childish recollections had been relegated to childhood things; Bill, I had " got over " as much as I would ever be likely to " get over " him. I had taken root in the country, with my own eyes and ears had learned about country things and had Adrian Bell and A. G. Street to amplify and enlarge that knowledge. There is no doubt that I was ready for such a friendship as that offered by Farmer L., that I was subconsciously prepared for it, but I accepted it without examination or analysis, certainly I did not ask in those days, where, if anywhere, it was likely to lead.

The three Territorials who walked out and found my cottage accidentally and who came again and again of a Sunday, to eat eggs and toast by its fireside, occasionally met Farmer L. when he made one of his unannounced visits. He would drive them all back into Yeovil, but entered into their conversation little.

I had known him more than twice as long as I had known these three birds of passage, but I knew far more about *them*, than it ever seemed likely I should about Farmer L.

The " Fairy-Ballet " as I had christened these three six-footers, sat by my fire on Sunday afternoons and discussed Tschaikowsky and war, and the country and film-making (one of them was an ex-newsreel cameraman). When Farmer L. joined us sometimes after tea, he seemed content merely to listen. He said very little about himself. I knew him eighteen months before I ascertained that his hobby was playing the violin.

The " Fairy Ballet " eventually dismissed him as " a dull dog ". " He has an owlish look, beneath those heavy eyebrows," said one of them. " Don't get too fond of him, Monica, he'll lead you a dull life," they advised me. " You want something different from that—he's the kind of man who thinks only ' cissies ' know anything about poetry! "

It was all too true, no doubt, I saw it clearly enough, and yet I was coming to believe that I did not want " something different from that ". It dawned on me slowly but surely, that I had found just what I did want in fact.

XXI

The Sixth Friend Bows Out

"——AS THE star of your next best friend rises, mine *must* in exact ratio, decline." So Mr. Gort had written. But he was not quite right about this. Now I felt the need of his friendship more than perhaps I had ever done. There were even times when had I the opportunity and means I would have taken a train to the North in order to see him. For there were times when the best of letters were unsatisfactory, when I felt that to be able to *talk* with someone who really understood me, perhaps better than I understood myself, would have helped me beyond measure.

As it was I never took that train, and I never talked with him for a second time. Our letters were all we had, and sometimes these letters seemed painfully insufficient.

I suppose it was natural for me in my early twenties to value deeds rather than words, and often I dismissed Mr. Gort's long, thoughtful and often beautifully phrased letters, over which he had expended much time, thought and affection, as just so many " Words! "

Only now perhaps, after the passage of time, can I fully appreciate the help he gave me, and how little he received in return.

Later when I had become fully conscious of the debt I owed him it was too late to thank him. The biggest return he might have seen for all his goodness, the publication of my books, was also denied him. He died three weeks before the first one was accepted.

In the same letter I have just quoted, he went on to say:—

" *You* know, as I know, that our correspondence, our association has been competely free from anything wrong or even questionable. I take it we have sought only to discover and to bring out the *best in each other*. But you could not get one person in ten thousand of the World, no matter how friendly they might be, to understand that and believe in it.

" Even your Dear Mother was, I believe, somewhat puzzled by the length and frequency of our correspondence, and may still be for all

I know. It would not be difficult for me to guess what your sister's opinion upon the matter would be.

"I do not think you will find this very difficult, and at least not nearly as difficult as it will be for me. You will be carried away upon the wings of a new association, the business of which, if things develop aright, should fill your heart and mind to the exclusion of everyone else. This should help you to put every experience in its rightful place."

Mr. Gort had been wrong about his own star declining in "exact ratio", and I think too he was wrong about the construction most people would have put upon this friendship-by-letter. He was a product of the Victorian Age and in spite of his intense humanity and wide sympathies he was too apt to consider public opinion as rigid and narrow as it had been in the days of his youth.

Some there are, of course, who find it impossible to accept anything outside their own circumscribed experience of life, and to whom the "unknown" is always highly questionable, if not absolutely "bad". But many people, young and old and of both sexes, have now had the privilege of sharing in Mr. Gort's letters, even as my four friends at the cinema had done, and I have found their import readily understood and their message shared. Only recently a highly valued young friend of mine wrote:

"I am sorry my letters must be so unsatisfactory, there is so much I always want to say, but I express myself so badly—oh for the pen of a John Gort."

It was true that my Mother was at first "puzzled" by the size and frequency of my correspondence with my unseen friend, but she soon came to accept it and after reading some of his letters, declared that "Mr. Gort is a very fine man."

He was right of course about my sister's reaction to the association—the "pick-up" had cut like a lash at the time and rankled long afterwards, but when I fully realised that some of our happiest and most worth-while associations can be the product of an initially "brief encounter", I ceased to let her facile phrases possess any influence over me.

But even as he decreed, Mr. Gort's letters now became less frequent.

At length he ceased to call me " Romany " and went back to " Dear Friend ", like any Quaker.

He had now retired from business and began to suffer long periods of ill-health when he wrote little. I also noticed the quality of his handwriting deteriorating slowly.

I endeavoured, as he wished, to let the friendship and the correspondence lapse, but there were times, very many times, when I ached for the spiritual presence of this old friend, and when I longed to lean upon his judgment and guidance more than ever.

There were times when I felt he had abandoned me in a leaking boat on a strange sea, while he stood safely upon the shore and I was able only to watch him receding from me.

For the sea was indeed strange and rough, and the boat anything but seaworthy. Mr. Gort had emphatically assured me that I was " Worth the best the best man can give you—that your rightful place is in a worthwhile country life, and you have but to step up and claim both in order to ' live happily ever after' ".

I had always believed implicitly in what he had told me before, but this was rather too much. He made it seem so easy. Had he forgotten what I looked like? how plain I was? (not that he had agreed to that—beauty of course, being in the eye of the beholder). Did he realise the apparent (to all but Mr. Gort and me) social gulf between Mr. L. and myself?

From now on I was *two* people. One recognised the rightness of all Mr. Gort's teachings and precepts, the other remembered only the treatment I had received from snobbish school companions and Bill's let down.

In one of his last letters to me Mr. Gort wrote:—

" Be quiet when you have really nothing to say—do not be afraid of any feeling of lack. Do not stress Mr. L's reticence and shyness, but accept them as matter of factly as possible.

" Be natural—above all be yourself—but there, I must not do your courting for you," he had concluded.

" Oh if only you *could*," I wailed inwardly. For the more I thought about the matter, the more was I afraid of doing right for fear of doing wrong.

Now why had I lost Bill? He had been so absolutely sincere, impossible ever to have accused him of being untruthful, and *he* had called me a girl in a million and swore undying love for me. Yet had I lost him. Now why? Why? If I knew the answer to that I should know how NOT to lose this "next best friend" whose star now shone so brightly in my firmament.

Why *had* I lost Bill? Had I been too backward or too forward? (My sister had declared I possessed no sex-appeal—was that what was really wanted to "hold" a man's interest?)

Had I been too ignorant or too much of a "blue-stocking". (Again my sister had assured me, more than once, that young men were not interested in girls who were fond of poetry.) And what had made Bill's parents dislike me so—the fact that I worked in a cinema? Then Mr. L's parents, when they eventually met me, would probably dislike me for the same reason.

Again, if I could not hold the allegiance of a young man who was so obviously suited to me in so many ways, how could I hope to gain that of a man whose background and outlook seemed so very different from my own; and who far from meeting me half way, was so very difficult to get to know?

Like an octopus the many tentacled inferiority complex seized hold of me and strangled constructive thinking. Only momentarily would I escape from it into the positive thought Mr. Gort had always advocated, and then only to dismiss it as impracticable madness. I must face facts, thinking "wishfully" would get me nowhere.

So I faced the facts, and what were they?

That I had never lacked for real friends of the opposite sex, but they had showed no sign of finding any "sex-appeal" in me, nor of thinking of me in terms of marriage, from Norman to Mr. Gort, I had been just a good companion, that was all.

My Mother had once expressed resignation to my employer at the cinema above all people, to the fact that I was "cut out to be an old maid".

I had been Bill's only girl, there was no "competition" there. Farmer L. on the other hand knew several other young ladies, at least one of whom possessed a fur coat and drove a car.

Bah! it seemed unthinkable that he should look twice at me, when there were those other girls, those girls who shared his tennis parties and who did not work in cinemas—who did not work at all!

Mr. Gort had of course declared that if Farmer L. had any sense at all, he would choose *me*.   Sometimes I believed Mr. Gort, more often than not however I believed the *facts*.

My friendship for Farmer L. had ripened so gradually that it had given me time for much thought on the way.   It was a matter of a word here and there; and then very occasional outings, when (I gathered) he had nothing better to do.   He did not care to visit me at my cottage, it being unorthodox and indiscreet, so I met him up on the high-road on those occasions when I was privileged to accompany him anywhere.   Strangely enough I soon discovered that in spite of a car, he knew rather less of the geography and history of Wessex than I had gleaned on a bicycle.

Ever since I had first entered " Romany Cottage " I had embarked on a long voyage of learning and understanding, necessary in order to be fully happy in a country life.   Never were lessons learned with greater delight, ease or love, but even so, a certain amount of readjustment was necessary.   I had of course, arrived at the conclusion that when my version of every girl's " Mr. Right " eventually appeared upon the scene, he would *have* to be a countryman.

As I gradually came to know Farmer L. I realised that he fulfilled *all* my requirements, furthermore I loved him.   But was it reasonable to hope that he should feel the same way about me?

My Mother had assured me I was argumentative and of an uncertain temper.   Boarding School had taught me that my values were all wrong, my sister had revealed my lack of sex-appeal and my total inability to make the best of my appearance.   Above all, I knew I was inclined to put *places* before people.

This was the evidence *against*, but I must be fair and submit the evidence *for*.

I was sensible, I could keep house, clean and cook (also type after a fashion).   I did not smoke, drink or go to dances.   If I was not good-looking, at least I took care of myself, particularly my hair and hands. I had a fair figure, although rather too short to carry clothes well.   I was never ill and did not mind being left alone in the dark or being confronted with awkward situations!   I was willing to give and take, had a sense of humour, and thought it neither smart, clever, nor a woman's special privilege to keep a man waiting, or pretend to make him jealous, or act the coquette.   I said what I meant.   I had also maintained some very long and sincere friendships with both sexes, so I could not be entirely lacking.

I sat on the steps of my humble dwelling (now humbled by comparison with a farmhouse) and tried to work out the pros and cons of the situation. At times they seemed almost to balance, and I could get no further.

Then one day, cycling to Yeovil, I caught sight of my own reflection in a plate-glass window. That settled it. I looked incredibly funny, I seemed to have been *born* with a double chin, and had not one redeeming feature. It appeared to be madness to continue further, as in Bill's case, I should only be doomed to disappointment in the end.

Farmer L. did nothing to remedy this state of affairs. How could he indeed, when I could hardly communicate to him the content of my thoughts?

Had he paid me a few compliments (even though I should not have really believed in them, having so few illusions about myself), had he just made me feel worth more to him, I should have been encouraged to continue, as it was, I decided to end the affair before it was ended for me.

Just a vision in a shop window brought me to that momentous decision. In the distance I could hear the other side of the argument going on all the time—" You have done well, you have made a success of running your little home and even your sister admits that you are intelligent and can converse admirably upon a number of subjects; why let a little thing like a funny face stand in the way of a happy life? "

The answer was never far to seek. A woman's duty is to be beautiful—at least easy to look at. She may need other qualities but all else are subsidiary to this. This was my belief and this is *still* my belief.

I have met men since who have sincerely tried to convince me that beauty or good-looks meant next to nothing to them—that to live with prettiness and nothing else can be boring. I would say " never ". Beauty is its own justification, other attributes may be very nice, but they are not absolutely necessary. Beauty is.

To me it is summed up in the terse remark of some Hollywood tough character who says:

" Baby, with that face and figure, you don't need to learn how to cook! "

Nothing would or will ever make up to me for possessing not one redeeming facial feature. That partly explains why I succeeded so with friendships that were nourished mostly by correspondence. With them I could be myself, the lack did not matter. Mr. Gort, for instance, saw me as he wanted to see me. The few snapshots I sent him were

Oats near South Barrow

One of the Dancing Class pupils

kind to me. Many of them had leafy, natural backgrounds and often Muriel was in them, her fairness proving a good foil for my dark colouring. Who says the camera can never lie? That in itself is one of the greatest untruths ever. The camera can be made to do almost anything *but* tell the truth, the whole truth and nothing but the truth—especially where the human face is concerned.

The war had now taken hold of us all in earnest, altering many values, levelling many inequalities and presenting life almost entirely shorn of inessentials.

Farmer L.'s father died suddenly, as I had reported in the letter written to " The Fairy Ballet " just after Dunkirk. Responsibility and work clustered thickly around him, the tennis-party girls were forgotten. He seemed to rely more and more upon the constant undemanding kind of friendship I offered him.

When business at the cinema grew very bad indeed in the chocolate line I was forced to change my occupation and took over the booking and accounts of a small business in the nearby town of Sherborne. I was not happy in my job in many ways. The hours were difficult for a girl with a house of her own to run, during the winter months I did not see my home in the hours of daylight, except on a Sunday. But I was still able to keep on the cottage. I missed the companionship of the cinema and my long experience of its manager. To compensate me however there was the unparalleled joys of periodic visits to Farmer L.'s home.

I joined in hay-making and corn-cuttings, and spent much of my spare time cycling along the road between Silverlake and South Barrow. Life was often full and good, if always difficult, but I determined not to think too much about the future. In the midst of such a war it was neither wise nor advisable.

On the last Sunday in September, 1940, Farmer L. asked me to marry him. It was neither well-set nor romantic. It happened in the " battery-house " where I was helping him to collect the eggs. It is a great wonder I did not drop them all. Instead I leaned against an upturned milk-churn and tried to keep my head.

It *did* seem too good to be true, but on the other hand, all those snags and difficulties I had once so carefully marshalled, still existed—nothing had changed, least of all my funny face. The war had perhaps made people less " choosey " in their mates, but the war would not last for ever!

Might I go back to my cottage and think it over—just for a day or so. I was gravely assured that I might.

The following day, Monday, was always a quiet day at my new work. I thought about my answer to the proposal a great deal, by the end of my lunch hour I had made my decision. With Mr. Gort, holding my hand " in spirit " I said " Yes."

The reply was written and posted. As I returned from the post office, the siren began to wail over the little town.

Of this savage, unexpected raid on Sherborne I have written in another book, and that I wrote truly is revealed by the numbers of letters which I received afterwards in which the writers say I have put their own picture of the time into words.

Although I escaped serious injury I was treated for shock and told to stay in bed for at least a month. A man who had been standing only a few yards from me was killed outright because he had not remembered to fling himself down in time.

This was the first time I had ever been ill and I lost my head entirely. I lapsed into long silences fraught with self-pity, which Farmer could hardly be expected to penetrate. Hitherto I had met him more than half-way—full of enthusiasm, talking of this and that, anxious to know and explore. But now I was afraid, and fear robbed me of my former high spirits.

The engagement was broken, he failed to understand what was wrong.

My illness cost me my job and when I obtained another it was too far away for me to maintain " Romany Cottage " and I had to find another home nearer my work.

When I had announced Farmer L.'s proposal to Mr. Gort he had written given me his blessing. Then his letters ceased. Try as I might, I could not bring myself to tell him how things had gone wrong. He might accuse Farmer L. of letting me down and that would hurt me, or he might realise that all his teachings had been forgotten in a moment of panic and that would hurt *him*.

I knew the danger that lay in regretting and moping, and made a great effort to keep on my feet. I found my new work in a civilian shoe-shop in a Service Camp, busy and interesting. Above all I found the companionship of a charming young man of my own age. We had a great deal in common. Presently, thinking to salvage something I married on the re-bound.

The action was indefensible, of course, but it is easy to be wise after the event. I thought our joint chances of happiness were good and did not make sufficient allowance for the fact that I had never really altered my feelings for Farmer L. though he had to all intents and purposes " jilted " me. I tried to be honest all round, my marriage broke up and the fault was entirely mine. It would be nice to say otherwise and to agree with those kind persons who always insist that in any broken marriage the faults are on both sides, but in this case it would not be true.

Just before my wedding I had written to Mr. Gort: " I am getting married next month—not to Farmer L. I'm afraid, but please don't worry about that. All you need to know is that I am loved as you have always wished me to be loved."

His reply was unexpected and yet perhaps typical:

" What will count in the long run is not who loves you but whom *you* love."

As usual he was right.

There were heart-searchings and mental-conflict on my part that went on for a long time. They started when I insisted to my Mother's puzzlement and even hurt, on an absolutely quiet wedding. This was to have been the wedding to make up for my sister's lack of pomp. But I was not even married in a church—a Registrar's Office for me. I could not say very much to other people but even by that avoidance I knew I was half licked before I started.

XXII

"The Chronicles of Church Farm"

M Y partner was such a good person that we were happier than I could have dared to hope, but all the time I felt I was wrong, that I was not being honest and that I was not in my rightful place.

I ended up in the house opposite the farm where I had so nearly gone as a bride. If the irony of it ever struck me, I had not time to brood about it. Farmer's dairy-farm was being turned almost overnight into an arable-farm. Implements were bought, borrowed, shared and crops were " trialled and errored " through fields that had not seen the plough in living memory. (During the 1914 war only one field at Church Farm had been ploughed.)

My choice was made, and the farm became my war-work. I found a tractor quite easy to drive and the pace (about three miles per hour) suited me perfectly. This work left the mind free, and the body open to all the airs of heaven, while the roar of the engine shut out all lesser sounds—even the throb of aircraft but rarely intruded. It was like working in a world of one's own.

While I worked I pondered my own private problem, a problem which involved others, but no easy solution offered itself. I longed for Mr. Gort's help and advice. He was a Victorian, would he not say " Marriage is for ever ". He was a Victorian and I could not, I dare not tell him that I was one of the many contemplating divorce. I wondered what he would say—perhaps he would be broad-minded and quote

" To thyself be true."

But to be true to myself meant being untrue to a person who had been unutterably kind to me.

My health deteriorated and when doctors had to be consulted they diagnosed nervous disorders though I led a healthy, orderly life and was not a normally " nervy " subject.

After all, Farmer L. had shown no inclination to marry anyone else. My own feelings in the matter had not altered at all, after years of wartime living and working which should have rubbed off the " glamour " and blunted romance, I felt him to be more my Mr. Right than ever. A time arrived when I asked my husband to release me and I tried to recover from the paralysing influence of my own short-comings and lack of confidence.

People who have read my country books or heard me lecture have sometimes approached me on this delicate, difficult subject. I am aware I behaved badly, selfishly, and yet they have expressed themselves towards me with charity and understanding. It is their attitude as much as the claims of truth that have helped me to report an episode which reflects no credit on me. If there be any credit it is that when I felt my mistake I tried to act honestly over it, because I believed ultimately it would prove in the best interests of us all. But it was hard at the time, hard all round and if I behaved selfishly I have paid for it in many ways.

For a long time I felt I deserved no good of anyone and did not merit any happiness, and yet it came to me in round-about ways—in watching the farm thriving about me, and above all in the happiness of other people—especially of children.

Remembering how much the opportunity to learn dancing would have meant to me as a child, I began a series of free classes for the children of the village. They proved most eager pupils, making up in zeal what they lacked in skill. Their enthusiasm was boundless and when they were good enough to put on " displays " and miniature ballets their excitement was infectious.

The war was still going on and we collected at the close of our entertainments for the Red Cross. I found myself planning and organising and contriving costumes from oddments that were veritably silk purses out of sow's ears. At the same time I made friends with a girl at Sherborne who had a natural talent for dancing though she had never trained seriously. She was evacuated from London and when she returned she went to ballet-school. By then she was eighteen and too old to make a complete career of it. But she was amply good enough for semi-professional appearances and on her frequent holidays to Church Farm, my class would watch intently to see " how it is done ". Honor became the vein through which new blood of technique and ideas flowed into my home-made ballet dancers. We even dated our concerts that our London member might dance the lead in them and her Fairy Godmother in the South Barrow version of *Cinderella* was a real pièce de résistance.

My camera which has always been my friend in the complete absence of any drawing or painting talents, now came to be used more freely than ever. Almost daily I would see something on the farm or about the village which needed "reporting". I also went "snapshotting" for the Forces in the Y.M.C.A.'s "Snapshots from Home" service, throughout Dorset and Somerset. I photographed many wives and babies and mothers for this service, and many pet dogs and cats as well; visiting many outlying villages and hamlets to send men overseas a small picture of the homes that they had left.

On these excursions I saw many other subjects I wished to photograph and keep forever—it might be winter sunlight among bare trees, or a cluster of corn-mows beneath the farmyard elms, but I soon found I had quite a collection of such pictured fragments of the country and country living.

I also met with (as well as temporarily housed) many evacuees, who had suddenly been thrown upon the utterly strange ground of their own countryside. Their ignorance of what I took to be the most elementary facts of everyday existence, upon which we all ultimately depend, so astounded, troubled and shocked me, that after trying to explain matters verbally I eventually wrote simply and plainly of the things that matter.

I remembered the sailor who had never seen a glow-worm and did not believe they really existed until I brought him one in a match-box. I remembered the children who thought milk came in bottles, and their mothers who did not know wheat from grass; and rushing in, where perhaps experts might fear to tread, I attempted to do a little educating in the things that really matter.

The result was my first book, *The Chronicles of Church Farm*. Of publishers or the correct procedure in book-publishing, I knew nothing, neither had I anyone to help or advise me. Looking through the bookcase, however, I saw that the firm of Hodder and Stoughton had published Walter Raymond's works, and as he was a Yeovilian and had always written of *my* countryside, I thought I would try them with my efforts.

The war was still at its height and publishing was not easy, but the book met with acceptance, much to my own astonishment. The courtesy and consideration always offered me by this old established firm, although I was very much a country bumpkin, is only one more reason for designating this particular book "An Autobiography of Kindness."

The poetry I no longer had the inclination or time to write, gave way to a kind of "reportage", and many country publications invited my contribution in spite of the paper shortage.

I found my views, the views which had first prompted my initial excursion into this type of writing, more than reinforced by my continued experience of townspeople.

A close friend of mine asked me, if as a favour I would give a country holiday to some friends of his. He knew we did not normally take in guests, but things were difficult, the seaside was hopeless, hotels were impossible, etc. I agreed to help them out. There was a young husband on leave from the Forces, a wife who had been working at a "Control Point" in London's Civil Defence, and an eight-year-old son.

The husband was quite happy. He asked for no entertainment, but spent most of his time walking round our fields with a gun, pottering over farm-machinery and giving his son rides on our pony.

The boy was deliriously happy, there was so much for him to do and see, that he could never have a long enough day. He loved all the animals and showed no fear of them, his idea of heaven was a ride out to the fields on a waggon.

The wife, on the other hand, was discontented. Even the fare of fresh eggs and milk, home-made butter and the legally forbidden cream and fruit did not impress her. She complained that she was left alone and also that there was nothing to do. Whenever I could spare a moment to join her in a deck-chair on the lawn, she would tell me how much she missed life at "The Control".

There they had knitted and played cards and gossiped, and it was all sociable and sometimes even exciting. She was pining to get back. I tried very hard to understand her—one can, I suppose, get used to anything. But she actually thought there was merit in the totally unproductive (if necessary at the moment) work of "The Control". Once regarding me closely, she said in effect,

"You must be dreadfully miserable here—how DO you keep going, with nothing much to do and nothing going on—especially in the winter?"

When I assured her that I did not find life dull, she sighed and suggested that—

"Well of course you don't miss what you've never had."

This struck me as most comical, and I did not tell her that I knew London probably better than she herself did, or that I had worked among crowds and known my share of city life. It would obviously be an unsolvable puzzle to her, she was so concerned with artificial values, with things that did not really matter. Her whole horizon was bounded by the false excitement and freedom the war had brought her.

What hurt me most was that I knew that she would laugh at the new-found contentment and happiness which her husband and son shared between them. She was already doing her best to belittle and discourage it.

" I can't think what you see in walking after a rabbit all the evening—it's not as if we liked it when you shoot one." She hated the smell of the farmyard and would never go anywhere near the milking-stalls if she could help it.

One morning the boy came over to the farm quite early, he was miserable and had plainly been crying. Farmer cheered him up by letting him accompany him in taking the milk to the factory.

When the mother put in an appearance she was vexed and irritable. " I've had to beat my boy," she said. " He is so tiresome, he WILL get up early—it's so silly on holiday—and then he went and broke my beads—broke my best beads. I tell you I had to beat him."

It made me wonder. I never wore " beads " myself, what did broken beads matter against a child's tears ? It seemed such a non-essential thing. One did not need beads, broken or intact, to be happy. She might have mentioned her displeasure perhaps and then left the matter. But the boy was treated to lectures on the broken beads for the rest of the day, and just when he was beginning to enjoy himself, his pleasure would be spoiled again at the sight of his mother's reproachful face.

No, I could not have explained to her what I saw in country life. I had begun to feel that the things which held importance for her have no real bearing on our existence. So wrapped up was she with the meaningless details of life at " The Control " that I saw it would be a waste of time to explain to her what I saw in country life—what her husband and son were beginning to see also.

Someone once asked me if I despised townsfolk and this was the answer I sent them:—

" If I do not, it is not because I have not good cause to do so. All my life I have suffered from their warped outlook so much. Not suffered personally perhaps, but most deeply in spirit, because I feel their outlook is largely responsible for the state of the world today, which few can view with equanimity."

That sounds rather emphatic, but when I was old enough to choose for myself I went to live in the country—the real country, none of your garden cities, or endless dreary suburbs—without the atmosphere of the true city, and without the individuality of the village, and in the real country I pray I shall live for ever.

On our very rare holidays, usually of a few days only snatched between haysel and harvest, we go deeper into the country, but occasionally we have been to London, Bristol, Cardiff, etc. It always seems to both of us that we can never get home quick enough.

I am young, fairly fond of the beautiful things of life, music, the theatre, fashion and the like, but *unlike* my city sisters I do not think these are the be-all and end-all of living.

Take for instance this interminable outcry about nylons. I am most frightfully sick of hearing about them. I value my legs as much as any woman but I would not waste a second of my precious time queueing for stockings likely to be laddered after a few hours of wearing.

Farmers' wives and daughters and many others contrived to exist without nylons, why pretend the world will come to an end if we can't get them? The newspapers may foster this idea, but the whole thing seems so out of proportion.

Now take my next bugbear—leisure. I've worked with town girls who have had so little heart in their work that they seem to spend all their time "wishing" their lives away. It is seldom indeed (never in my experience) that a person engaged in the care of livestock, or the welfare of the land, is heard to voice such sentiments as "Roll on the week-end", etc., etc. Country people I know, of every class and condition, seem to find their days rather too short for all they *want* to do. They may grumble about overwork sometimes—heavens, I do myself, but they aren't discontented at their work—they take a pride in it, even though, in the case of the village housewife, it starts where the towns-woman's leaves off. Often we literally have to make the straw to make the bricks to make the house. By the time the townswoman is free for the rest of the day we are still trimming oil-lamps, fetching water, getting in fuel or feeding animals.

When the town housewife has finished what happens—does she do any good with her leisure? can she pick blackberries or mushrooms, bottle fruit or help with the milking? Does she do any good with her days? Very often she does not. Oh the few who have hobbies are exempt, or the few who plan to improve themselves and their " entertainment value " to their husbands by attending lectures, classes, etc. But most of the young, town, married women I know personally (and they are quite a few and of a cross-section of the community) are bored to death half their time. They worry me to go to tea with them, or to take them out or accompany them on some jaunt to the sales. They spend hours in hairdressers, and absorb seas of print in popular journals which are never meant to be remembered.

Some of them have not even the safety valve of the care of a child or even a garden. There is nothing creative in their days—it is no longer the thing to bake bread or cakes or make one's own clothes. Often, often they have no topic of any real interest to offer their husbands when they return home and chronic boredom on both sides is the result, especially where there is not sufficient money for non-stop *purchased* entertainment.

The countrywoman on the other hand whether she be Vicar's wife or cowman's daughter, Lady of the Manor or Land Girl, has plenty to do; most of which benefits other people besides herself. Much of it benefits the nation as a whole—taken directly and indirectly. The war has left the world in an unholy mess, and she is busy doing her tiny bits to put it straight, to help the lacks and losses right themselves. It is a round-about way sometimes, making jam, picking the harvest of field and hedgerow to see nothing is wasted, making patchwork garments out of scraps, gathering rose-hips for vitamin syrup, organising sales and shows. They may be only little things but they are all helping in a world short of the necessities of life because there are too many people producing *nothing*, nothing of any real value that is.

The farm-worker's wife who makes her rugs out of old stockings, dresses her children in cut-downs and makes their handkerchiefs from bleached flour-bags, is in her way contributing as much to world supplies as the man who originally grew the silk, wool or flax. *Something saved is something gained.*

Furthermore she contrives to be very happy although so occupied— perhaps because of it. On the whole I think faces of country people are more comely and contented than those of their counterparts in the town. Yes, I know it is a shame to generalise, and I know there are exceptions. But these are my convictions on the whole, and I have as many town friends and acquaintances as country ones, if you count my " fan-mail " then more so.

Life is real, life is earnest and first things should come first. I know the townswoman has much to put up with, and I know there are countless good, hardworking mothers of families, who never waste a thing—but even they would be better for knowing a bit more about their own countryside.

Many townspeople seem to dismiss the farming community as inefficient " bumpkins ", almost unnecessary to modern economics. So they continue the hunt for nylons and the heated controversies about exact length of skirt and miss the most important, the most lasting and happiness-promoting things in life.

I have yet to meet the countrywoman or man who wanted to change their existence for that of the town. But on the other hand I have met hundreds of townspeople who ache for the country. It is their growing nostalgia that accounts for the popularity of country publications, and the comparatively new fashion in books on the countryside. Before the Industrial Revolution such writers as Street, Bell, Massingham and Co. would only have been declaring what everyone already knew and the entertainment value would be practically nil.

I don't know if this has answered your question outright. There are so many good people, brave people, hardworking people in the towns, how can I say I despise them? Let me rather say I despise the line of thought which can permit a long war to be fought saving fundamentals or the things that matter, only to chase after Will o' the Wisps once peace is established.

Did our men give their lives for nylons, plastic ash-trays? They will fight a war but will not fight red-tape, racketeers, shoddy workmanship and all the belittling things left in the wake of war. Country people are not nearly so easily " fobbed-off ". They know the real value of things so much better. That is what I call *real* education.

I had noticed too that the man who makes his money in the cities invariably retires to the country. The American millionaires do more, so keenly do they feel the lack of roots so essential to well-being, that they come to Europe to buy homes with a history. It is not just a matter of snobbery, I am convinced it goes much deeper than that. It is some inrooted need in the human animal for an existence a little closer to nature than your city flat can offer.

What type of Christmas cards and calendars sell best? Stand for a moment during the season at any store-counter and watch them going out—the oh-so-cute pictures of thatched cottages, of sheep in the moonlight, of country gardens by the sea, of fisher-folk, and harvest-homes. The townsman loves to see them on his mantelpiece. The countryman buys them as a matter of course. To him they are the only real pictures. He is the happy man whose work is also his hobby and recreation.

While I was writing my early books, the government were exhorting the farming community to grow more food and save the country. Here is an extract from an editorial in one of our dailies:—

" —Ploughing is the Maginot line of our food-front, and we must work on it night and day so that we may resist any assault by submarine, mine or bomb. Less than two months remain for farmers to make the greatest effort in history to get their land ploughed up and under crop. They have a heavier responsibility in this war than in any other, for on them falls the burden of producing every ounce of food they can to prevent any possible risk of defeat by starvation. —there is a note of drama in the present agricultural situation, Farmers are working against time and as they work they should bear in mind these words,

" A field of oats may save a ship——"

This belated recognition of the importance of agriculture must have amused many farmers (if indeed they stopped to read it). The royal " We " at the commencement is particularly entertaining. At first I thought the newspaper editor and his staff must be coming down to lend a hand on the land as it were, but when " the greatest effort in history had to be made " the word " farmers " was employed again.

All this propaganda about farming has had some little effect on the average townsperson. They have begun to know that their land is their concern, that it affects them personally, that without it indeed they may be " sunk ".

Thus I found my task easier, my first book was an unhoped for success and the amount of favourable publicity accorded it amazed me. But I felt that I was still largely preaching to the converted. So many people took the trouble to write me, but they were naturally largely people who thought along the same lines as myself.

I have never taken the success of my self-imposed mission for granted, I know too well the forces that oppose me, and the welter of urban politics that will always, in my lifetime at least, block the progress of true education.

But the friends made for me through my country books have been an unceasing source of happiness to me. Most of them I may never meet, some are from the other side of the world, but they have all served to strengthen my faith in the kindness of humanity in the *individual*. There is the cowman's wife from Winchester, a woman who we should take it is of limited means, but who yet contrived to send me a 10/6 book about Hampshire on my birthday as a token of her gratitude for the pleasure my books had given her. She had taken the trouble to notice my birthdate which, I understand from her letter, is mentioned in *Romany Cottage, Silverlake*. She added that she and her husband were very fond of their adopted county of Hampshire, and they hoped that in due course and with the assistance of their little gift, I should come to know it as well as I did my own Dorset and Somerset.

From a farmer's wife and daughter in the Shetlands came the gift of a beautifully executed Fair Isle beret and glove set, followed by some stockings for Farmer, together with stocking-boards to ensure they dry in good shape!

From Tasmania I have had books, from South Africa a gift of fruit and confectionery, and from Canada a tin of biscuits.

I do not think any biscuits ever tasted so well as those from across the Atlantic. As I ate them, going about my work, or sitting at my desk (according to the advertisements one can keep going on biscuits) I dwelt long upon the kindness of these strangers, expressing their appreciation (for something it had been a pleasure to do) to a person they are not likely to meet.

I always answer these correspondents, because if they have taken the trouble to write then I feel I should likewise to reply. If I do not always do so at the length I should like, may I quote the following from a book upon writing by Vera Brittain?

" —even minor public figures receive an amount of correspondence, of requests to do this or that, which is quite literally impossible to cope with if private life and work are not to be abandoned altogether, and there have been very few successful men or women energetic enough to answer every irrelevant letter and accept every invitation— When people talk of a celebrity as being 'unspoiled' they nearly always mean that he suffers bores gladly——"

As a very minor public figure I can vouch for the truth of that statement and if the day ever comes when I cannot reply to all my correspondents I suppose I shall have the accusation " spoilt " hurled at me as I have heard it hurled at many well-known writers. Some of the trouble is of course, that so many people fail to consider writing as work—until they try it, that is. These same people simply loathe the thought of letter-writing, and avoid filling in forms whenever possible. The fact remains that except to a few geniuses (or perhaps to them more so, I do not know!) writing is very hard work indeed.

Vera Brittain makes another plea for the woman writer when she says:

" Only those who appreciate the different qualities of work produced by complete and by partial concentration can ever estimate the extent to which women's performances suffer from constant and small interruptions, and petty and time-wasting tasks. The triumphant enquirers who put their hackneyed question ' Why have we never had a woman Shakespeare, Michelangelo, Rembrandt or Beethoven? ' need look no further than the ill-adjusted burdens of the average household for their answer. . . ."

Visitors to Church Farm have not infrequently asked me when and where I write my books.

The answer to the last is " in the dining-room ". There are enough rooms in the house for me to have a study, even as I have given our paying-guest a study of his own in which to do exactly as he likes. But of what use is a room miles away from the door and the telephone. The vet might ring up with an urgent message and I should never hear it, the baker might forget to leave enough bread, the butcher might accidentally admit a cat, *with* the meat, the postman might wait for ages unheard while he hunted for someone to sign for a registered envelope. The lorry man might knock unheard while waiting to know where to put the new consignment of cow-cake, lime or fertiliser.

Lastly, if I made myself so comfortable and peaceful in a little den of my own with " do not disturb " on the door I might forget to come down and cook the lunch. No, it would never do. Were I a man my work would of course be taken completely seriously. But then of course he would be called a " breadwinner ", while I only keep myself and help those nearest and dearest to me.

To the first question " When? " I can only answer " I do not know." The times I spend writing are so infinitesimal compared with the hours I spend washing-up or cooking or cleaning, that they leave no mark in the mind at all.

When I had finished my novel of Monmouth's time, which had taken me the better part of four years to complete, I found myself actually asking myself: " When did I write all this? " I had no recollection of getting through so much work at all. I suppose it grew like knitting (or like ploughing does), one goes up and down a line, and slowly it grows!

But when I survey my books published, and someone like my mother says:

" They do look nice—books to be proud of," I think: " Yes, but how much of my life has gone into them, what do they represent of which you know nothing? How many sunny hours have I spent indoors when I longed to be out amid the fragrance of the fields? How many parties, picnics and outings have they caused me to miss, how many invitations and holidays refused? Because of them, how many *good* books have I to leave unread, how many films, and plays unseen, how many symphonies unlistened to! How much self-discipline do they represent, that after an ordinary day's work when relaxation comes to most people I have begun my real work of the day? "

There is no self-pity in this. I write both because I want to and because as Mr. Gort would say I have felt " under orders " to do so. But how many bright young things who probably think I look old for my age and have not much fun in me, realise that nothing is purchased without its attendant price, even when it is a price one is happy to pay?

XXIII

The Badger's Bequest

ONE of the most noticeable things about my life so far is that whenever I have been in need, that need has always been met.

When all my faith in life was shaken by an unhappy love affair, which was not the less real to me for being immature, Mr. Gort appeared upon the scene and brought lasting good out of what had at first seemed to be a chastening experience.

And when, more recently my faith in human nature was shaken in an unexpected, but no less real way, the same kind of help was forth-coming, the same kind of need was met, and good grew out of an experience which at the time I thought could be nothing if not wholly evil.

Perhaps ever since the days when I listened horror-struck to *Reynard the Fox*, the *thought* of cruelty has troubled me more than any other, next to war—which is a branch of the same evil. I am fully aware that as a race we are much opposed to cruelty, and that in many ways we are more humane to the animal kingdom than almost any other nation. Most sensible people however recognise that much cruelty still exists, but as their impotent anger or grief can do little for the victims, they adopt the reasonable, sensible attitude of *resignation*.

I have indeed tried it myself, though I found it very difficult. When I saw the milk flowing from overstocked udders in the local market, while some little hungry calf butted its muzzled snout half insensible against its mother's teats, I wondered *why* unmuzzled calves, and "milking-out" could not become the *accepted* thing. If the same conditions were imposed on all cattle for sale, the advantage would be equal among farmers, the cows would not suffer discomfort, nor the calves the torture of thirst and famine in a land of plenty—in a land where their sustenance ran to waste upon the floor of the sale-ring.

I found it difficult to adopt an attitude of resignation over matter of long overdue market or slaughter-house reform. Farmers in the main do not treat their charges badly, if only for the reason that they are always valuable, but often drovers, and unauthorised persons, including

The New Face of Britain ?

The Old Face of Britain

mischievous boys, through ignorance and stupidity or a mistaken belief in the rights of man over the animal population, are unnecessary cruel and occasionally even wantonly brutal.

Inferior intellects are frequently cruel of course. The Nazis when they found themselves in power, used that power irresponsibly to boost their own superiority. Defeated in one great war, when they found themselves winning in the next, their attitude was—

" We are the top-dogs NOW—you shall feel our power." If they had feared the great power of Russia lying on their borders, their reaction when they thought they had her by the throat was typical.

Man has, with cause or without, long feared the domination of the animal kingdom, and often, when animals are in his power, he makes up for his own sense of fear or inferiority by exerting that power to the full, whether consciously or not.

Children often appear to enjoy superiority because, having been chastised themselves, they have the power to do the same to some almost defenceless pet who is in their charge. It is a natural, if unworthy reaction. Fear begets cruelty and cruelty fear, and so the circle grows, viciously.

As I have said before, many people turn a blind eye to existing cruelty—" It is a pity of course—and if they actually saw it happen, they might do something about it—but try to bring about a reform? let someone else do that."

The attitude is understandable, but I am more inclined to agree with Doris Langley Moore when she writes:

" Were it not for this universal inertia of humble, patient acceptance, the worst human evils—war, cruelty, poverty, the oppression of the penniless and the persecution of the weak—could be destroyed tomorrow. I have come to recognise *resignation* as the deadliest of the seven deadly sins; to see it as a positive menace to the civilisation which only some tremendous renaissance of initiative can rescue from doom."

" Initiative " is a dangerous word. Those who use it may find themselves unpopular. The herd-mind seeks safety in numbers. To depart from a current line of expression or action is to be marked out among one's fellow-men. It means being reviled and often accused of the worst possible motives.

This happens to those who question organised religion, or advocate disarmament. It happens to those who question the practices of almost any set, long-established body, society, or sect, which has the backing of usage, custom and tradition behind it. Yet I agree with Alyse Gregory when she says that at least once in each of our life's time, we owe it to ourselves and the world in which we live, to examine freshly, in the light of our own knowledge and experience, every precept, code or belief that has been " handed down to us ".

As cruelty has always been my Achilles heel, as I am more vulnerable to it than to religion or even war as controversial topics, it was perhaps inevitable that I should fall foul of society—the society of " resignation " some time or other.

Now until the incident which I shall shortly relate, I had never presumed to inflict my views upon my hunting neighbours, unless particularly asked for them, when I said my piece with rather a few blushes and we agreed to differ.

My sympathies however have always been with the fox, the deer, the otter and the hare. And it has always seemed to me that their slow death, of being hunted to a " beaten condition " and then dispatched (and not with a humane killer) was not really essential to the happiness of those who would hunt.

Riding and point-to-points can supply the exercise, and a well-laid drag-hunt, the thrill. Furthermore a " drag " can be laid with regard to cultivated or stocked land in the vicinity, and a good run may be had without offence or damage. Lastly the field may be sure of their sport, and a skilled drag-man can make it good sport indeed.

I live in hunting country and did so at Warminster and Whitestaunton both. Before I lived here, Farmer hunted. He has said that he hardly liked to set his pleasure against the cry of the doomed and terrified hare, or the fox, stiff with fatigue, heart and lungs failing, dragging his brush through the mire a few yards ahead of the pack.

He thought only of the exhilaration of the chase, never of " the kill ". When he thought about it, he did not like it, yet he is a fine horseman and the thrill of riding to hounds was his greatest pleasure.

But since the days he hunted regularly, he has not only looked at the sport from the point of view of ethics, but of common sense. Since those days he has become a much better farmer, and good crops and increased milk-production have come to mean more than idle sport. A farm of newly-sown expensive leys, and sensitive pedigree cattle, of new-dug ditches and freshly-laid hedges is not improved by the passage of scores of horses, however careful their riders may be.

We have come to wonder who does the most damage, the fox or the hunt? The hare or the hunt? It has been said that hunting is carried on in the interests of food-production, but during the war, when hunting ceased, we were untroubled by foxes. On the other hand, our spaniel was once driven out of a cover in case he destroyed some young cubs being reared for the pleasure of hunting. Now these young cubs were supposed to be the enemies of egg-production, and in the interests of food supplies should have been exterminated before they could do any harm! These potential chicken-thieves were destined however to be carefully kept until they were a fit age to offer sport.

All this puzzled me as it hardly seemed common sense or clear-thinking, and I began to examine this established tradition of hunting more closely. I was not to be put off by my Mother's remarks after hearing Masefield's poem, that such things had always been, and it was no use hoping for them to be altered.

I had also heard that some young children took a rather doubtful view of the ritual honour of being " blooded " and had even been known to ask, " Do you think the fox minded very much, Mummy? " Only to be told that the " fox expects to be hunted".

To bring children up on such fare, is, in my opinion, tantamount to teaching them to accept violence and cruelty as inevitable. That is bound to have some effect on their conduct in life towards another creature's pain, even if that creature be a fellow human being.

Now I hold that pain, and the spectacle of another's pain, especially when avoidable is not ennobling at all, it is degrading, and lowering to the best values of human civilisation.

We are of course inconsistent, we have banished the stocks and the pillory, the spectacle of public whippings and executions, and the mob-amusements of bear and bull-baiting. These were eventually " cleaned up " by humane-minded persons, always a minority, who at the time were reviled as cranks and reformers.

It has long seemed to me that the tolerance of cruelty to animals begets tolerance of cruelty to humans, and breeds an acceptance of the cruelties of war.

" Worse things were done at Belsen and Büchenwald to human beings."

And worse things will of course always be done, while violence is easily condoned. One builds a house, or a temple, from the ground upwards. A beginning is made from the foundations. It seems to me a good foundation is to bring up children to respect wild life that shares the earth with us.

If this wild life threatens our well-being in any way and has to be killed or kept down, let us do it as humanely as possible, and never, never make a " Roman holiday " of it, disguising a lust for power and blood and excitement (occasionally I believe as a substitute for sexual excitement) under the guise of " duty " to food production.

Let us above all not invest any necessary killing (where it is proven by agricultural experts to be necessary) with all the panoply of the old blood-sacrifices. We are growing up, let us reveal it in our conduct to our fellow-creatures. There are so many people who grown-up physically retain the mind of the child teasing the kitten, tormenting the puppy. Of one of these Llewelyn Powys has written:—

" he was always troubled by something beautiful in the victims he so ruthlessly pursued and killed—he was one of those men of undeveloped minds, so common in cricket-pavilions, regimental messes and rural district councils, whose highest happiness is in its essence identical with that of the simplest farm boy, whose joy it is to dig out badgers in a midnight copse."

The beauty of the Exmoor deer is something never to be forgotten by those who have been fortunate enough to come face to face with them in their natural haunts. But it is not beautiful to see them crashing through the undergrowth, tongue lolling, eyes staring, flanks painfully heaving, hocks bleeding from the teeth of hounds, the sweat caked upon their fine coats. And after them come the belling, reverberating tongues of the pursuers, through the bright waters of the Doone Valley, and up the opposite slope, struggling, toiling, panting, the gap between bright life and a cruel death slowly narrowing.

To spend the last morning of one's life on Exmoor crashing through the oak woods of Horner with antlers bleeding and shattered. Is that beauty? I find in it death and ugliness. And sometimes across the neighbouring Quantocks, as a last resort the hard-pressed quarry turns to the sea. Relentlessly the " sportsmen " follow. There is no choice, the stag or the hind (sometimes in calf) goes over the cliff, bright life spurting away among the rocks below. Sometimes the momentum of the close-pressing hounds is such that some of them follow, and there is weeping and gnashing of teeth as they can be seen dragging maimed and mutilated bodies across the lonely beach.

What a great deal of suffering and ugliness, and how absolutely unnecessary! Here is Man *making* something he has pledged his life to destroy—sheer barbarity.

And from barbarity to badgers, which are clean, courageous and even lovable creatures. They may lack the shy beauty of the deer and the hare, but they combine almost all the characteristics which in our national life we have come most to respect. Even those who hunt the fox and the hare would spare the badger. More than one fox-hunter has told me they " love badgers ". When I found the badger was threatened with extinction in our part of the country I looked up Bewick's *History of Quadrupeds* which says:—

" It is harmless and inoffensive, there seems no better reason to consider it a beast of prey than the analogy between its teeth and those of carnivorous animals.

" Few creatures defend themselves better—on that account it is frequently baited with dogs trained for that purpose. This inhuman diversion is chiefly confined to the *indolent* and *vicious*, who take a cruel pleasure in seeing this harmless animal surrounded by its enemies, defending itself from their attacks—in this manner this singular creature is able to resist repeated attacks of both men and dogs from all quarters, until being overpowered with numbers and enfeebled by many desperate wounds, it is at last obliged to submit."

Today badger " baiting " is *illegal*, but the " indolent and vicious " have got round the law by the sports of badger digging and hunting which *result in exactly the same sort of* scenes as those described above. The badger, because of his pluck is always like King Charles " an un-conscionable time a-dying ". It takes many hours digging, many attacks from sharp-toothed terriers, and many blows from the humans on the scene to finally put an end to his game fight.

If he were an agricultural pest it would be just a trifle easier to under-stand such persecution, but as he is classed as " the farmer's friend " absolutely *unanimously* by all authorities, such cruelty is both inde-fensible and against the interests of agriculture.

The badger eats many farm pests, above all does he love to dig out litters of young rabbits. The most damage he does on a farm is to take an occasional roll in a field of growing corn. I am told this does not do irreparable damage. Occasionally one hears of rogue badgers, but they are very rare, few cases are proven, and usually it is a fox, sharing an earth with the badger who is to blame for the signs of roost-robbing upon which Brock is condemned.

Modern writers like Ralph Wightman, who are easy-going about other forms of hunting, are strong in their indictments against persecution of the badger.[1] Indeed from all quarters the conclusion appears to be almost unanimous. " It is not *sport* at all, it is long-drawn out, very bloody and demoralising murder."

The exception is of course the badger-hunters themselves. These " indolent and vicious " persons as old Bewick would have designated them (and I wish to be associated with his remarks), continue to turn a deaf ear to the voice of authority. They have never read any book on natural history, they turn a blind eye to letters to the Press confirming Brock's innocence and usefulness, and a deaf ear to the country-life broadcasts which have sought to tell the truth about the badger. They discount the evidence of men like Ernest G. Neal[2] who have spent their whole lives studying the habits of badgers, or of men like F. Howard Lancum whose documents upon badgers amount almost to a Royal Commission.[3] They also discount the most important fact of all, namely that all these experts *agree* on their verdict—namely that badgers are innocent and should be encouraged rather than persecuted. This is a verdict reached by many well-known farmers and agriculturalists from Ralph Whitlock among his Wiltshire downs to Colonel Garton among the woods of Pylle. From Essex to the Cotswolds, the tale of the enlightened, of those who have troubled to look into the matter, is the same.

Their verdict—the verdict of the specialists—was not my excuse or reason for interfering with a cruel practice when it happened in our own neighbourhood. They have since made my position stronger—have indeed done all my fighting for me, but I should have continued alone—even as I began alone.

Many people came to watch this hunting of the badger—people from as far away as Bristol, people I might add who were in complete ignorance as to its habits. Drinking was, of course, an integral part

1. *Moss Green Days.*
2. *The Badger.*
3 See also his book, *Wild Animals and the Land*, and his official Ministry of Agriculture leaflet.

of the evening's entertainment, and I have heard even the participants declared that many were " well boozed up " before the " sport " began.

I was not present, therein lay the weakness of my case when I presented it to the R.S.P.C.A. But some of those present were of like mind to myself in the matter. They at least had gone because they did not know what to expect, because it was a " new thrill ". They kept silent afterwards, not wishing to lower themselves in the eyes of public opinion, or not wishing to let down their friends who had been the ring-leaders.

When Farmer who is phlegmatic enough, being indeed the exact opposite of the " crab " species, and rarely troubled inwardly, came home from market (where the " hunt " had been the topic of the day) obviously upset over something, I was greatly surprised. As little upsets him I knew that whatever this was it must have bitten very deeply. When he refused to tell me " Because your blood would boil and there is nothing you can do about it", my woman's curiosity not to mention my apprehension was aroused sufficiently to make enquiries. The story was not long in forthcoming.

A badger after a long chase was beaten to death—all the lads of the village took a " swipe " at it. Out of fairness to the " master " of the hunt it was said that he could not get at the job for the pack of people. Men were the worse for drink, women were screaming and hysterical, villagers were kept awake by the " shindy ".

It has taken me months to piece together the whole story, for now, gradually people concerned have told me their views coincide with mine, but that they were either " carried away by the heat of the moment " or else that they were ashamed to say anything at the time.

The townspeople of course " knew not what they did ", though they are hardly to be forgiven on that score, ignorance is no excuse for cowardly murder.

By bringing the R.S.P.C.A. into the case (after openly acquainting people of my intention) I drew upon my head, venom, malice and of course the usual anonymous communications.

A fully-grown badger of fine proportions was left in a tea-chest on my doorsteps, no doubt in the hopes that its steely jaws would give me something to remember the badger-hunters by.

We took the animal down to one of our lower fields and let it loose. We have not seen the poor creature since. It appeared to be uninjured as it loped off into the darkness, but a badger carries its disabilities amazingly well and there was no way of knowing how the intrepid hunters had managed to " bring it back alive ".

Those days were miserable indeed for me. Those who have read this far will be able to guess how I suffered. If it had been my own dog who had been beaten to death I could not have felt worse. And here was this sort of thing going on all over the country every night—had not this particular hunt boasted that they had exterminated by these slow, painful and barbaric methods over twenty badgers in as many nights.

Our astute " lodger " from Norfolk declared that part of my grief was at my disillusionment over the human beings in the case—that people in Somerset *above all places* could descend to such practices, it was this that had so shaken me, kept me awake at night and put me off my food.

He was partly right of course. How I wished it had never happened. What good could ever come of it? I had thoroughly upset myself and I could not spare the badger his pain thereby, I had made myself many enemies, got myself thoroughly disliked in my own neighbourhood, and got myself into a place of prominence painful in the extreme.

The R.S.P.C.A. were excellent. I had stated that I wanted no conviction in the case because punishment of the offenders would hardly mend matters, but there was no question of that. The body of the badger could not be found, impossible to say just how he met his death, the " Master " could state " as humanely as possible under the circumstances," which was one way out of it. The witnesses, all badgerhunters to have witnessed the occurrence at all, gave conflicting evidence as to time, etc. The evidence all pointed to cruelty but beyond convicting 300 people, little could be done.

I was told, " We shall go out all the oftener for your interference."

This, while the logical outcome of argument against such minds, was the last straw. I felt the cause of humanity had fallen upon evil days in this district.

But slowly the tide turned—letters began to turn up, none of them were from " cranks " nor from members of anti-hunting societies, they were from ordinary decent people, and from those with an expert knowledge of badgers.

When I was living down the unpleasantness, and hoping I should not take a gun to any hunters found on our land I saw an excellent letter in defence of badgers appear in our local paper. The signature Littleton

Powys was not unfamiliar to me. I had read much of his brother Llewelyn, who is greatly praised in many of H. J. Massingham's books. I have always respected Mr. Massingham's judgment and in spite of some controversy over the religious views of some of the literary members of this great family, I knew they had their roots deep in the Somerset and Dorset countryside.

This letter to a local newspaper which had so impressed me was backed up by the testimony of a Ukrainian professor who said he was at a complete loss to understand our attitude to an animal most valued and respected by farmers in his own country.

I was invited to come to Sherborne and report on my own badger case to Mr. Powys who was the representative of the R.S.P.C.A. in North Dorset. And thus began a friendship whose worth I find it impossible to over-estimate.

Of Littleton Powys, his friend H. J. Massingham might well have written:

" In our own lives here in England, we do meet with people who love beauty and peace and the face of nature, who do not walk in the ways of the world, who have no professed religion, but whose presence is a benediction.

" Free in mind themselves, they seek in no way to restrict the liberties of others, while their only form of criticism is to follow their own grassy paths, serene and undismayed. They are like quiet places through which city pavements do not run."

How strange, how unpredictable are life's compensations when the cruel death of a badger could be the means of bringing me such a friend; a friend whose unfailing encouragement and support had something reminiscent of Mr. Gort. Yet, high as I place this friendship, and great source of happiness that it has been, I would still rather it had not come my way than that a badger should have met such a barbaric end.

Of the Powys family so much has already been said and written, especially during the decades between the wars, that little can be added by me. Mr. Massingham's writings had prepared me for Llewelyn's gallant fight against ill-health, had told of his boundless zest for living, and his understanding of our Wessex countryside. But I was not prepared for the sweetness, the quiet understanding and the deep spirit of Alyse Gregory, his widow. Nor was I prepared for the poet, the independent spirit that was Philippa, his sister.

Nor, in my wildest dreams of a free, untrammelled life such as I had lived at " Romany Cottage ", could I have pictured a house like the cottage on the downs between East Chaldon and the sea. There, high in a dry valley running towards the shore, cupped deep in the topmost downs, and almost within sound of the breakers so far below, I found Alyse, and Philippa and the eldest sister Gertrude. Gertrude looked exactly like the clergyman's daughter that she was, gentle and grey-haired, serene and blue-eyed, softly spoken, a real " gentlewoman " in country woollens. But that same Gertrude had studied art and held exhibitions of her work, had illustrated her brother's books and hung the walls of their homes with her portrait paintings of themselves and their families. That same, frail looking person walked the lonely primeval track from the village to the house above Bat's Head, heavily laden, in all the wild weather this coastline can know.

This house, hidden in the downs, unapproached by any hard road, out of sight of any other human habitation, made my " isolated " cottage at Silverlake positively metropolitan in comparison.

The brother and sister, Littleton and Gertrude, I found to be alike physically and temperamentally. A close friend had written of Littleton, something that equally well applied to Gertrude:—

" You have the secret of happiness in yourself beyond anyone I have ever known. It is an open secret, for it can hardly help being shared by anyone who consorts with you."

I found the house near East Chaldon permeated with Gertrude's spirit which Massingham might have called a " benediction ", and which brought an atmosphere of sheer goodness, kindness and right-thinking which envelopes the stranger almost immediately, leaving them no longer a stranger.

The badger had also led me to the gentle, courteous wisdom of Theodore Powys whose Dorset " Fables " have a style entirely their own. No other west-country author approaches Theodore, he stands alone. Littleton said it was one of the happiest moments of his life when the Government awarded a pension to his brother for his services to literature.

Theodore surrounded by the countryside he has immortalised, loves to " bide and stud " beneath his central Dorset hills—the frowning Bulbarrow, the shaggy heights of Milton Abbas, the prehistoric Rawlsbury, or meditate in his ancient church at Mappowder.

The eldest of this amazing family, John Cowper Powys, has settled in North Wales, delving day by day, deeper into his Celtic forbears' history to the days of the Mabinogion and of Owen Glendywr. Close on eighty years of age he has just published a very well-received translation of Rabelais, from the original, mediæval French. Many young authors and poets have owed him a great deal for his selfless advice and encouragement. He still strides his "ancient mountains" with an unflagging appetite for life and letters.

Arthur Mee in his Dorset book in *The King's England* series, has paid tribute to yet another of the Powys brothers—A. R. Powys, to whom we owe the preservation of so many fine West Country buildings.

In the section devoted to the village of Winterbourne Tomson Arthur Mee writes:—

"Those who enjoy the delight of the recovery of this old place may spare a tribute of homage at one of the graves in the churchyard, for in it lies the man who accepted the responsibility for saving and restoring an immense number of places in England, Albert Reginald Powys. For a quarter of a century he was the energising Secretary of the Society for the Protection of Ancient Buildings, which owed its origin to William Morris, but its inspiration to Mr. Powys through all these years. No man knows how many old cottages and old buildings have been saved through his enthusiasm and example, for not only did he save them through his Society, but by his counsel and advice, and by his writings. If there is a better understanding of old building in the world today it is greatly due to this untiring man who died all too soon, after a devoted life in which his recreation was, as he used to say, seeing country things."

When through marriage with Littleton in 1944, Elizabeth Myers entered the family she brought a further contribution of good writing, clear thinking and unselfish work, to the name of Powys. Her *A Well Full of Leaves* was acclaimed as one of the books of the year in which it was published (1943) and to many it was a landmark in the history of the English novel. In 1947, her untimely death from tuberculosis cut short a brilliant career, both as novelist and short-story writer. Her writings were more than pure entertainment, they carried the age-old message of the brotherhood of man, a message I could appreciate and understand, and one that must have cheered and

The Walnut Tree

encouraged thousands. Her last published novel (her volume of short-stories *Good Beds, Men Only*, was brought out posthumously a little time ago) *Mrs. Christopher* is being made into both a play and a film. Its "human-appeal" should be unfailing.

To all these wide sympathies, these tolerant understandings, these brave personalities was the martyred badger responsible for introducing me. But even now I do not care to think of that September night in the fields and covers of South-east Somerset when he was hunted and beaten to death by those who should have known better.

Yet it is a great joy to hear Littleton say:

"This is my friend, Mrs. Monica Hutchings—I have the greatest possible admiration for her, her work and her way of life—and how do you think we met? It was a badger that introduced us!"

268

XXIV

"The New Face of Britain"

IN May of the year 1947 the following letter appeared in the columns of the *Observer*:

" Sir,

" I am engaged in research work for a film on the preservation of rural England and would ask anyone who can quote concrete examples of flagrant misuse of land which should have been reserved for its agricultural, scenic, historic or scientific value, to write to me—the cause is I feel a vital one."

The letter was signed by A. Essex-Lopresti of Eclipse Film Productions. My Mother who takes the *Observer* had forwarded it to me, marked with a cross. I read it carefully and then put it by. I was too busy, let someone else tell them about Imber, or what was happening in the Isle of Purbeck, what commercialism had done to Cheddar, or how the White Horse of Westbury was threatened by a cement factory.

I had enough to do—more than enough, I was tired and busy, let someone else tell them. A. Essex-Lopresti! I pictured a large, fat foreign gentleman, smoking a cigar and sending his minions to make a picture of Rural England—from an address in Dulwich Village. Pah!

This was the sort of thing with which real country lovers had to contend. But wait, he did say the cause was a " vital " one. It did seem the gentleman cared a little.

When I had time to think about it, which was several weeks later, I decided to send a reply to the letter, after all it might do some good, and if good to the countryside cause I held so much at heart was to be the result, I must not let a name like a brand of sardines put me off.

I wrote the letter and scrawled my signature at the close of it. The " i " in Monica slipping towards the end, the " a " looking like a badly finished " e ". No wonder the recipient thought the country author was Maurice Hutchings!

The reply came back " Dear Sir ". And yes, they had had a number of letters, but nothing about Imber. They were quite interested in the fact that I was the author of several country books too. Perhaps I could assist them over the script?

I positively snorted—from an address in Dulwich Village? I was tempted to use Eliza Doolittle's reply—" Not ' Pygmalion ' likely! "

Ah, but that was perfectly all right, Eclipse Film Productions understood my feelings completely (did they, by Jove?), they were all young and presumably impetuous but willing to consider advice on how to proceed with this urgent, vital, delicate and important subject. If I would have them, they would come down for a discussion.

Late in June, Maurice M. Hutchings, Esqr., met Essex-Lopresti off the London train. When I saw him, my heart sank. True, the information that the firm was young, had killed my preconceived notion of an elderly, fat, foreign gentleman smoking a cheroot—but this—this was going to the extreme.

He was a dark, untidy, faintly nervous young man. He had no poise and no assurance and, I judged, very little personality. Something about him made him look even younger than his declared twenty-three years, yet his face was hardly that of a schoolboy's, it was lined and slightly worried-looking.

In spite of the very ordinary English accent (he might have come from any county between Cumberland and Kent) the " sardine " part of his name was plain enough. His colouring and wiry dark hair (which wanted cutting) were definitely un-English. My heart stayed in a sunken position. He looked a bit of a funny mixture to me. His fingers were badly stained with nicotine and I saw at once that he smoked too much, this fact hardly served to endear him to me.

I decided he looked too young to know what he was about and that I was a priceless fool to let myself get mixed up with any half-baked incompetent Bohemians who really did not know a thing about " the things that matter ". I was angry with myself and tried to hide it by being extra friendly and polite.

He responded with a positively disarming smile, but I found no occasion to revise my initial opinion of him. I moaned inwardly at the thought of a country film being made by one so ineffectual, so young, so inexperienced, so half-baked, by one above əll, who lived at Dulwich Village!

" My plan," I said in a famous-author business-like manner, " is to show you what we have—both beauty and vandalism—if you can use any of it then we'll consider the script and you can send for your cameraman."

He agreed politely. Indeed I had the feeling he'd agree to almost anything. Some of the day was left, I would make a start by taking him to the woods and lakes of Stourton and Penselwood. The sooner I began, the sooner would I be rid of him.

Among the Stourton tracks I got stuck with the car. I knew all the trails and rides, but had tried to be clever and take a short cut, against the young man's advice too. When he told me he did not drive I considered his advice impertinent, and continued on my way.

It took us both, with a jack and the help of a woodlander to shift the thing. I was no better pleased for my companion refraining from saying "I told you so".

In revenge I took him to the top of Alfred's tower, which is dark and steep and ascended by more than a hundred steps. Half-way up I wondered at the wisdom of my course, after all I was almost a decade older, and not in the best of health, my breath was already coming in short pants. My companion was young and only just out of the army. I struggled on. My revenge was good enough, he was more breathless if anything than myself. He was plainly out of condition. He smoked too much.

The countryside was spread like a map below us, on a level with our eyes a pair of buzzards wheeled and banked. I pretended to have a head for heights and leaned well over. This was *my* countryside, there was nothing like this at Dulwich Village.

The day following, I had promised to take Littleton and a friend of his to the Mizmaze. I decided that if Anthony would behave himself he might as well come along. He took the hundred-mile journey almost without comment and I could not make out whether he was "taking things in" or just dead from the neck up.

On the way home we stopped at the Pitt-Rivers Museum, and I tried to force the study of a couple of thousand years into about half an hour. We all came out with mental indigestion—except possibly Anthony. He showed very few signs of life one way or the other. Littleton was kind to him and called him St. Anthony, and was heavily encouraging over the prospects of a country film. (He had never seen a " talkie " himself and had not been inside a cinema for about thirty years!)

The Mizmaze on a midsummer day is an enchanting experience and everyone seemed happy but faintly dazed by such a surfeit of beauty and interest. In one journey we had seen the clear chalk streams and the lovely summer flora of the downs, the superb village street of Rockbourne, the barrows and dykes of Cranborne Chase, the woods of King John's Tollard Royal, the noble sweep of hills about Shaftesbury, the treasure-trove of 'Pitt-Rivers' and the haunted maze itself. It was almost too much. Anthony took it in his stride however and seemed a good deal older than Littleton, who enthused like a boy.

The following day we went to Wells, Wookey Hole, Cheddar, the Ebbor Gorge and the Mendip plateau at Priddy. My companion still appeared to live in a world of his own.

The next day was my birthday, it was July the third and I was thirty-one. It was a year ago I had begun *The Walnut Tree*, a work that had been interrupted by the advent of this " film-director ". I thought as a final resort I would show him Exmoor. It was a grey rainy day, and the countryside hardly looked its best. Cleeve was grey and Dunster colourless, the moor looked dead or dying. What a stupid waste of time and petrol I thought, as the car took the almost vertical Porlock Hill, and the chocolates which my Mother had sent me, fell out of the dash-board pocket and scattered themselves all over the floor.

What a way to spend a birthday!

At the top of the hill I swung the car round to face Wales. A gleam of sun crossed Porlock Vale and I pointed out land reclaimed from the sea—land which now grew prize crops of barley. If my companion was impressed, he succeeded in hiding it.

The sun stayed out and the moor enfolded us. We stopped for a drink where a torrent crossed the road, and I saw the would-be film-maker peering under the old stone bridge and gauging where the light would fall when the sun was at its best. It was the first real signs of life he had shown and I felt heartened. He had an eye for a picture after all.

On Sunday, in the intervals of getting meals and doing the house-work, I tackled the script with him. At once, he was a different person. He knew just what he wanted, all he really needed was his ideas backing up by someone of a like mind. The purpose of good agricultural land was not to lay out camps and aerodromes or race-courses and fair-grounds, speedways, stadiums or even housing estates.

It seemed he had the right idea and really knew where he was going. I began to take heart. On Monday the camera-man arrived. He was a few months younger and in direct contrast to Essex-Lopresti. Tall, Saxon, phlegmatic, the product of a public school who now lived in an old rectory in Surrey. He was a bit of a countryman and was interested in falconry.

They made an odd pair, Anthony now galvanised into action and responsibility; nervy, dynamic, idealistic. And Ricky, good-natured, able, matter of fact and materialistic. Between them they got things done. I was less than nothing—I was " comfort for the troops " and " general factotum ". When the truck broke down which was fairly frequently, as it was an ex-Army vehicle, I drove them, miraculously finding the petrol from my meagre allowance. I cut sandwiches, and filled flasks, almost in my sleep, guided them to tattered castles and ruined abbeys (as the script demanded), carried the data-sheets, and " liaisoned " with landowners and curators, custodians and farmers, in order to achieve the " shots " required.

In the evenings after the light was gone I talked to young Anthony about the countryside, while Ricky went out with Farmer's gun to shoot rabbits as a change from shooting film.

I pointed out that the great earthworks were accomplished without bull-dozers or steam-shovels, and that Wells and Exeter, Sherborne and Cleeve were constructed without cranes and steel and the modern building equipment. I pointed out that with our new and shoddy standards of architecture we were fast being put in the position of the present-day savages who look upon the temples and statues of their forefathers with ignorant amazement, as the undoubted production of giants and demon.

It had even been put to me that our great West Country earthworks were " natural phenomena " and not achieved by the hand of man at all. Anthony chuckled.

Those South Sea natives by the way, who stared at their forefathers' works were incapable of anything better than grass-thatched huts, themselves. Are we not almost following suit, as we run up " pre-fabs " amidst the Roman and Regency splendours of Bath? Anthony agreed it was a shocking thing. And amazing, too, how the Roman roads had lasted without tar-mac! Why we asked each other do we destroy ancient and beautiful bridges when we might by-pass them? Why do the Forestry Commissioners plant only conifers in a country intended for hardwoods? Why does the War Office pick the most fertile sites for its camps and ranges and training grounds? Why does

London have to have a reserve reservoir that drowns the life of a whole rural community, when she already has more water per head than any part of the country? Why not a little piped water for the homes and farms that have *none*, before London has any more?

Why should Enborne die that London might drink? (Only a *reserve* supply note, in addition to the normal, and at the moment, adequate one.) Why should Imber die that the size and range of modern weapons might be tested and maintained?

Here I said, "I will get you into Imber, I know the way." We entered Imber, although the War Office had not granted us permission, and we filmed it through like a newsreel; each forlorn and empty house, each gaping roof and ruined thatch, each overgrown, neglected, *wasted* acre of it.

The road was mined, we had no pass; we sweated while we worked. Both Imber and the day were ominous and we were relieved when at last we were out of the danger area. Afterwards the War Office said they would not suppress our work since we had accomplished it, but they had not wished us to go in. I thanked the stars that had sent me to Warminster as a child, enabling *The New Face of Britain* as we had christened the film, to contain this cinematographic "scoop".

The whole course of the filming was something like the film itself— beautiful and ugly, a mixture of pleasure and pain.

Two things emerged from this venture, besides a documentary film which so far has been very well received.

The first, is the help with which we met from the "natives" everywhere. In the main, government departments and large concerns (particularly works and factories) were not helpful, but "private-enterprise" stopped work everywhere and assisted and co-operated and advised.

We shall remember the Enborne Valley postman, who declared he "had the prettiest round in England, though I says it as shouldn't!" And the Jesuit Priest of Wardour who came to our rescue when we ran out of petrol and who showed us the way to the magnificent ruin of the Castle. We shall long recall the farmer whose name *really was Giles,* and who swore that if he won a football pool and took a house at Bournemouth (why Bournemouth above all places?) that he would mope to be back home and working.

"What should I do with meself all day—No I tell ee I'm happy as

I be. What's ten thousand pounds if you can't be doing the things you suited for and happiest at? "

What indeed?

There was the Exmoor farmer who roused himself from his Sunday afternoon's siesta to go out on the windswept hills after his flocks for us, and did not tell us until *afterwards* that he strongly opposed my views on stag-hunting which he declared

" Is *our* pictures."

There was the schoolmaster at Wells who took us among the local quarries during his dinner-hour and showed us the vandalism that is endangering his fair city in what was once an unusually fair setting. He afterwards contributed a dedicatory poem for the film, which in its direct simplicity was exactly what we required.

We shall remember the farm-staff and especially the carter who waited with a loaded waggon until the sun came out, and the man with the " combine " who stopped for a close-up.

We shall remember the cottagers and the official guides, the people in village stores and post offices, who were always ready to give their services freely because they had the same cause at heart—the preservation and defence of our natural heritage.

The New Face of Britain took shape and was eventually completed, although the going was never easy as we lacked adequate resources and equipment. But when it emerged, to those who made it at least it was more than thirty minutes of documentary film with a very earnest and vital message, it was a great experience and something of a human-document.

To Anthony Essex-Lopresti, his first completed film was a revelation, for it opened up a new world for him. It was a world he knew existed and whose importance he had recognised when he had first had the urge to make such a film; but not until he entered into the new kingdom, did he realise how extensive and how important it was.

I did not have to teach him, he discovered it for himself. Soon he was teaching me! Did I know how many sacks of barley had come off that little bottom-field? No? Well, he did and it was absolutely incredible. And out would come paper and pencil for facts and figures.

Did the average towns person know how much food there was in one English field? And we looked at each other with something of stout Cortez's " Wild surmise ". There was another film there—*One*

English Field and all its life and growth from seedtime round to seed-time.

Almost everywhere we looked, there was a film subject in the countryside.

Littleton Powys smiled on and encouraged us, and I began to realise why Sherborne preparatory schoolboys return again and again all through their lives to visit their ex-headmaster. I saw him teaching Anthony about birds and trees and the importance of field study in education, and then they would soar off into the realms of literature and poetry and discuss making Elizabeth's books into films and plays. And I thought of her dedication in *The Basilisk of St. James'* to Littleton and his brother John. " —Two men with whom one could talk and feel that the world was boundless, who would say nothing to limit one's vision, or constrain one's imagination."

The great kindness done me by that poor old badger, I now passed on to Anthony.

The second thing that grew out of this experience was my regard for the young film-director. I often thought of Mr. Gort's words about the difficulty of keeping one's heart in anything, even once you had firmly put it there. I saw how Anthony fought against all kinds of odds to keep his heart in this film and its admirable theme. Nothing and no one should side-track him or turn him from his appointed course—neither financial considerations, nor concessions to popular appeal. He did not even care if he made any money or not, as long as he might continue to make good films that would do *good*.

He won my grudging admiration and although I often subconsciously felt that being older I should know better than he, I found myself even deferring to his opinion.

We discussed all aspects of country life and among other things I pointed out how the towns laugh at our innocent pleasures and recreation and the scorn frequently pointed by the sophisticated at such organisations as the Women's Institute.

I pointed out the inestimable good they do, bringing all kinds of interest and culture to the countrywomen and recounted how on one of my visits to the nearby branch one of the members demanded sanitation, etc., equal to those in the nearby army-huts!

"If adequate water can be found for the camps to have a piped supply and proper flush-lavatories, how is it the authorities say sufficient isn't available for us to have it in the village?"

Anthony was often amused as well as enlightened! I took him to the Powys eyrie above Bat's Head and during our few hours "off" we talked shop, and indulged in a "busman's holiday" by picking out sites and themes for future films.

I found myself doing my cooking and housework before dawn or after dark, but it was all worth it. I still retain a childish love of picnics, and in the true sense of the word making *The New Face of Britain* was one long picnic. We rarely bought a meal out, for one thing time and convenience were against it, and for another I think hospitality should be given freely and freely accepted. I have *always* felt that; somehow I hate paying for service and loathe hotel meals for that reason.

And so we discussed many things, from broadcasting (I had read some of my own stories in the West Regional programmes) to the effects of army life on the individual. (Anthony had suffered rather more than a little on that score.)

We travelled many thousands of miles all told, and both learned a very great deal. For my own part, I learned, yet once again how kind people can be, and how many give freely, asking nothing in return.

I also learned to trust young Anthony Essex-Lopresti with my most precious possession—my countryside.

XXV

Comment and Conclusion

THIS morning I awoke as the light was growing and the insistent crowing of the rooster out in the yard told me the time of day. Presently other birds began—thrushes, blackbirds, robins. It is still winter, but the birds sound like spring. The season has been mild so far, and though the boughs are leafless, it can plainly be discerned that last year's leaves were pushed away by the new buds. There is a continuity in nature that forbids the giving up of hope.

It will be months before the cuckoo flings his echoing challenge over the blossoming orchards, dominating the territory of the birds. It is still winter, and that amazing glory of the " dawn-chorus " is as yet far off, but Hardy's " Darkling Thrush " pours out his contribution to the joy of living, and there are many other bird voices, so although the " sedge hath withered from the lake ", one cannot say that " no birds sing ".

I have been thinking how empty would our world be if there were only human beings in it. How we should miss the sight and sound of the other creatures we now take so much for granted—the cats and dogs, the little domestic pets, the horses and cattle of the fields, the white-scutted rabbit, the birds and butterflies, the webs and wings, the very crickets chirping merrily from the tall grasses, and those delicately striped snails of brown and white and pink and yellow, which so delighted Elizabeth Myers.

Once again, as I have done from my early days at Walnut Tree Cottage, I beg leave to wonder at the blindness of Man that he so often misses or passes over the beauty and importance of these minutiæ of life.

How wrong it is that many town children are brought up to believe that all wild life should be destroyed. When they come into the country their natural reaction is to catch and kill. All the things they do not understand, from butterflies to badgers, must be killed. There is nothing so delightful as badger cubs at play, or the mad antics of the graceful leverets, or the puppy-like games of a vixen's litter. All, shy, wild young things are a joy to watch, but it is so come near them. They are aware, from an instinct born diff and bitter experience, that the greatest, most ruthless of all enemies, is Man.

Man is the Great Fear. It is one of the blackest entries against us that it should be so and a grave blot upon the human race. Yet everywhere, all along the centuries, where Man has won the trust of some animal, he has been well rewarded.

The late George Arliss, a humanitarian as are so many artists, once said:

" Surely it is something more than sentimentalism to feel that animals have rights as well as human beings. What of the boasted superiority of Man, if he can be more cruel than the cruellest beast, torturing to death where the beast of prey slays at one stroke? "

The beast of prey slays also for existence, not for pleasure. To kill of necessity is one thing, but to add to the slaughter from wantonness, is another.

In one district, badgers were recently exterminated with gas and broken glass, for the sin of digging up a golf-links. Now it seems to me more fitting that they should have been allowed to continue their useful life as the farmer's friend, than that all be perfection for men who wish to spend their time hitting a little ball about.

Similarly I know of a fishing-club who put a price on the head of every heron in the district. One member who was also a bird-lover and naturalist, resigned, for as he said :

" The heron fishes for a living, we do so only for pleasure, and anyway there should be sufficient sport for the heron and the fishermen if the *latter* are not too greedy in their demands."

Cruelty, ignorance and stupidity are all closely related, and they are all things which Man should fight (instead of himself) if he wishes to improve his happiness in life.

Unfortunately cruelty goes deep in human minds and make-up, a legacy from the " survival of the fittest " days. It is associated too with sexual stimulation which may account for its momentary attractions for those who in " cold-blood " are afterwards ashamed of their indulgences.

This may or may not account for some of the cruelties of the victors in war, upon victims who are helpless to defend themselves. But it goes deeper even than sex and is rooted in the age-old fears of Man.

" There but for the grace of God and different circumstances, goes

I," says the tormentor, in effect. " Yesterday I was the und.
today I am on top—tomorrow—well, who knows? Today, it is yo
turn to suffer, while I, praise be, can feel nothing but superiority."

Meanwhile children who seem to possess unusually cruel traits of
character are often children who lack security and assurance in their
home-life. Love begets love, and kindness kindness. If kindness
were the universal law in dealing with all creatures, not only would
avoidable cruelties disappear, but Man's inhumanity to Man would be
a thing of the past.

We do make progress, of course, in spite of many backslidings
accelerated largely by the renewal of force in each disastrous war.
Public conscience *is* slowly being awakened, we move slowly, but on
all fronts. I say slowly, for although we have banned " bread and
circuses " we still permit murder-trials to be made public, and although
we condemn other nations at their sport of bull-fighting, we permit
the more unequalled combat of one hind versus the pack and the field.
But we *have* improved from the days of wholesale hangings, drawings,
and quarterings, or the burning alive of so-called witches. Mob-rule
while still dangerous and uncertain has progressed since the days of
public executions.

The improvement is painful and slow, but it does continue, and I
believe will do so, as long as thought continues.

It is a slender, distant hope to offer but I do believe that the day will
come when war, and political imprisonment, and hunting will become
unthinkable.

" If we wish to test the strength of transition's influence on us, it is
only necessary to imagine how we should regard any time-honoured
institution, if we had *never heard of it before*, but were asked to consider
it in the light of our ideas at their present stage of development. What
reception, for instance would be accorded fox-hunting *as an innova-
tion*? The great troup of horses, hounds and men after one small
animal, the ceremony of rubbing the freshly killed victim's blood on
the face of a beginner, the ridiculous jargon (pink for scarlet, taboo
upon the use of such obvious words as ' dogs ', ' barking ', etc.) all
designed to give a feeling of exclusiveness, like certain kinds of schoolboy slang, the damage to crops, the fantastic expensiveness? I fancy
the question of cruelty would hardly need to be debated, so swiftly
would the sport be condemned for stupidity. And can it be supposed

that otter-hunting, beagling, pig-sticking, not to speak of a large number of ritualistic slaughterings, would seem more intelligent? "*

I know that many fox-hunters while defending their own sport, consider stag-hunting to be very cruel, while there are stag-hunters who would not beat a badger to death. But where is one to draw the line? Unfortunately many of the people who at least got as far as discriminating over their cruelties have now made a firm stand *for* all kinds of hunting and cruel-sports because the abolition of them has been made into a political issue.

It really has nothing whatever to do with politics. Many Socialists care little or nothing for animal welfare, while many Conservatives have always disliked the cruelties attendant on hunting, but where once they were outspoken in the matter, are now silent lest they be considered traitors to their political party.

I find this particularly stupid—because one wishes to be an humanitarian, it does not mean that one must necessarily be a Socialist, or because one happens to be a Conservative, it does not follow that one approves of hunting.

Tradition leaves us good and bad things, it is for us to discriminate and neither reject nor accept in a wholesale, unthinking manner. While upon the subject of cruelty, let me return to the market. I do not advocate the better treatment of newly-born calves because I am a sentimentalist. It would be difficult to get sentimental over a calf which is hardly an engaging creature like a lamb or a kitten. They are awkward, irritating animals with the disconcerting habit of " scouring " at the wrong time. But their treatment lacks common sense and is to no one's advantage. A calf exposed, foodless and comfortless, at a tender age in market and sale-ring, often needs quite a bit of coddling when it gets back to the farm for which it was purchased, sometimes it never recovers or does well. Lastly, I hate waste, and milk running from an over-full udder while a weak calf totters alongside seems wrong and senseless.

Of course it is said that a cow with her " bag " stocked-up, will sell so much better. But if it were the habit by law to let the calf run naturally, all sellers and dealers would be in the same position. As it is, an unscrupulous man can perpetrate a fraud by refraining from milking the cow for a whole day beforehand, if needs be, so that her

* Doris Langley Moore, *The Vulgar Heart.*

bag may look better than it really is.

By those who do not know me it has been suggested that I must be an arrant sentimentalist. Yet the true sentimentalists have accused me of hardness because I would kill a trapped rabbit rather than set it free, and because when my dog Spry, ill with an incurable disease, was eventually shot, I immediately adopted another dog.

So it seems I fall between two stools. One friend said to me, in a tone of hurt reproof,

" I *never thought* you'd have another dog, after Spry."

I believe sentiments of this kind are also voiced to those who marry a second time! If the " once bitten, twice shy " theory is to be believed, then a second marriage is the greatest compliment that could be paid to the first. I can give the same answer regarding the adoption of a new dog :

" I was so happy with the first, that I would not now be without one for anything."

Spry taught me the value of a dog's companionship to such an extent that I would not now readily forgo it. Yet I will not say that it did not cost me a pang to say " good-bye " to him. He was the first dog I had ever called my own, I had brought him from a rickety puppy, he had shared so much of life with me, from Romany Cottage to Church Farm, he had been through good times and bad times with me, known air-raids; and holidays on the farm. He had never been very demonstrative or fussy—I daresay he was not everyone's idea of a " pet ", but I knew him and liked him. I hated to hear the shot that ended his brief, enthusiastic eight years. I am glad that I do not know the motorist who ran over him and left him in the ditch in agony without reporting it. Of course Spry took that, as he took everything—as if it did not matter. Only living mattered. He went on the same, rabbitting, watching the road, ruling the roost, even with a leg in plaster.

It was when we discovered later that there was something wrong internally, something that no treatment would remedy, the canine equivalent of the fatal " Bright's Disease ", that I had to make my decision. He would gradually suffer more and more, losing his old *joie de vivre*. So the shot rang out and he lies buried near the rick barton.

Bob is a fine dog. He was not wanted where he was, he needed a good home, and he was very thin when he came to us. Now he sleeps in Spry's haybed, tolerates the cats and the spaniel Sandy, impartially; and delights to follow the farm-work. He is as friendly and faithful as his forerunner, and since he was a working dog, far better trained; but the sentimentalists would have me mourn over an empty kennel!

Bob has only one fault that I can find, and that is that he is not Spry. Of course he may think I am not a patch on the man who trained him to leap five-barred gates, before I became his owner, but that is by the way.

And here cruelty and ignorance almost meet and overlap, for it is surely a kind of ignorance which decrees that because one has given one's heart to one dog (or human being) there is nothing left to offer any other. There are many kinds of love and affection, just as there are many qualities in people—or dogs.

Another kind of ignorance was displayed by a recent B.B.C. speaker when he referred to some land in the country as:—

" Land rateable only for agricultural purposes."

This glib remark coming from a townsman, gave me food for thought, even though it is unlikely to put food in his larder, or anyone elses. The primary purpose and use of *land*, is for agriculture. How else shall we live? I take exception and gravely object to the use of the word " only " in this context.

Here are ignorance and stupidity if ever I saw them. It seems to me that the more clever we become, the less we know.

W. J. Perry, in his book on early man *Children of the Sun*, has stated that :—

" It is commonly thought that the only hope for the student of society is the acquisition of knowledge; more facts and still more facts is the common catch-phrase. But what is really needed is more *insight* into what facts have already been gained. The mere accumulation of knowledge in itself, is of little use: what really is needed is some means of using that knowledge."

I find it significant, that

" during the pre-war years, our rulers declared that they could not find the money for this or that social advance, but we go on spending 685 millions a year on drink, 548 on tobacco and 750 on gambling, in contrast with not more than 38 millions on books."*

* J. W. Robertson Scott, *England's Green and Pleasant Land.*

It would also seem that in many ways, the more we produce, the poorer we become. We have wonderful wireless in our homes, but insufficient nourishing food in our larders. We can sit in the comfort and safety of our wonderful cinemas and see men killing each other in some distant land.

I may be a very simple person, as I said at the beginning of this book, but to me this does not seem to constitute progress. It also appears very stupid to buy foreign vegetables at a high cost (though as a nation we are supposed to be so impoverished) while we plough our own produce back into the soil.

Trade pacts, Whitehall farming, agricultural politics, call it what you will, seem to have little enough in common with common sense. Efficiency is a good servant but a bad master. Mr. Massingham says,

> " It is a purely economic conception and as such has become our master. So it comes about that we feel compelled to go on producing more and more cheaply; for whoever is more efficient can undersell him who is less so. We are forced to go on striving to reduce costs, and to do so, so to speak, at *all* costs, even the cost of the *quality of the product*, the independence of the producer, and the fertility of the soil which makes production possible."

I began to learn these things at Warminster and Whitestaunton, and my lessons continued at Silverlake and South Barrow.

Upon the other matters mentioned in the course of this story, I have found little cause to alter my mind or outlook. As a girl cycling doggedly from one place to another, I would often be tempted off my rightful road by some inviting signpost, by some shape of hill or wood, by some gleam of river or glimpse of thatch.

And it still happens. Last spring Mr. Ralph Whitlock and a friend set out to follow on horseback in " The Steps of King Alfred ". They made Church Farm their headquarters, and although work kept me at home, I followed the progress of their tour with interest tinged with envy. Oh to be abroad in Somerset in the bridle-paths and lanes of May. They followed the great Saxon King from his monument on the hills at Pen Selwood above Stourton to Aller where he baptised the Danish Guthrum, to Athelney where he burned the cakes, to Edington which some authorities say was the old " Ethandune ", and about the woods and meadows of Somerset where the Saxons burned the " ashen-faggot " to hearten themselves for battle against their heathen enemy.

When they had finished I drove them back to their home the other side of Salisbury. It was a glad May day, and no one wanted to go straight home. Ralph directed me through the by-ways of the lovely Nadder Valley, to investigate tithe barns and ancient yews at Tisbury and to admire the serene beauty of Teffonts Evias and Magna, and the lake at Fonthill Gifford.

They had opened up a new country to me, and one I was to store in my mind and use later in our film of the English countryside. By the time I deposited my guests and was prepared to return home there were precious few hours of daylight left, and the usual insufficiency of petrol in my car's tank, but I still found myself coming a longer way home, just to explore a further corner of Wessex not too well known to me.

Having crossed the beautiful Avon, and left Salisbury's slender spire behind me, I found myself in a corner of Cranborne Chase and Salisbury Plain which was the missing piece in my jig-saw puzzle mind-map of this interesting territory.

The other pieces of the puzzle had been put into place when I searched for, and eventually found, the medieval Mizmaze, as is related in *Hundredfold*.

Now I was rewarded by beginning to feel I had mastered the lie of this time-haunted land perfectly, and by approaching it from another direction and crossing the hitherto neglected corner, the map was complete in my head to the very last piece.

I was driving into the setting sun and the skyline was scalloped with barrows. On one side of my road was the Ox Drove, probably the oldest road in England, on the other were the dykes of Bokerly and Grim, and the camps of the Romans. All about were Celtic fields and the remains of British settlements. Massingham has called this country " The land of the living dead " and I can think of no title that suits it better.

Few linger to explore it, most people do as the Romans did, and march straight across it on the highway from Salisbury to Blandford— the Roman Sarum to Blandford Forum.

It was a strange experience that night. There was little traffic on the road, and I felt as if my car was a time and space machine, so that I was in one age and dimension being carried through and across another.

At Handley Cross I had completed the survey of the unknown land, and the last piece had fallen into place. I stared at the familiar signpost :

" 6d. Handley."

How original but how lacking in dignity! Had the powers that be written it out fully as Sixpenny Handley it would have been better, but not nearly so funny.

I reflected how the old Saxon " Hundreds " of Sespenna and Hanlega had been united under one overlord, to become the territory of Sexpenna-Hanlega—today 6d. Handley.

To work these things out for myself is still a joy, as much as ever it was when my bicycle was my only form of transport. I can still find happiness in pausing to think of the peoples who inhabited this ancient land before me, even as I did when I leaned on my bicycle in the high pass in the Downs above Maiden Bradley. I can still look at the West front of Wells Cathedral and say with the poet Wordsworth, " They dreamt not of a perishable home, who thus could build."

And still, as in the days of Whitestaunton I can take delight in the woodnotes wild of the lyrical Grieg, hear the rain and the butterflies in Chopin or feel the great, puzzled yet gallantly articulate soul of Tschaikowsky close to my own experience and understanding.

I do not go to symphony concerts, to me the antics of the conductor " interpreting " the great master, the sight of the soloist poised for his entrance, the proximity of so many other people in the audience tend to separate me from the truest enjoyment of great music. Nor do I advocate taking wireless or gramophone into the country to listen amid sylvan surroundings. Nature has her own music and it is a shame to drown it even with the best that can be composed by man. No, the proper place in which to listen to Paganini speaking through his violin music, Beethoven giving us his " Moonlight " Sonata, is by the fireside on a winter's evening, with all interruptions shut out and nothing but our own selves quiet with the wonder of the music.

Change is all round us, and as I said at the beginning of this book, the rate of change and decay has been speeded up out of all proportion to that of other centuries.

The buzzards may not always nest in Whitestaunton wood, nor the wild daffodils remain unravished at Stourton. I may not always be able to go to the exact spot where the oxslips grow so tall; and one day the Folly of Warminster, or the Yarty of Whitestaunton may find themselves piped into concrete culverts on some great Government undertaking which is to make day of night, or produce food without soil, or do away with the necessity of sleep, or something equally fantastic and wonderful! Then these little brooks will not know the paddling feet of care-free children, children who were told there could never be another war. The Yarty will not sing within the copse so that some other schoolgirl may read Shelley's *A Dream of the Unknown* in a fitting setting,

> "I dreamed that as I wandered by the way
> Bare Winter suddenly was changed to Spring,
> And gentle odours led my steps astray,
> Mixed with the sound of water's murmuring
> Along a shelving bank of turf, which lay
> Under a copse, and hardly dared to fling
> Its green arms round the bosom of the stream,
> But kissed it and then fled, as thou mightest in dream."

Again and again, in some village street, on some upland earthwork, in a hayfield surrounded by blue hills, watching a leveret play, or village children coming back with wild flowers, I have thought—

"Some people would declare that poets, painters and musicians have 'over-done' life and Nature; that they have idealised it and made the blue bells more blue, the sunsets more fiery, or have exaggerated the call of the cuckoo or the music of the storm. But the fact is, no artist could possibly give more than a shadowy glimpse of the beauty of life or the wonders of nature when compared with the original."

There are great floods and great droughts, earthquakes and pestilence, plagues and the eternal threat of starvation and misuse of the earth's wealth. These are the things against which Man should band himself in one great brotherhood. Man should not waste his energies and resources in fighting himself.

I cannot help feeling there should be enough for all and room for all. Even after the wars and calamities down the ages, the world remains glorious and wonderful and full of challenge and Man could yet claim his full birthright from it. Cruelty and stupidity and our still colossal ignorance are the only real enemies we have to fight.

THE END